MW00649000

INDOCHINA HAND

Casemate books by Barry Michael Broman

Risk Taker, Spy Maker: Tales of a CIA Case Officer
The Spy from Place Saint-Sulpice: A Novel

Other books by Barry Michael Broman

Old Homes of Bangkok: Fragile Link
Myanmar: Serenity and Transition in Burma
Bagan: Temples and Monuments of Ancient Burma
Faces of Myanmar: A Photographic Mosaic of Burma
Irrawaddy: Benevolent River of Burma, with John Stevenson
Myanmar Architecture: Cities of Gold, with Ma Thanegi
Spiritual Abodes of Thailand, with William Warren
Cambodia: The Land and its People
Myanmar: The Land and its People
7 Days in Myanmar, with assorted photographers
Thanakha: Nature's Gift to Myanmar, with Ma Thanegi
Naga: Celebration of Identity, with Ma Thanegi
Nats: Spirits of Fortune and Fear, with Ma Thanegi

INDOCHINA HAND

Tales of a CIA Case Officer

BARRY MICHAEL BROMAN

CASEMATE
Pennsylvania & Yorkshire

Published in the United States of America and Great Britain in 2024 by
CASEMATE PUBLISHERS
1950 Lawrence Road, Havertown, PA 19083, USA
and
47 Church Street, Barnsley, S70 2AS, UK

Hardcover Edition: ISBN 978-1-63624-441-9
Digital Edition: ISBN 978-1-63624-442-6

A CIP record for this book is available from the British Library

Printed and bound in the United Kingdom by CPI Group (UK) Ltd, Croydon, CR0 4YY
Typeset in India by DiTech Publishing Services

For a complete list of Casemate titles, please contact:

CASEMATE PUBLISHERS (US)
Telephone (610) 853-9131
Fax (610) 853-9146
Email: casemate@casematepublishers.com
www.casematepublishers.com

CASEMATE PUBLISHERS (UK)
Telephone (0)1226 734350
Email: casemate@casemateuk.com
www.casemateuk.com

The Prepublication Classification Review Board (PCRB) of the CIA has reviewed the text and approved it for publication.

All images from author's collection unless otherwise credited.

Cover image: The image was taken by Associated Press Bureau Chief for Cambodia Matt Franjola after the battle for Oudong in Cambodia in 1974.

Contents

Dedication

This book is dedicated to the memory of:
Jennifer Barton—my sister
Bob Peterson—my buddy
Neil Hollander—my partner in Adventure Film Productions
John Stevenson—my editor and friend

"I love to sail forbidden seas, and land on barbarous coasts."
Herman Melville

Preface

This book is a sequel to my memoir *Risk Taker, Spy Maker: Tales of a CIA Case Officer*, published by Casemate in 2020. That book followed a chronology of my life, notably my quarter-century as an officer of the Clandestine Service of the Central Intelligence Agency. This book consists of stand-alone stories, most of them dealing with my years in the CIA. I have made every effort not to repeat any of the stories from the first book in the second.

I retired from government service in 1996 after 30 years in the Marine Corps and the Agency. I was 53 years old when I retired and took advantage of a "buy out" by the Clinton administration where the CIA was somewhat ignored and the collection of intelligence from live sources (human intelligence) was not in favor.

I joined the CIA in 1971 straight out of the Marine Corps. I entered a career in intelligence largely because I wanted to spend my working life in Southeast Asia. The CIA made that happen. The work was interesting and important; the pay and benefits were good. I was also looking forward to a life of adventure and was not disappointed. Often, the truth is more unbelievable than fiction. I viewed the CIA as a vocation and was privileged to work with some of the best in the business, male and female. And also with brave men and women who often put their lives on the line in support of the free world during the Cold War and had a yearning for a better life in a better world. I tried to make that happen and usually succeeded.

The timing was good for me. Thirty years of stressful government service was sufficient. Our sons were both born outside the United States, and neither had the opportunity to grow up in the United States as an American. Seth, our oldest son, graduated in a senior class of 10 in an international school and was anxious to begin college. His senior essay talked about his growing up abroad, where he lived a life of privilege with servants, cars with drivers, and dinners with ambassadors, princes, and generals. But he had few friends and had to seek new ones at every posting.

My wife, BJ, had forsaken careers not taken, including writing for television, and a lucrative catering company she founded with my sister, Jenny, that had to be left when I was posted overseas for the fourth, but not last, time. She was ready to resume life as a teacher in the United States after teaching in two international schools abroad. Young Brendan knew very little of the United States and needed time with his grandparents in Seattle and Hawaii.

This book consists of stories covering my life span and most of them are tales from my days at the CIA. A few of the stories are from friends and colleagues, who I thank for sharing. The book has been approved by the CIA and, where possible, I have used true names. Many people assisted with the book and some, for security reasons, cannot be named.

These days I am writing more fiction than fact, and find it challenging and liberating. In recent years, I have focused on assisting Ukraine *pro bono* in its defense against fascist Russia's invasion, and am putting skill sets from my days in government service to use. *Slava Ukraini!*

Acknowledgements

I want to thank the people who helped me with this book. Some of them unfortunately cannot be named.

Thanks especially to the folks in the CIA's Prepublication Classification Review Board for their help in reviewing the text.

Sadly, my friend and partner in Adventure Film Productions, Neil Hollander, has passed away and did not see this book. He encouraged me to write. I thank him and his wife, Regine, for more things than I can count.

I also want to thank my mentor, Ambassador Timothy Carney, Ambassador Manfred von Nostitz, Fred Kroll, James Mullen, Lynn Peterson, Isobel Escoda, Chris Andrew, Sanjar Rasulov, Steve Richards, Armen Agas, Cletus "Charlie" Foote, Art Kim, Matt Ward, Regine Hollander, David Eubank, Suwat Soysingtong, Paul Strachan, Kim McDevitt, and the late Dan Arnold.

I want to also thank Ruth Sheppard, Daniel Yesilonis, Lizzy Hammond, and Declan Ingram at Casemate, and Seth Broman for his help in designing the cover.

And thanks to BJ, my wife, for her tireless support and encouragement.

CHAPTER I

England

I was a military brat. For years my younger sister, Jenny, and I followed the flag with my father, Harry Broman, an officer in the United States Air Force. I was born in Louisville, Kentucky, in 1943 when Pappy, as my father liked me to call him, was assigned to Bowman Field nearby. Jenny was born in Seattle four years later. We lived in six states and two foreign countries while Pappy served as a civil engineer. An architect by training at the University of Washington, Pappy was short but athletic. His Swedish father, Frank, a custom tailor, taught Pappy to shoot and fly fish. As a freshman, Pappy was the coxswain of the Washington crew. He was also head of the Washington rifle team which won the PAC-8 trophy while he was captain. In 1935, Pappy was commissioned a second lieutenant in the United States Army. He went on active duty in 1941 had served as a glider pilot in World War II.

My mother, Hilda Foley Broman, was a Canadian farm girl from British Columbia who emigrated to the United States on her 18th birthday. Her father, Thomas Foley, was born on Prince Edward Island and married Regina Marquette from Quebec. The lure of gold brought Thomas to the Yukon around the turn of the century and he eventually settled on a farm in Dudney, not far from Vancouver, where my mother was born. Family lore states that Thomas, a tough Irish scrapper and onetime constable, fought world champion boxer Tommy Burns for three rounds in an exhibition match in Nanaimo BC and didn't get knocked down.

Hilda met Pappy in Seattle while she worked as a film splicer for MGM and he was a member of Kappa Sigma fraternity driving a Stutz Bearcat sports car. They married in 1934. Pappy called her "Booge," for reasons we never knew. She was a smart and pretty lady, proud of her Irish and French-Canadian heritage. She had a dry wit, was an avid gardener, and little fazed her; she was the perfect military wife.

Pappy led a flight of gliders across the Rhine River on March 24, 1945, in Operation *Varsity*, the largest glider invasion in history. After the war, he returned to architecture as a partner at Edwin J. Ivy and stayed in the reserves. In 1948, he was recalled to active duty for the Berlin Air Lift for a year, and again for the Korean War in 1950. Life for Jenny and me changed in 1954 when the Air Force, in an effort to retain him in the service, offered Pappy his choice of any assignment.

An Anglophile since 1944, when he served in England prior to moving on to France and Germany, Pappy chose the job of base engineer at Royal Air Force (RAF) Manston in east Kent on the English Channel. The base was very busy during the

Washington Governor Clarence Martin presents Harry Broman with the trophy for best rifle team in the Pacific Eight conference. Harry was captain of the University of Washington ROTC (Reserve Officers Training Corps) rifle team, *circa* 1934.

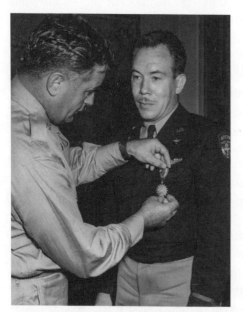

Captain Harry Broman being presented with the Air Medal in 1945 after Operation *Varsity*, the crossing of the Rhine River in Germany.

Hilda Foley "Booge" Broman in Seattle, *circa* 1932.

Harry and Booge in London, *circa* 1957.

Battle of Britain in 1940 when Manston was the closest RAF fighter base to German-occupied France and right on the flight path of the Luftwaffe on their way to bomb London.

We lived in the seaside town of Herne Bay about 18 miles from the base in a large house called "Deepdene" on the Canterbury Road. It had four bedrooms, a ballroom, a formal garden, an orchard, and a very large vegetable garden complete with an aged gardener, Old Fred, who worked two days a week as part of our $90 monthly rent. But the house had no central heating and I quickly became a proficient coal fire maker.

Barry Broman in Herne Bay, Kent, England, *circa* 1955, wearing the uniform of Eddington House boys' preparatory school.

Jennifer Broman in her ballet tutu at Girdler's School for Girls, Herne Bay, Kent, England, *circa* 1956.

I enrolled as a day boy in Eddington House prep school and Jenny attended Girdler's School for Girls, where she studied piano and ballet and quickly developed the distinctive accent of the English upper class to which we did not belong. We were the only Americans in each school. I played cricket, field hockey, and soccer along with learning French, Latin, and more about colonial British history than I wanted or needed to know. On Thursdays I rode horses with a few classmates who owned their own horses and "rode to the hounds" at home. Early on, Pappy warned me never to say how important the United States had been in the World War II victory. It was sage advice. My peers were mainly critical of the United States taking so long in joining the war against Hitler.

Jenny and I loved our English schools and our new English friends. I quickly gained a first-hand appreciation of global politics. The Cold War was in full spate and Manston was home to two USAF squadrons of F-86 Sabre jets, the finest in the world at the time. Most of the pilots were recent veterans of the Korean War, where the USAF ruled the skies. While Manston was still an RAF base, all aircraft were American, including some helicopters for air-sea rescue in the English Channel.

We rarely visited the base but made a number of English friends locally. Chief among them was our physician, Dr. Quentin-Evans, who lived nearby in the ancient hamlet of Herne, about five miles from Canterbury. The doctor's wife, Barbara, was once the ladies' badminton champion of Kent and had served in the war as a nurse in the Royal Navy's Women's Royal Service, commonly called the Wrens. She was assigned to Dover, where her job was to provide medical assistance in recovering air crews shot down in the English Channel. She plied the waters, usually alone in a small open boat with a young sailor at the helm. She was armed with a Webley revolver. Often, her boat fished out more German air crews than downed RAF Spitfire and Hurricane pilots. Barbara told me she could have been overpowered by Germans and the boat taken to nearby Calais in France. "But that never happened," she said. "They were happy to be out of the war and always polite to me and grateful for being rescued."

I learned to play tennis at school and had my rackets strung at Swan's sports shop on Herne Bay's high street. It was a quiet shop owned by Mr. Swan, a quiet, thin, greying gentleman who brought to mind a retired cleric. How wrong I was. One day, Mr. Swan asked if my father was stationed at Manston. "Yes, sir," I replied.

"Is he a pilot?" Mr. Swan asked.

"He was a glider pilot in the war," I answered, "but is now the base engineer."

"Step into my office," invited Mr. Swan. "You may find it interesting."

The wall was full of photographs from the war. Mr. Swan had been a pilot in the RAF. I recognized the ribbons for heroism in the air on his tunic in several photos which I examined closely. Then I saw a photo of Mr. Swan with a man I recognized.

"Did you know Douglas Bader?" I asked. Like many schoolboys in Kent in those days, I knew a lot about "The Few," the young airmen who protected England from the full strength of the German Luftwaffe. I knew of the legless RAF pilot Bader, who lost his legs in a flying accident before the war but insisted he would fly with tin legs when the war came and became one of the RAF's greatest "aces" against the Germans.

"I knew him," Mr. Swan said. "Excellent pilot, but a bit full of himself. When Jerry shot him down and took him prisoner he kept trying to escape so at night they took his legs away from him. Douglas flew Spits; I was a night fighter in Mosquitos."

I was in total awe with Mr. Swan, who seemed bemused by a young Yank who knew a lot about the RAF and the men of whom Winston Churchill famously said: "Never in the field of human conflict was so much owed by so many to so few."

When America got into the war after Pearl Harbor, English skies became full of B-17 Flying Fortress bombers. Thousand-bomber daylight raids to Germany became common, so the runway at Manston was extended to handle shot up B-17s that were limping home to England. Manston had the longest runway in England.

In 1957, it was decided that I should leave Eddington House as I outgrew prep school. A new school was opened at Manston, so I enrolled in the 9th grade class of 14 students. The only classmate who had attended an English school was Bob Starkey. Together we joined the Manston soccer team, where all the other members were USAF airmen who knew nothing about the game. We lost every game and only scored two goals in the season; Bob had one and I had the other. One of our classmates was an African American girl named Gloria Tyree. She was the first African American I ever met. She was extremely intelligent, somewhat shy, and a head taller than me. Her father, Major Eugene Tyree, was a veteran of the famed Tuskegee Airmen, an all-African American flying outfit in the war.

I was taken to school by taxi every day, 18 miles one way, and returned in the evening with Pappy. It worked out very well and usually involved a stop at the officers' club for a drink for Pappy, or more commonly a stop at one of the pubs that he frequented along the way home. In the public houses, I, at the age 14, could drink a "shandy", half beer and half lemonade. My parents would host dinner parties on Saturdays. Many guests were fighter pilots, who flew hard and partied hard. I kept the coal fires going and served as bartender. Often the parties would end at dawn and included a walk in the grounds and orchard, while Booge made scrambled eggs and coffee.

I witnessed the British press in action one day and learned a lesson on how they can and would skew stories to fit their own agendas. I was the only passenger in my taxi through an arrangement the U.S. Air Force made with the Herne Bay taxi company. Most of the students at the Manston school went by buses from nearby Margate or Birchington. One day, an enterprising Fleet Street hack bribed his way onto a school bus and interviewed the young Americans about what they disliked most about England. Many of the kids knew little of England and had little real contact with the English. With not much effort, the journalist elicited a number of quotes that were generally anti-British in tone. That was the purpose of the story which ran the next day in a major London daily under the headline "The Wayward Bus." It caused a minor furor but was an eye-opener for me. It was also a cautionary tale for the need to tread carefully when dealing with a hostile or opportunistic press, both foreign and American.

In 1957, the University of Washington (UW) crew team visited England to row in the Henley Royal Regatta, the premium rowing venue in the world. When Pappy attended the UW, he was the frosh coxswain. He only quit when he was accepted into the School of Architecture and told he had to give up sports. Harold Pebbles Jr., the son of Pappy's best friend, was manager of the crew, so I got to see rowing for the first time. Pappy took me to Henley, a town he knew from the war and where he still remembered some pubs. He wore his British tweeds and I wore my Eddington House uniform. We looked the proper British pair taking in the regatta. Sadly, the Americans lost to a Soviet crew at Henley, but they got their revenge soon after in a rowing event in Leningrad.

My first visit to the European mainland came the following year when the World Fair was hosted in Brussels, Belgium. It was a short ferry ride from Dover to Ostend, and I finally got a chance to practice my French. We drove with Air Force friends in two cars and enjoyed the fair. Then we drove up to Breda in Holland, where Pappy was sent after the Rhine crossing in 1945 to regroup with other glider pilot survivors of Operation *Varsity*. The bartender at our hotel informed Pappy that it was legal for me to have a beer, so Pappy ordered a local beer for me—and presented me with the bill. "You have to pay to play," he informed me.

It was a rough crossing back across the Channel in fog and high seas. I was reminded of the headline of a London newspaper years before that perfectly described the English view towards Europe: "Fog in Channel—Europe cut off." Our stateroom was requisitioned by the boat's crew for a woman who went into labor and gave birth while we drank in the saloon bar. The ship's skipper picked up our tab.

We said a sad farewell to England in 1958 when Pappy was assigned to Wright-Patterson Air Force Base in Ohio, where he attended the Air Force Institute of Technology and earned an MA in civil engineering. One of his fellow attendees was an officer of the Royal Thai Air Force, Captain Sudhi Lekhyananda. They quickly became friends. Sudhi was not your average airman. He was from a very prominent family, close to the royal family, and a graduate of Tufts University in Boston. Sudhi's father, a future Minister of Justice, was a student at Harvard Law School with Prince Mahidol Adulyadej, the 69th child of King Chulalongkorn and the father of modern Thai medicine. Mahidol was also the father of King Bumiphol Adulyadej, who was Sudhi's childhood classmate and close friend.

Sudhi always had a smile on his face, and was witty as well as smart. He was the first Thai I ever met and he became a fixture at the Broman house. I still wonder if Sudhi had a hand in Pappy's assignment to Thailand in 1962 as a civil engineer advisor to the Royal Thai Air Force, where Sudhi was very well connected.

After Ohio, Pappy was assigned to Scott Air Force Base in southern Illinois, where I attended Mascoutah Community High School about twenty miles east of St. Louis, Missouri. In 1961, I won a four-year scholarship to the University of Illinois, where I was a fraternity brother of future Chicago Bears football star Dick Butkus and a photographer on the staff of the college paper, *The Daily Illini*, and worked for night editor Roger Ebert, later an acclaimed film critic. When Pappy was assigned to Thailand in 1962, he asked if I would like to drop out of college for a year and experience Asia. Surprised, I immediately said "yes" and gave up my scholarship and status as a midshipman in the Naval ROTC. My life changed again when I headed for Indochina.

CHAPTER 2

Associated Press Photographer

In the summer of 1962 I was a teenage college dropout in Bangkok facing a return to the University of Illinois if I didn't find a job. My lifestyle was not what my father had in mind when he invited me to spend a year in Thailand, where he was assigned as an advisor to the Royal Thai Air Force. He told me that if I didn't find a job, I would be heading back to Illinois in the fall.

With few skills and no connections, I began looking for work as a photographer, armed with clippings from the University of Illinois daily newspaper. Following a few leads, I approached Tony Escoda, bureau chief of the Associated Press (AP). I was braced for rejection but my timing was perfect. American troops were arriving in Thailand in the wake of a political crisis in neighboring Laos. The AP needed an English-speaking photographer. Tony looked at my clippings, smiled, and said: "Can you start tomorrow?" I said "Yes." Tony apologized that he could only pay $10 per day, plus expenses. I didn't care. I didn't need money. I was living at home with my parents and Jenny, my sister. I needed a job and Tony took a chance on me.

After a few assignments, including a trip "upcountry" to document the arrival of U.S. Army troops at Korat Air Force Base, Tony put me in charge of photos. "You will deal with Tokyo Photos," he informed me. "I don't want to hear from them." The center for AP photos in Asia was in Tokyo, under the command of Harold "Hal" Buell, who happily noticed an uptick in photos from Bangkok. Tony was a newsman and didn't want to be involved with photos. Although only a "stringer," not a staff AP employee and paid only when I worked, I was a member of the AP team in Bangkok which included Guillermo "Gil" Santos, who was, like Tony, a Filipino.

Tony also gave me another responsibility: I was to deal with all Japanese clients of the AP who might be in Bangkok, or any Japanese in general. I found this strange. Only later did I learn that Tony's parents had been killed by the

Japanese in Manila in World War II. Tony's mother, Josefa Llanes Escoda, founded an underground resistance movement against the Japanese occupiers of the Philippines together with her husband, Antonio Escoda Sr. They were both turned in to the Japanese by Filipino collaborators, tortured, and executed. Their bodies were never found. Tony's mother is commemorated on the 1,000 Philippine peso banknote, along with two other World War II war heroes who gave their lives for their country and the United States.

In Bangkok, Tony lived with his wife, Isabel "Betty," and their two young daughters, Carrie and Tina, in the penthouse apartment above the AP office at 103 Pat Pong Road, so commuting to work was not a problem. In 1962, Patpong Road was not the tawdry nightlife scene it became a decade later. It was privately owned and housed the American USIS library, Shell oil, AP and UPI offices, and a number of high-end bars and restaurants, starting with the classy Keynote Club, Bangkok's top live music venue. My personal favorite was The Red Door, an upscale bar/restaurant that offered the best Shanghai fried noodles I ever tasted. Also, its owner, a Shanghai-born lady, let me run a tab, quite a treat for a 19-year-old AP stringer.

One early assignment put me into a less-than-pleasant encounter with the U.S. Marine Corps. I was covering a joint USMC–Royal Thai Marine Corps exercise in jungle-covered hills on a beach south of Bangkok. I was in a jeep with a couple of Thai journalists covering the exercise when our vehicle was stopped by a ragged-looking Westerner in civilian clothes carrying an M-14 rifle. He ordered us out and picked me, the only Westerner in the jeep, for interrogation. We were initially surprised and a little concerned, but it quickly turned out that the gunman was actually a Marine working with the Thai Marines as an "aggressor" opposing U.S. and Thai Marines making an amphibious landing nearby. He accused me of being a spy for the Marines.

The misunderstanding was quickly explained by an accompanying Thai Marine officer. The aggressor apologized for his error and disappeared into the jungle. A Thai photographer with us photographed the aggressor manhandling me, and the photo appeared in a Thai newspaper the next day. Tony laughed when he gave me a copy of the paper and said: "You are supposed to be covering the news, Broman, not making it."

Despite low pay and growing responsibilities, I loved my new job. It had a few perks, one of them being given the rank of lieutenant colonel for billeting and flight seniority when on the job with U.S. military; a fact I never mentioned to my father, a major. He would not have been happy. A bigger perk was given to me by Tony when he showed me a stack of invitations that were extended to the AP to a variety of events, including from embassies for national days and a bevy of events that were seeking press coverage. If Tony and Gil did not want to attend any of the events, I was allowed to represent the Associated Press.

One of the events I attended was from the British embassy that was hosting a reception for RAF pilots who were participating in the Southeast Asia Treaty Organization (SEATO) military exercise. I bumped into my British friend, Harry Mason, a sub-editor at the *Bangkok World* newspaper and a seasoned "Bangkok hand." In his late 20s, Harry showed me Bangkok by night, including the infamous Mosquito Bar, located just outside the port of Bangkok and famous for its raucous maritime clientele, many of whom had not touched liquor for days or weeks before arriving in the city. We were present when a drunken young Norwegian seaman, encouraged by his equally soused shipmates, tried to approach the naked young lady who was performing for the crowded, smoke-filled, room. As the youth approached her, she sidestepped him, took off a stiletto shoe—her only apparel—and planted it in the head of the young seaman, who collapsed on the floor. The girl ran offstage and the band played on. The Mosquito was that kind of place.

Harry and I, in true journalist form, viewed the occasion as an opportunity to eat well, have a few gin and tonics, and pick up any newsworthy gossip. We hit it off with the young British airmen, the evening's guests of honor, who were eager to enjoy the delights of Bangkok after drinking gin and tonics on Her Majesty's shilling before disporting themselves into the night.

An elderly and distinguished-looking gentleman in black tie uniform joined our little group, where Harry was suggesting several places to visit after the reception. His first choice, of course, was the Mosquito Bar, a suggestion that was approved by all. As we were about to make our move to leave, the old fellow who had been listening intently piped up: "Perhaps I could join you chaps."

"And who you might you be?" asked one of the more inebriated Hawker Hunter pilots.

"I am your host," said the British Ambassador, rather coolly. "I hope you are enjoying the evening so far."

"We are, indeed your excellency," spoke up the senior pilot present. "Many thanks. But we wouldn't want to take you away from your guests. Perhaps another time."

"Another time it is," Her Majesty's Ambassador Extraordinary and Plenipotentiary said, clearly disappointed at not being invited along on the RAF sortie through Bangkok after dark.

Tony was the first Filipino and the first Yale graduate I ever met. After the war, an American couple who had lived in the Philippines and who knew the

Escodas made Tony, who was 14 when the war ended, and his elder sister, Bing, their wards. While Bing studied at Barnard, Tony went to Phillips Academy-Andover, Yale University, and Columbia University's School of Journalism. After he won the Borden Award and Pulitzer Travelling Fellowship at Columbia, he was hired by the Associated Press and worked his way up the ladder to become the AP's first Asian bureau chief.

I learned a lot from Tony. In addition to getting my journalistic feet wet, he taught me to drink martinis and play poker Filipino-style. In that he was assisted by Gil Santos, a seasoned newsman. Gil helped me write my first published article, "Filipino Entertainers in Bangkok" for the *Philippines Free Press*. The fee was negligible, but I became a hit with the best musicians in Thailand, all of them Filipino, starting with Narcing Aguilar at The Keynote Club not far from the AP office. *Downbeat* magazine rated Narcing the top jazz pianist in Asia and the Keynote Club featured Narcing's trio.

Across the street from the Keynote Club was Mizu's Kitchen, a restaurant known for its steaks and run by a Japanese named Mizutani, who was said to have deserted from the Japanese Army and stayed in Thailand after World War II. The restaurant was the unofficial headquarters of the Foreign Correspondents Club of Thailand (FCCT), a group numbering no more than a dozen members from the wire services stationed in Thailand, starting with the AP and followed by UPI, Reuters, and Agence France Presse.

I was the youngest member of the FCCT. Probably the oldest was Jorges Orgibet, an American who pitched up in Thailand at the end of the war with the U.S. Office of War Information and established the U.S. Information Service (USIS) office. He later became the first AP bureau chief in Bangkok. Jorges was a crusty old fellow from California and a founding father of the FCCT. He prided himself on not being able to speak a word of Thai after decades in the country and referred to the local currency, the Baht, by its old name, the Tikal, or "ticks." The exchange rate at the time with the dollar was 20:1. "Easy to remember," he told me, "a Tikal is a nickel."

The senior Thai in the FCCT was M. R. Kukrit Pramoj, an Oxford-educated politician, leading man of letters, and founder of *Siam Rath* newspaper. He was a great grandson of King Rama II. At our first meeting at Mizu's Kitchen, Kukrit directed me to stand on a chair and sing a song. I sang "Tom Dooley," poorly, and was never asked to sing again.

Years later, Kukrit became the prime minister of Thailand and while in that post wrote the foreword to my first book, *Old Homes of Bangkok: Fragile Link*. Kukrit's home, an attractive blend of Thai and European architecture, was featured in the book. Before Kukrit became a real prime minister, he played a prime minister of the fictional country "Sarkhan" in the 1963 film *The Ugly American*, starring Marlon Brando. I covered the world premiere of the film. It was the only time I wore a coat and tie while shooting for the AP.

My last visit to the FCCT was in 2019 at the world premiere of the documentary film *Who Killed Jim Thompson, the Thai Silk King*, a film I made with my partner, Neil Hollander. The room was full and included many old friends. The FCCT has grown to over seven hundred members, including about seventy who are working press, a far cry from our infrequent gatherings at Mizu's Kitchen.

Tony rarely had time for FCCT meetings. He was busy 14 hours a day keeping the world informed of events in Thailand. We often traveled together covering stories upcountry. From time to time we would cross paths with Sergei Sverin, the correspondent for TASS, the Soviet news agency. Tony warned me to be careful around Sergei. "He is a KGB officer," Tony said, "a Russian spy. Never give him any information." I didn't ask how Tony knew Sergei was a spy, but years later I checked and learned that Tony knew what he was talking about. Sergei was indeed a Soviet intelligence officer.

My father was busy helping the Royal Thai Air Force build runways, radar sites, and a few secret projects I was not cleared to know about. With him

Barry, right, with Marlon Brando at the world premiere of *The Ugly American* in Bangkok, 1963.

Jock Mahoney as Tarzan, with a Lisu girl near Chiang Mai, Thailand, 1963, during the making of *Tarzan's Three Challenges*.

every step of the way was his good friend Captain Sudhi Lekhyananda. Among their projects was the construction of U-Tapao air base south of Bangkok. It is the longest runway on the mainland of Southeast Asia and built for B-52 bombers. On the wall of his office at Don Muang, Pappy had a framed poem by Rudyard Kipling that he required all of his subordinate Americans to learn by heart. It read:

> Now it is not good for the Christian's health to hustle the Aryan brown,
> For the Christian riles, and the Aryan smiles and he weareth the Christian down;
> And the end of the fight is a tombstone white with the name of the late deceased,
> And the epitaph drear: "A fool lies here who tried to hustle the East."

Wise words to live by in Asia. Earlier, Pappy had a shorter and less profound statement framed over his desk at Manston with the message:

> Don't start vast projects with half-vast planning.

When I was a teenager, he showed me a small, framed message from World War II he said that he displayed in his office in Melun, France, for the benefit of the young glider pilots under his command. It read:

Flies cause disease. Keep yours zipped.

We were treated royally by Sudhi and his English-educated wife, Siripong, known to her Western friends as Sue and Thai friends as Au. Her father was a member of Thailand's supreme court. Sudhi's father, Phra Suth, was a Harvard classmate to the king's father and served as Vice Minister of Foreign Affairs. Sudhi and Sue were members of a small and select group of King Bumiphol's inner circle of friends and were frequent guests at the king's jazz evenings at Chitralada Palace. Sudhi included the Bromans in family weekends at beach houses in Pattaya and Hua Hin, and introduced us to Thai and Chinese cuisine. The whole thing was a rare treat which we all appreciated.

We kept in touch over the years, and when our first son was born in Bangkok in 1978 we asked Sudhi for help naming the baby. He pondered and came up with the name Seth, who, according to the *Bible*, was the third son of Adam and Eve. Sudhi noted that the name also has a positive meaning from Sanskrit involving wealth. So Seth it was. Sudhi had his own naming issues when his first son was born. Because Sudhi was connected to the royal family, the boy's name was decided by Brahmins in the royal household; a great honor but also slow in coming. In the interim, the boy was called Ake, indicating that he was a first-born son. The name, Piwat, eventually arrived from the palace, but he is still known by friends and family as Ake.

Life in Bangkok in 1962 was an adventure in itself. Our house was not air-conditioned, but Pappy and Booge's bedroom was. Jenny and I made do with fans. We lived in a spacious house on the northern outskirts of Bangkok which made Pappy's commute to work at the military side of Bangkok's international airport, Don Muang, easier. However, the road in those days was a paved two-lane road with canals (*klongs*) on both sides, a drive made challenging for Pappy's 1957 Cadillac with the steering wheel on the left. The Thai drive on the left lane, like the British.

Jenny attended the International School of Bangkok, and in the rainy season ran through ankle-deep water to catch her school bus. Even running, she had to pull leeches off her legs when she got to the bus. When the yard filled with water, I tried, without success, to shoot cobra snakes with a crossbow. Then there was the problem with *kemoys* (burglars). They were a perennial hazard, but rarely resorted to violence. One night, Pappy woke me up quietly with a rifle in his hand. "*Kemoys*," he whispered, "downstairs. Get your sword and follow me." I quickly unsheathed my 2-foot-long Thai fighting sword, which was functional as well as decorative. Pappy switched on the lights as we surprised two burglars in the living room. They immediately ran, and as we watched them reach our perimeter wall and the barbed wire on top, Pappy fired a bullet into the air. Lights came on all around us. Minutes later, police arrived from the Bang Sue station nearby. We were not troubled by burglars again.

Our house, like most in Bangkok, was home to little geckos known as *chinchuks*. They were effective at killing mosquitos and harmless to humans. One of them, named Archie by Pappy, became a sort of pet. Pappy's favorite after-work libation was a cocktail called an Old Fashioned, a drink made with bourbon whiskey and bitters and a slice of orange. Archie would brazenly approach Pappy's drink and quietly lick the whiskey from the swizzle stick that Pappy used to stir the ingredients. Archie often did this and Pappy told his Thai friends about his pet. No one believed him, so one day I filmed Pappy and Archie enjoying an Old Fashioned together with Pappy's 8mm camera.

My boss was Tony Escoda, but when Horst Faas came to town I was under his command. He was the only AP staff photographer in Southeast Asia and was based in Saigon. Horst was an experienced war photographer from assignments in the Congo and Algeria before being posted to Saigon in 1962. One of the first things he did was triple my pay, having learned that I could handle the job along with my darkroom skills. Although American ground forces didn't arrive in Vietnam until 1965, Horst went to war on a daily basis with the South Vietnamese Army (ARVN) troops, often going into battle in American-piloted helicopters. He spent more than a decade in the war zone, was wounded numerous times, and won two Pulitzer Prizes. He was an early mentor and arranged for assignments for me to cover stories in South Vietnam and Cambodia.

In the summer of 1963, my year in Asia was over. I did a lot in my drop-out year, including work on a Tarzan film as stills photographer, and had to turn down two offers to work on films in Cambodia and Malaysia. A deal was a deal; it was time to go back to school. I enrolled at the University of Washington in 1963 with plans to become an expert on Southeast Asia. I kept in touch with Tony Escoda and we visited him in Manila a decade later when I was working for the CIA. It was BJ's first trip to her father's homeland. Horst Faas had introduced me to collecting Asian art, and in the Philippines

AP Bangkok bureau chief Tony Escoda, left, with AP photographer Horst Faas in Korat, Thailand, in 1962.

Tony arranged for his sister, Bing, to take us to see the exquisite and private Ongpin ceramic collection in Manila. It was a real treat.

Following the footsteps of his father, Antonio Escoda, Sr., Tony left the Associated Press and returned to the Philippines, where he became the Managing Editor of the *Philippines Herald*. Sadly, he passed away all too young from cancer. Horst Faas passed in 2012. I remember them both fondly as the men who gave me my start at becoming an Indochina hand. And also Hal Buell, who rose to become vice-president of the Associated Press and hired me for three summers while in college to work as an AP photo editor in Chicago and twice in New York. I was poised to return to AP after my stint with the Marine Corps, but the CIA made me an offer I couldn't refuse.

CHAPTER 3

The Girl from Pepeekeo and a Quantico Wedding

When I was a sophomore at the University of Washington in 1964, I met and wooed a cute young lady fresh from Hilo High School on the Big Island of Hawaii. She was Betty Jane ("call me BJ") Apilado, the daughter of a Filipino father and Japanese American mother. Her maternal grandfather was Tomonojo Nagai, the black sheep of a samurai family who encouraged his emigration to Hawaii, where he worked initially as a sugar cane cutter. He married a "picture bride" from Japan, a mail-order situation that was common and worked out well.

BJ's father was Simplicio Apilado, a Filipino from the Ilocano ethnic group of the northern part of the island of Luzon. The late president of the Philippines was an Ilocano, and many Ilocano emigrated to Hawaii. Simplicio was one of them, arriving in 1928 as a cane cutter for 10 cents an hour, 10 hours a day. He met and fell in love with Yachiyo Nagai, BJ's mother, and they were married in 1943.

That was a bad year for marriages between ethnic Japanese and Filipinos in Hawaii. The Imperial Japanese Army invaded and captured the Philippines in 1942, and bad blood existed between the two ethnic groups. In BJ's family, the situation was dire when her Samurai grandfather refused to recognize the marriage. This sad situation continued until BJ was born in 1945, when Tomonojo fell in love with the baby, forgave the wedding, and made her his favorite grandchild.

Japanese Americans in Hawaii during World War II were generally not put into concentration camps as their mainland friends and kin were, but old Tomomojo was kept out of sight of the authorities due to his undying loyalty to the Emperor of Japan, even when two of his sons joined the 442nd Regimental Combat Team of the U.S. Army, an all-ethnic Japanese unit whose motto was "Go For Broke." They gained wartime fame and recognition in combat in Italy and France, but at a high cost in casualties. The late Senator Dan Inouye, from Hawaii, lost an arm in combat and was awarded the Medal of Honor. I was told that when Dan was a freshman congressman, he was taken to meet Sam Rayburn, the famed 43rd Speaker of the House. "Mr. Sam," as he was called, greeted the young Hawaiian veteran with the words, "People are going to take notice of you on the Hill."

"Why is that Mr. Sam," Inouye asked.

"We don't get many one-armed Japs around here."

Dan went on to serve as a distinguished senator from Hawaii from 1963 until his death in 2012.

BJ was a conscientious student at Hilo High and an avid reader. She was accepted at a number of top universities, but the UW was one that the family could afford and she flew to the mainland in 1963 with a small number of Hilo High School graduates for the first big adventure of their lives.

Before she left, BJ's aunt took her aside and encouraged her to find a nice Japanese American boy to marry. Her father also had a quiet word with the college-bound BJ, expressing his hope that she would find and marry a nice Filipino boy. Both parents warned her against going out with a "*haole*" (white) boy. Enter Barry Broman, *haole* boy and ardent admirer of BJ Apilado. Her parents' hopes were dashed when BJ was "pinned" by Delta Tau Delta fraternity man Barry. She became a Delta Tau Delta "girl," which unofficially meant that she was engaged to be engaged. Marriage would often follow.

After my chance encounter with BJ on the quad in full cherry blossoms in the spring of 1964, when I photographed her (with no film in camera) and learned her name and phone number, I followed up when I learned we were both taking Anthropology 280 (Theories of Race), a popular elective two-hour course. There were at least two hundred students in the class. The Delts were well represented by me and several pledge brothers. BJ was among a bevy of Hawaiian *wahines*.

It was an interesting class in which questions were never expected or sought. The "prof" was a young anthropologist with a specialty in the people of Melanesia in the South Pacific. All went well until he asserted that the 19th-century English writer and poet Rudyard Kipling was a racist. I am an aficionado of Kipling and his works and concede that he was an arch-colonialist, but not a racist.

After hearing a number of anti-Kipling comments, I lost patience and raised my hand. The prof was taken aback. Questions were rare in the large class, but he acknowledged the raised hand and I spoke in defense of Kipling. I cited a passage from the poem *Gunga Din*, the story of an Indian Army water bearer,

Midshipman Broman at sea in the Strait of Juan de Fuca, 1967.

or *bhisti*, named Gunga Din, as told by an English soldier, in which the water bearer dies carrying water under fire to wounded Englishmen:

> Of all that blackfaced crew
> The finest man I knew
> Was our regimental bhisti, Gunga Din …
> An' just before 'e died,
> I hope you liked your drink, sez Gunga Din.
> So I'll meet 'im later on
> At the place where 'e is gone—
> Where it's always double drill and no canteen …
> And I'll get a swig in hell from Gunga Din! …
> By the living Gawd that made you,
> You're a better man than I am, Gunga Din!

I sat down. There was silence. The lecture resumed. I felt I had made my point and was playing to Miss Apilado as much as to the anti-Kipling professor. I don't regret my remarks, although years later BJ later told me my comments had little bearing on our courtship.

While at the UW I was accepted into the Naval Reserve Officer Training Corps (NROTC) program that offered a commission in the Navy or Marine Corps upon graduation from college.

Barry walking on a log at his Lake Union houseboat, Seattle, 1967.

Barry in Mexico, 1966. (Photo by Neil Hollander)

I had a double major in Political Science and Far Eastern Studies, was the chief photographer for the student newspaper and yearbook, and was the only student studying Thai.

When I received my BA in 1967, I was commissioned a second lieutenant in the Marine Corps Reserve. The Corps, in its wisdom, decided that I should have a master's degree in Southeast Asian Studies before going on active duty, and the university agreed. While in grad school, I grew a mustache and goatee, probably the only second lieutenant in the Corps with such facial hair. It caused a little consternation with the Marine Guards at the main gate of Sand Point

Marine 2nd Lieutenant Barry Broman while in grad school in Seattle, 1967.

BJ Apilado with Senator Warren Magnusson, when she worked as a Senate intern.

Naval Air Station in Seattle, where I frequented the PX (Post Exchange) and officers' club. I had proper documentation but I am sure I was suspected of being a malefactor of some sort. No *real* Marine would wear a beard.

BJ also majored in Political Science and put it to good use when she was appointed a Congressional summer intern for Senator Warren G. Magnuson (D-Wash). While I was studying Thai, BJ learned Japanese, a language she often spoke with her mother, and while I worked on my master's degree she worked to get her teaching certificate. We enjoyed our time in a condemned houseboat on Lake Union in Seattle with our roommate, Neil Hollander, who was working on a doctorate in communications. We split the $80 rent for our three-bedroom, condemned boat with an outside moorage looking at Seattle's Space Needle across the lake.

This came to end in the summer of 1968 when I received my MA, about the same time I was promoted to First Lieutenant of Marines. I headed to Quantico, Virginia, minus beard and mustache, and with a "high and tight" haircut that was approved by the guards at Sand Point, a sure sign that I was indeed a Marine and probably heading for war.

I checked into The Basic School (TBS) at Quantico, where Marine lieutenants were taught to lead men in battle and kill enemies of the United States. I was the only first lieutenant in Class 1-69. Instruction was excellent and training was rigorous. With America at war and Marines dying daily in Vietnam, the focus of training was on preparation for fighting. The instructors were invariably Vietnam veterans and often heavily decorated. There was little time for the parade ground and sword drill.

One young captain had been an advisor to the Vietnamese Marines on his second tour. They were tough fighters but there weren't many of them. The unit was surrounded and recon reports were that the North Vietnamese were massing for an attack. The advisor spent the day arranging "on call" artillery support on all sides with allied arty units. When the attack came, he calmly called in fire with devastating accuracy that killed hundreds of the enemy as the assault failed. We all noticed the captain's Navy Cross ribbon that he won that day. It is second only to the Medal of Honor.

Early on, I remembered my journalist background and thought that TBS would make a good feature for a professional magazine such as the *Proceedings of the US Naval Institute*. TBS leadership agreed and I proposed the idea to the *Proceedings* at Annapolis. They liked the idea, so I went to the field with my rifle and field gear, and also my Nikon F camera with several lenses. The result was my photo essay, "The Basic School, Quantico: Core of the Corps." It was published in the March 1969 issue while I was fighting in Vietnam.

During my Quantico sojourn, I thought, and BJ agreed, that we should get married. We had co-habited for a couple of years and despite the actuarial numbers on the survival rates for Marine infantry officers in Vietnam in those days, we made the move. We announced our engagement. This was not met with unanimous glee by our parents, but we moved ahead with plans for a Quantico wedding when my class graduated. Because of the short timeframe and distance from our families, we decided on a small wedding with only a few guests.

I chose Bob Peterson, once my roommate and a *LIFE* magazine photographer, as my best man. His wife, Lynn, was BJ's only bridesmaid. My former boss at AP, Hal Buell, gave the bride away. We had a traditional military sword arch comprised of my Quantico classmates. For many it was the first, and probably only, time they would carry a sword in the Marine Corps. We saved money on a military wedding. The chaplain's services were free but I spent $10 for the sheet music of the "Hawaiian Wedding Song", money well spent. A fellow lieutenant lent us his apartment at Quantico, where I carried my bride over the threshold while Bob, my photographer as well as best man, recorded the moment. Other lieutenants had the same idea. Weddings at the Quantico chapel on November 30, 1968, were held every 15 minutes.

My most dangerous moment during my Quantico months came off base and off duty. The night before our wedding, I was driving down to Quantico from Washington, D.C., where Sam Angeloff, a writer at *LIFE* magazine and an old UW friend, hosted a dinner party for us. After leaving the party, my little Fiat 850 Spyder was hit broadside by two youths in a stolen car fleeing police. My head went through the window on the driver's side, and BJ was banged up but nothing broken. While a doctor sewed up a cut on my scalp, a nurse cleaned the blood off my dress blue Marine uniform. Thankfully, I was not wearing whites, a summer uniform. It would have been ruined by the blood. Bob Peterson picked us up at the hospital and put us in a hotel room. Six hours later we were married. A few days later we limped across the country in my battered Fiat with a new gas tank and windshield. That was our honeymoon.

CHAPTER 4

Hard Times in a Hard War

I served as an infantry officer in the Marine Corps in Vietnam in 1969. I began as the platoon commander of the 2nd Platoon, Company H (Hotel), 2nd Battalion, 5th Marine Regiment (5th Marines), usually referred to as Hotel 2/5 (Hotel two five). After six weeks I became the company executive officer (XO). I served on the "line" for seven months before finishing my 13-month tour as a Civil Affairs Officer (G-5) at the Headquarters of the 1st Marine Division near Da Nang. I then extended my tour for six months, half of which was spent as the MACV (Military Assistance Command Vietnam) liaison officer in Bangkok.

In my memoir, I wrote about the highlights of my Vietnam and Thailand tours. Here are some of the "lowlights" about which I have never written and rarely discussed. Some I am still trying to forget.

Most of my bush time was spent in and around the An Hoa Combat Base about twenty miles west of Da Nang, where the 5th Marines was based and supported by the 2nd Battalion of the 11th Marines, magnificent artillerymen. In a sweep between An Hoa and a strongpoint at Phu Loc 6, a village located at Liberty Bridge on the Son Thu Bon River on the road to Da Nang, we made contact with the enemy, the North Vietnamese Army (NVA) troops and their southern communist allies, the Viet Cong (VC). They were well entrenched around An Hoa, especially in the so-called Arizona Territory, a much-fought-over piece of terrain through which NVA infiltrators passed heading for Da Nang. Most died in the attempt.

The contact required close air support from the Marine Corps Air Wing, part of the air-ground team. I saw F-4 Phantom jets streak in low and drop bombs and napalm in support of the grunts on the ground. One day something went wrong. They were not supporting Hotel Company, so I never learned the details, but the bombs fell on Marine positions, not the enemy. This was known as "friendly fire." That day, six Marines died. It made me think twice before calling for close air support after that, but that was the only time I ever saw Marines killed by Marines.

I joined the 2nd Platoon in early February, replacing a lieutenant who had been medevacked for malaria. I only learned many years later that he was replaced for poor performance in the field. The platoon was blessed with a very experienced and totally squared-away Staff Sergeant Dunbar, whose bush name was "Robin." I became "Kiwi," a flightless bird.

Robin had been in the Marine Corps a long time. He once told me he was a private first class (PFC) for years, and while stationed in Hawaii was finally told he would be promoted to lance corporal on the Monday morning. We went into Honolulu to celebrate, missed the last bus back to Kaneohe Bay on Sunday evening, and missed formation on Monday morning. He was called in to see his captain tear up his promotion certificate. That was the old Corps. The Vietnam War brought several promotions, all deserved. Robin always carried 50 blasting caps with him in the mountains in case we needed to blow trees to get a medevac chopper in. We got along fine.

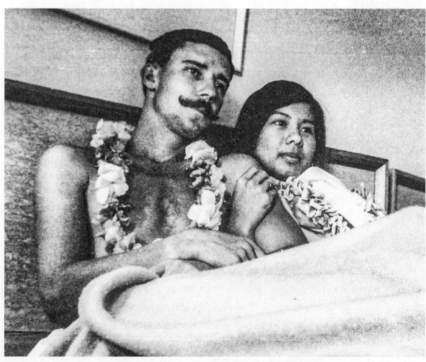

Barry and BJ on R&R in Honolulu, 1969.

The normal complement of a Marine infantry platoon is 46 men. My platoon had 25 men, including machine guns attached and one Navy corpsman. All corpsmen were called "Doc" and invariably set aside from other "squids," and universally respected and appreciated. Corpsmen were often targets of enemy snipers and many were killed in action going to the assistance of wounded Marines. The missing 25th man was in the brig in Da Nang charged with murdering a Viet Cong sniper during the Tet Offensive in Hue City in 1968, where the battalion took heavy casualties. The story of Hotel 2/5 in Hue was told in Stanley Kubrick's film *Full Metal Jacket*. The accused Marine was never convicted; there were no witnesses in country.

On my third day with H 2/5, we left the safety of An Hoa and went to the bush. We were part of Operation *Taylor Common*, a large operation aimed at halting NVA infiltrators from Laos where they left the Ho Chi Minh Trail to attack Da Nang, and especially the Da Nang Air Base, the most active airfield in the world in 1969. They never took it, thanks to the Marine Corps. The 5th Marines were the tip of the spear and the closest regiment to Laos.

We were airlifted into the mountains along the Vietnam–Laos border in CH-46 Sea Knight helicopters from An Hoa. Other Marines rappelled in before us and blew down trees on a hilltop that allowed our choppers to hover over the downed trees. We jumped out loaded with gear, extra food, water, and ammunition. I was in the war. We established a defensive perimeter around the hilltop as a mini bulldozer was carried in, suspended from a chopper, and in short order cleared off the hilltop, allowing 105mm artillery from the 2nd Battalion of the 11th Marines to set up a fire base from which we operated.

On my first patrol we were ambushed.

Two NVA trail watchers opened fire on the 2nd Platoon as we quietly crept down a well-worn jungle trail in search of the enemy. As we moved north, we kept in contact with the company through my excellent radio man, Lance Corporal Anthony "Tony" Cordisco. As soon as we were fired on, the lead squad returned fire. I heard the cry, "Kiwi up!" and had my baptism of fire. Most of the danger around me was from a panicked Marine firing his M-79 grenade launcher randomly. My first order was for him to cease fire. Then I moved forward to learn that we had one casualty, an African American Marine with a bullet in one arm and another which had gone into his belt buckle without breaking skin, so he had some good luck to go along with the bad luck of being hit.

We needed to medevac him quickly and called for a chopper. There was no place to land so we asked that a jungle penetrator be dropped through the triple canopy. This was dangerous, as the CH-46 helicopter was a sitting

Marine CH46 helicopter with external load, An Hoa, Vietnam, 1969.

duck for any enemy rifleman, or machine gunner, nearby as the bird hovered while winching up our wounded Marine. As we loaded the Marine into the penetrator's pod, he handed me his Zippo lighter: "I won't be needing this for a while, Kiwi. You need it worse than I do." I thanked him and the chopper began winching him up.

It was the ride of his life. The oscillation of the Marine inside the penetrator pod caused him to hit trees as he moved slowly upward. Seeing this, the pilot swiftly lifted the helicopter higher to move the pod out of the trees and the helicopter out of small-arms range. We watched in sympathy for our wounded comrade as he dangled a thousand feet above the jungle and finally into the rescue chopper. He survived the ordeal but we never saw him again.

We were in the mountains for about a month. We didn't see many NVA, who probably sought sanctuary in Laos nearby, a country they had invaded and a country that our political leaders declared off limits to U.S. military forces. But that's another story. It was surprisingly cold in the mountains at night in February, but the Marine Corps provided us with wool shirts which helped a lot.

The lack of combat didn't mean we were safe in our arboreal sojourn. The Annamite Cordillera, as the mountains were known, was notorious for malaria. We took tablets that prevented two strains of the fatal disease. Less deadly but

Wounded Marine being evacuated by air, Quang Nam province, South Vietnam, 1969.

probably more feared were leeches. These nasty little critters would drop on us from trees or jump from the ground and suck blood until they became engorged and dropped off. Removing leeches was relatively easy if they could be seen. Bug juice, mainly used to discourage mosquitos, was effective against leeches, but even better was the application of a burning cigarette. Leeches loved to enter human orifices and stay there. To counter this, we called on the Marines' friend, the condom. Many Marines found an alternate use for the "French letter," as the British called them, or the "*Capote Anglaise*" (English overcoat) to the French.

There were a few tigers in the mountains, but we didn't see any. We did see barking deer and plenty of wild pigs, but never killed any. For a month, no one bathed and no one ate hot chow. We kept in shape by walking up and down steep jungle trails, usually carrying heavy packs. Hotel Company was the last unit to be withdrawn after the artillery guns and gunners were safely lifted off. The intense heat caused by burning wooden artillery crates prevented all of the company getting off together. The 2nd Platoon was detailed to remain on the abandoned fire base until a chopper could be sent to get us in the morning.

It was a tense night as we formed a tight 360-degree perimeter and waited for an attack by the NVA that never came. No one slept, kept alert by wild boars that rummaged through old garbage pits seeking Marine Corps C-rations, which they seemed to relish more than the grunts did. At first light, a big CH-53 arrived to lift us off and return us to the hot rice paddies and booby traps. Twenty minutes later, we were back "home" in An Hoa.

A few weeks later, the company ran into a "buzz saw," a sharp fire fight with the North Vietnamese Army, in the Arizona Territory on a sweep. The NVA were waiting in fighting holes and ready for a fight. They occupied a pro-VC hamlet where every house had a bunker. Some contained NVA and VC;

others contained civilians. We could not call in artillery or close air support. We cleared the bunkers one at a time, taking casualties doing it.

The best weapon against bunkers, in my opinion, was the CS gas grenade. It was actually a non-lethal micro pulverized powder that was much stronger than tear gas, CN. No one without a gas mask could remain in a bunker when a CS grenade was thrown in.

In the course of a hot day's work, one bunker was fragged by Marines after cries in Vietnamese to come out went unheeded. There were no armed enemy in the bunker; only an old lady, dead, and a badly wounded child. The corpsman said the little guy was in bad shape. We took him into the command post and circled the wagons, expecting an assault in the dark. I sat up with the doc, who administered morphine to the boy. The boy died at dawn and the skipper, Captain William Fite, ordered the lieutenant whose platoon had fragged the bunker to return the body to his family.

The lieutenant asked that another platoon return the body. Fite was firm: "You killed him, you take him home." Our Kit Carson Scout (KCS) went with the platoon to express our regret. He was a former VC who rallied and worked with a Marine program to help locate booby traps and weapons caches and debrief prisoners. Most of our casualties were caused by booby traps set by VC sympathizers. Little kids would ask for food or cigarettes as we passed through their villages, and might help their dad plant booby traps at night. It was that kind of war.

In the spring of 1969, the company was assigned to defend Liberty Bridge on the main road linking An Hoa with Da Nang. It was good duty, mainly defending a well-fortified piece of high ground known as "The Alamo." Patrols would sweep the countryside during the day while swim parties would bathe in the river under the protective guns on the hill. At night, small charges of C4 explosives were dropped from the bridge to explode in the river and dissuade enemy swimmers from trying to blow the bridge.

The enemy, known widely as "Charlie" by Marines or sometimes "Mr. Charles" by respectful African American Marines, was a cunning foe and attempts to blow the bridge had been tried, always unsuccessfully. One night, a Marine whose bush name was "Mouse," a riff on his real name, Fouse, prepared to drop a quarter-pound charge of C4 into the river. He lit the fuse but did not see it burn, and the charge went off in his hand. He was blinded and both hands were blown off.

We immediately called in a chopper, and in minutes Mouse, a popular Marine, was an emergency medevac. Within minutes he arrived at the Navy hospital at China Beach in Da Nang. An hour later we received a radio message: Mouse's dog tags were blown off in the explosion and in the rush to get him in the chopper he was sent without identification. I was dispatched in the company jeep at first light to identify Mouse, who survived the blast and was in intensive care.

I checked in at the hospital and was told that the unidentified man was in a stable condition in intensive care and that I needed to wait before I could see him. I sat down opposite the ICU ward to wait. A few minutes passed and two wounded men, one American and one Vietnamese on gurneys, were wheeled down the corridor to wait for treatment in an operating room. Both were awake, naked, catheterized, and bandaged. They were parked near me and the American asked in a tired voice: "Could I trouble you for a cigarette, lieutenant?"

"Of course. Are you a Marine?" I asked, feeling for a four-pack of cigarettes from my morning C-Ration meal. I lit it and put the cigarette in the Marine's mouth.

"Who are you with?" I asked. "What happened to you?"

"I'm a lance corporal with 3/26," he said. "We got in a firefight with Charlie and that guy was wounded by the same Chicom grenade that hit me."

"Is he an NVA?" I asked.

"Sure is, the only one left alive. He gave me my Purple Heart and hopefully my ticket home."

Just then, a group of Vietnamese women approached them. They were the local char force, and seeing the handcuff that the Vietnamese man wore probably led them to conclude he was the enemy. They started talking to the very embarrassed young man. One woman started tugging on his catheter, which made him moan in pain.

"Lieutenant," the Marine said, "can you shoo them away? I don't like the way they are treating him."

I was taken aback. I was surprised that the NVA was alive and being treated. But I was more surprised that the man he had wounded was now trying to help him. I walked over to the women. I was wearing a flak jacket and a shoulder holster with my Colt .45 pistol in it. I put my hand on the weapon but did not draw it.

"*Dee dee mau len!*" I said in a menacing voice (Get out of here). They drew back. A Navy lieutenant walked up and asked what was going on. I explained why I asked the women to leave the prisoner alone.

"You need to understand," he said, "they are all widows of ARVN killed in action. They would probably kill the POW if we gave them a chance. Thanks for stepping in."

At that point the door to the ICU opened and a Navy nurse ushered me in.

I stepped into a dark, air-conditioned room filled with maimed men, some near death. Everyone spoke in low voices. It looked like a well-appointed American hospital; we were lucky to have such a superb facility so close to the action. Helicopters were coming and going from chopper pads outside. It was a room I never wanted to see again, especially as a customer.

The nurse took me to the bed where a man with his head totally wrapped in bandages was sleeping under sedation. Both arms were similarly bandaged. Both hands were missing.

"His hands were blown off," the nurse said. "We removed his eyes. His nose can be replaced. He is deaf but we think that is temporary. He was brought in around midnight. Can you tell me what happened?"

This was Mouse. No doubt about it. I explained what had happened and the nurse took notes.

"He will be medevacked stateside when he is stabilized. You guys might want to think again about dropping explosives in the river."

She was right. Changes were made. But that didn't help Mouse.

Just before I was transferred to G-5 in the summer of 1969, the company was on an operation in the Que Son Mountains south of An Hoa. An incident occurred that almost resulted in the court martial of an officer. As it was explained to me, the man walking "point" detected a strong odor. He stopped and walked to a nearby stream, where he found a badly wounded NVA soldier in a hammock strung across the stream with a tin cup so he could drink from the stream. A corpsman was called up. The wounded man was near death and was crawling with maggots. He was suffering from serious wounds and there was no telling how many days he had been there with no medical attention or food.

The first thought was to get a medevac chopper in. It would be difficult, as there was no plausible landing zone anywhere close and the NVA were in the area. It would be dangerous for a chopper to come near. The issue was moot, as no chopper would be put at risk for a wounded prisoner.

A shot was heard and the company moved on.

Days later, I was informed of the incident. There was a policy in the 1st Marine Division that if a Marine took a prisoner he was given a three-day in-country R&R at China Beach. The idea was to encourage Marines to take prisoners, who were always in demand for current intelligence on enemy units and their intentions. Only in this case there was no prisoner, and the point man made a formal complaint that his prisoner had been killed.

The notorious case of the My Lai massacre was fresh in the minds of Marines, and especially the Marine brass. In 1968, a platoon under army Lieutenant William Calley Jr. was found guilty of the murder of 22 Vietnamese civilians. He was an infantry officer in the 23rd Infantry Division in Quang Ngai Province, south of Da Nang. Initially, Calley was sentenced to life in prison, but he served only three years before being pardoned by President Nixon. The Marine Corps may have been influenced by the Army's initial attempt to cover up the massacre and decided to charge the Hotel Company officer with murder.

Memorial service for fallen Marines from Hotel 2/5, An Hoa Combat Base, South Vietnam, 1969.

But there were no witnesses and no body. It would have been difficult to prove a killing took place at all. Furthermore, one of the Hotel Company men made contact with the renowned defense attorney F. Lee Bailey, who expressed interest in taking the case. Perhaps as a result, the Marine Corps decided not to proceed with a court martial and the officer was returned to duty.

During my time on the line, I wrote condolence letters to the families of 34 fallen Marines from Hotel Company, usually in the name of the company commander at the time as the officers were engaged in combat operations. I knew some of the men personally and their loss is never far from my mind. Early on in my tour, I noticed that my commanding officers were not interested in being too friendly. This was completely correct. Distance had to be maintained. At any moment they might have to give me an order that would result in my death or the deaths of other Marines. Those orders needed to be obeyed. Sentimentality has no place in combat.

CHAPTER 5

Combined Action Marines

One of the unsung stories of the Vietnam War is that of the Combined Action Platoon (CAP) program. Born of battlefield necessity by the Marine Corps, it was one of the most effective and least costly initiatives to come out of that unhappy war. The CAP program was the brainchild of a Marine battalion commander in 1965. It was a way to improve security in villages in the area of tactical responsibility not far from Hue, a former royal capital of central Vietnam. The concept was to combine a 13-man rifle squad of Marines (including a Navy corpsman) with a platoon of Vietnamese village defense militia, the Popular Forces (PF). These were villagers too young (or too old) to be drafted into the South Vietnamese Army (ARVN). They were poorly armed and poorly trained, and as a result were marginally effective. That changed when they teamed up with the Marines.

While I never served as a CAP Marine, I did work with them when I was a G-5 Civil Affairs officer in 1969 with the 1st Marine Division. Before that, when still in the "bush," I was on one operation with PFs when I was the XO of Company H, 5th Marine Regiment, on an operation in the Que Son Mountains southwest of Da Nang. Hotel Company helped defend a hilltop manned by a platoon of PFs under the command of an old sergeant who had served in the colonial French army a generation before. I spoke with him in French. Together, we gave the NVA a nasty surprise when they attacked our position and I came away with greater respect for the PFs and the impression that when properly led and armed they could fight.

Early combined action efforts worked well when Lieutenant Colonel William Taylor, commanding officer of the 3rd Battalion of the 4th Marine Regiment, assigned Marines to work with PFs in six villages around the airfield at Phu Bai, not far from Hue in central Vietnam. The idea gained traction when it came to the attention of Major General Lew Walt, a veteran of the

Marine Combined Action Platoon sergeant with Popular Force South Vietnamese militia near Da Nang, 1969.

"Banana Wars" in the Caribbean where Marines worked effectively with security forces at the lowest levels in Nicaragua, Haiti, and the Dominican Republic. That experience in working closely with local populations was unique to the Marine Corps. General Walt immediately saw the value in putting combat Marines together with PFs and the program grew in size, mission, and success.

After seven months in the 5th Marines, I was assigned to G-5, Civil Affairs at 1st Marine Division HQ near Da Nang. Among my duties, I was named the division Personal Response Officer. My mission was to get Marines to get along with our South Vietnamese allies, and especially the civilians in areas where Marines were operating. It was not an easy job. The primary mission of Marines was to find, fix, and kill NVA and their VC allies. Most of our casualties came from booby traps, often placed by civilians sympathetic to the VC or forced to help them. This bred distrust and dislike of the civilians by Marines. At that time, the division was losing one Marine leg a day to booby traps. The kid you gave chow to this morning might be setting booby traps tonight.

The CAP program put Marines in direct support of villagers and I worked to support them as part of my G-5 duties. CAP Marines were an inspiration to me and helped focus my efforts to change Marine attitudes. I wish that the CAP program had been larger, and had put more Marines in contact with Vietnamese to improve their security while building the mutual trust that is critical for success.

I visited CAP villages near Da Nang near Highway One, Vietnam's main north–south highway. At the wheel of my jeep was Sergeant Ray Bennett, an outstanding Marine. In mid-1969, the area was pretty much secure from large enemy units. We saw Marines instructing their young Vietnamese buddies how to care for and operate their small-arms weapons. Each CAP had a Navy corpsman, always known as "Doc," who ran med caps for civilian Vietnamese from their village, often the only medical professional in the area.

I was particularly taken with the performance of the Marine sergeant in charge of the platoon. With only a rudimentary grasp of the Vietnamese language and aided by an interpreter, I was happy to provide the unit with copies of a Vietnamese–English handbook dictionary I produced as one of my G-5 duties. The young man was mature beyond his years and was impressive in his understanding and respect for Vietnamese culture and ways. He worked very closely with the village elders and was meticulous in weapons training and in leading his team.

The corpsman was clearly one of the favorites of the villagers. He was the "doc" not only to the Marines and Popular Forces, but all the village kids lined up for medical attention. There was a palpable sense of mutual respect and affection. The young NCO observed his men closely, relaxed with kids around him, but was all business when it came to planning patrols. I wish I knew his name.

CAP Marines were not always lucky enough to work in a pacified and friendly area. A friend of mine, former Corporal Cottrell "Cot" Fox, was a CAP Marine not far from Hue City in early 1968. His unit, CAP Hotel 8, came under intense attack by a large and heavily armed NVA unit making their way to Hue, the former imperial capital of Vietnam at the onset of the Tet offensive of 1968. Cot's small unit was in deep shit from minute one. He wrote in a letter home from a hospital bed in Cam Ranh Bay on February 3:

> Briefly, 400 NVA attacked us at 400 AM from all sides—maybe 100 penetrated the compound—mostly sappers ... we had to fall back to the center of the compound around the radio bunker ... Finally, we called the deadliest anti-personnel artillery of all on ourselves ... Plus 50 rounds of 155mm high explosives around the compound itself.

The Marines and PFs fought off the NVA while guarding a key bridge. Cot continued:

> My rifle was so hot that I had to take off my shirt and hold the fore stock with it ... We kept praying for dawn to break—and it seemed to take forever ... I found 25 bodies that we had killed. I knew there were beaucoup dead—everywhere you shot you hit them ... When dawn broke we had 2 dead Marines and 3 dead PFs.

The Marine Corps summary of the action of Hotel 8 on the night of January 31, 1968, has less emotion. It reads, in part:

> A multi company of NVA/VC opened the assault with a simultaneous mortar and sapper attack ... that quickly penetrated the perimeter and led to the hand to hand, life and death struggle of several hours described in this recommendation of award for Corporal Cottrell Fox and Corporal Charles Brown ... More than 40 enemy bodies were found in and around the compound which was badly damaged and subsequently abandoned.

Years later, Cot Fox, a retired business executive in St. Louis, received the Silver Star Medal for his actions which saw him badly wounded. His buddy, Corporal Charles Brown, received the Navy Cross.

Cot informed me that his CAP platoon was saved by the timely intervention of Hotel Company, 2nd Battalion, 5th Marines, the unit I served with a year later. He has abiding affection for Hotel 2/5.

As Brigadier General Gary Brown, a skipper of mine in early 1969, put it, "If the CAP concept had been implemented and fully supported early in the war, the outcome could have been much more positive than the April 1975 TV debacle." I agree.

More than five thousand Marines participated in the Combined Action program. More than five hundred of them were killed in action. It was an innovative and successful program, but it came at a price. The lessons of the program should be remembered; and the men who paid that price.

CHAPTER 6

My Buddy Ralph

Ralph Bertelson was born to be a combat Marine. But a peacetime Marine, not so much.

Ralph and I were classmates in the Marine Corps' The Basic School Class 1-69 which graduated at Quantico, Virginia, in late November 1968. A native of Spokane, Washington, Ralph was a hunter and hellraiser in his younger years. His idea of fun was starting, or ending, bar fights. He was big, boisterous, and for reasons I never fully understood, liked hanging out with me. And I with him. He was the kind of guy you want to have on your flank in the attack. He would never let you down.

Barry, left, with Marine 2nd Lieutenant Ralph Bertelson at An Hoa Combat Base, 1969.

Ralph was in our sword arch at the Quantico Marine Base chapel where BJ and I were married on November 30, 1968. We were both officers of infantry and to no one's surprise were ordered to Vietnam. Our trip across the Pacific was delayed by 30 days to undergo prewar training at Camp Pendleton for conditioning and visits to the mock Vietnamese village that was full of surprises, most of them lethal.

While at Pendleton, we were each put in command of 164 enlisted Marines of every military occupational specialty (MOS), from rifleman to aviation technician. Our only shared item was orders to the Fleet Marine Force, Pacific, and the aircraft headed there carried 165 passengers. The focus at Camp Pendleton was to get everyone in shape to survive a combat tour in the tropics.

The days were long, with conditioning hikes through the rolling hills of Camp Pendleton, located between Los Angeles and San Diego with 21 miles of pristine oceanfront. But we had weekends off. On one of the free weekends, Ralph and I decided to visit nearby Tijuana, Mexico. I had good Spanish in those days and some experience in Mexico.

Marines were discouraged from crossing the border; danger and naughty women were reported to be found there. One of Ralph's men was found in Tijuana, naked and crawling towards the border early on a Sunday morning. His only possession was a handful of Polaroid photos of one of the naughty women, nude, which he refused to relinquish. The Mexican authorities turned him over to the U.S. Navy Shore Patrol at the border, who, in turn, returned him to the welcoming arms of the Marine Corps at Camp Pendleton. There was not much they could do with him. They had already shaved his head and he was already under orders to Vietnam. I don't know what legal issues faced him, but do know he didn't miss his flight.

Before Ralph and I crossed the border, we got our stories straight: we were college kids from southern Cal, although our high and tight haircuts suggested otherwise. I advised putting our cash in our socks, leaving credit cards at home, and putting $20 in cash in our pockets. Tijuana is an unappealing city at any time, but had a lot to offer visitors from north of the border. We arrived in time for lunch at the famous Caesar's Hotel, where the Caesar salad was invented. It tasted fine, but not as good as BJ made.

We walked around the old town, bought a bottle of rum that we sipped from a brown paper bag, and saw the sights. We kept the drinking down, knowing that we would have to drive back up to Camp Pendleton, and the Corps frowns on DUI (driving under the influence) arrests. We enjoyed some excellent street food for dinner, hoping that Montezuma's Revenge would miss us. A Mexican policeman stopped us and informed us that drinking in public was illegal. His English was better than my Spanish, and I suspected he had done this before.

Taking charge, I politely informed the officer, grossly overweight but not unkind, that we were college students and asked if it would be possible to pay the fine to him directly. He nodded.

"How much is the fine?" I enquired.

"How much you have?" he responded.

"$40," I answered, referring to the cash in our pockets.

"The fine is $30," he informed us, and we fished the money out of our pockets and paid the officer. In return, he gave us back our unfinished bottle of rum and wished us well in our studies. The rest of the evening was uneventful. We made it an early night.

For my last weekend before flying to Vietnam, BJ flew down from Seattle for a planned quiet, subdued farewell at the Coronado Hotel in San Diego.

Ralph had other ideas. He was married, but not for long, and his wife stayed at home in Spokane. Ralph decided to drive up to Los Angeles, in uniform, with a gunnery sergeant who was in Ralph's temporary command. Those were the days when many Americans were against the war in Vietnam and anyone in the military; hence the order to stay out of uniform. But Ralph was proud of the Corps and of his uniform. The "gunny" had been to Vietnam before, and Korea before that. He was decorated and tough, as was the second lieutenant with him.

Ralph told the story when I saw him on Sunday evening. He and the gunny found a quiet blue-collar bar somewhere in LA and started to drink. Ralph wasn't looking for a bar fight. He had plenty of fighting coming soon. No one said or did anything offensive, and the two Marines focused on having a good time and talking about what was in store for them "in country," as Vietnam was known.

A middle-aged, heavy-set, African American then entered the bar and sat down next to Ralph. He ordered a drink, noticing Ralph's summer service Marine uniform with one service ribbon (National Defense Medal) and his shooting badges for rifle and pistol. Ralph fired expert for both.

"You fellows been in 'Nam?" the black gentleman asked Ralph.

"Going on Monday," Ralph responded.

"I tried to join the Corps in '44 but they wouldn't take me."

"Sorry to hear it," said Ralph. "Plenty of blacks in the Corps now. Not too late to enlist."

The black man laughed and said: "If the Viet Cong didn't kill me, my wife and daughter would." Then he put a crisp $100 bill on the bar. "Let me buy you Jarheads a drink."

Ralph and the gunnery sergeant ordered drinks, as did their host, and they drank to each other's health. They drank in silence and Ralph said: "We've got the next round."

"I don't think so," said the black fellow. "Let's just drink up my hundred dollars. Or you can fight me." Now Ralph loved a fight, but he probably loved to drink more. He also saw that the fellow just wanted to treat a couple of men going in harm's way to a few drinks. So they drank, and when the hundred dollars was spent up, Ralph and the gunny thanked him quietly and drove back to Pendleton. A day later, we went to Vietnam.

But not directly.

We flew to Kadena Air Base on Okinawa, where we staged our civilian gear and picked up camouflage utilities and combat boots. We were there for a couple of days before "heading south." Ralph and I enjoyed our first look at Japan. The food was excellent, along with the beer, and the locals were pleasant if not exactly friendly. Marines had killed a lot of Okinawans in 1945 and lost a lot of men themselves in the last big battle of the war in the Pacific. I picked up a used Nikonos underwater camera for $60 in a pawn shop. It served me well in the bush.

I was billeted in a room with another officer, whom I didn't meet when I checked in. I saw his gear on one bed and didn't meet him until about three in the morning the next day. I was sound asleep and he woke me up when he collapsed on the floor, severely drunk.

"You goin' north [home] or south [Vietnam]?" he asked.

"South."

"You poor motherfucker. I'm going north. You can have Vietnam; I hope I never see it again."

He was a chopper pilot and obviously happy to be heading home in one piece. I hoped I would do the same one day.

Not all my classmates were grunts. Some of the best and brightest went into the Air Wing, where they flew choppers or fighters, saving the lives of many of us on the ground by flying us out wounded or flying close air support against the enemy. One of these was African American Charlie Bolden, a graduate of the U.S. Naval Academy who flew more than a hundred missions all over Indochina as an A-6 "Intruder" pilot. Charlie retired as a major general after becoming an astronaut. He later served as the head of NASA.

Ralph and I made it to Da Nang without incident and went our separate ways. I was sent to the 5th Marine Regiment at An Hoa, engaged in action daily with North Vietnamese Army regulars infiltrating from "neutral" Laos. Ralph went to the 26th Marine Regiment further north. He was the only one of my TBS classmates that I saw in Vietnam.

One day in the spring of 1969, I was pleasantly surprised to see Ralph on crutches making his way to the company office of Hotel 2/5 at An Hoa Combat Base, where I was the XO. Ralph's right leg was in a cast. He had been hit by inaptly named "friendly fire" from a short U.S. Marine artillery round and was temporarily out of action. Technically UA (unauthorized absence, Marine talk for being absent without leave, AWOL), he left the air conditioning, soft beds, and safety of the China Beach Navy Hospital in Da Nang and somehow hopped a chopper ride to An Hoa, where there was no air conditioning, men slept on cots—an improvement over soggy rice paddies—and "incoming" enemy rockets were a nightly annoyance.

He stayed with me a couple of days and regaled me with stories from his time with the 26th Marines. His personal "body count" was 12 NVA killed by the time he was hit. One story he told was about an ambush that his rifle platoon laid near a well the NVA were suspected of using. Just before dawn, three NVA in uniform, with rifles and carrying a bunch of canteens, quietly moved to the well. The squad leader wanted to open fire, but Ralph told him to wait.

"I will be the first to fire," Ralph told the squad leader. "When I fire, open up."

"OK Lieutenant."

Ralph waited until one NVA leaned over the well to fill a canteen. "Then I fired," he told me, "at a range of about one hundred and fifty meters in a prone position. The NVA dropped into the well as the squad opened fire and killed the other two North Vietnamese. We recovered three rifles and maybe twenty canteens. A good morning's work."

Ralph was medevacked to the United States for further surgery soon after he visited me in An Hoa. He later wrote that he was in the Navy hospital in Bremerton, Washington, not far from Seattle. I wrote to BJ asking her to check on Ralph. When she called the hospital, they discovered that he had gone UA. It was not the first time, nor the last.

When Ralph's time with the Corps was up, he joined the Spokane Fire Department and rose to the rank of captain. We kept in touch, and when I was posted to the Pacific Northwest for three years we saw him a lot. He had a vacation house on the Priest River east of Spokane, where he taught our sons, Seth and Brendan, to shoot, ride dirt bikes, drive cars, and steer cigarette boats on a nearby lake.

Ralph stayed in the Marine reserves at a unit based in Spokane. One day he took a bunch of reserve men to his riverside cabin in the woods for some practice with a .50 caliber machine gun from the reserve unit. This led to a house call from the local sheriff.

"Jesus Christ, Ralph, if you're going to fire automatic weapons out here, call me first. I'm getting calls about right-wing crazies on the warpath," the sheriff told Ralph, a drinking buddy.

"My bad, Sheriff. It won't happen again." And it didn't.

Ralph passed away a few years back and I miss him.

CHAPTER 7

Air Wing Invitation

The Air-Ground Team is a time-honored mantra of the Marine Corps. The Corps has its own air force, specially trained to support troops on the ground. It is the Air Wing and I have seen it in action. Marines flying helicopters carried men into battle and ferried wounded Marines to medical care, saving lives in the process. Other Marines flying F4 "Phantom" jets flew close air support, dropping bombs and napalm on the enemy nearby.

I once cowered in a bomb crater as an F-4 dropped 250lb "snake-eye" bombs on top of NVA dug in less than one hundred meters away in a tree line. A piece of shrapnel from a bomb landed on the pack of a corpsman next to me. Fortunately, the corpsman was not wearing the pack. Unfortunately, the pack contained whole blood for transfusions. Soon, the bottom of the bomb crater was covered in blood. That is about as close as I would like to see close air support get.

The mystique of the Air-Ground Team may have come from the fact that all Marine lieutenants attend The Basic School at the Quantico, Virginia, base regardless of their final military occupational specialty. All Marine officers are infantry officers first. Theoretically, a Marine pilot can bail out over a battlefield and take over a Marine platoon on the ground that is lacking an officer. I have never heard of it happening and doubt many "Airedales," as Marine aviators are affectionately known, would want to be put in that situation; but if they were, they would know what to do.

It is rare that the infantry comes to the rescue of the Air Wing, but I witnessed such an event in the spring of 1969. Hotel Company, 2nd Battalion of the 5th Marines was on a sweep operation in the always-dangerous Arizona Territory of western Quang Nam province west of Da Nang. We were spread out, moving carefully through heavily mined terrain, when out of the blue, literally, a Marine chopper gunship set down in the middle of our formation. We quickly established a security perimeter as the pilot got out.

"Am I glad to see you guys," he said. "I am having a little mechanical problem and hope I can fix it myself without having to call for help from Da Nang." I introduced myself and said we would be happy to provide security while he was on the ground. The lieutenant was jovial, and rightly so. It would not go well for him if the NVA or their Viet Cong brethren got to him. We ensured that they did not.

The pilot pulled out a small camera and asked me to photograph him in front of his bird, flanked by two Marines with full fighting gear, including flak jackets and M-16 rifles. "The guys are not going to believe this," he explained with a grin. Then he went to work on his chopper and a few minutes later said he thought he could make it back to Da Nang; 10 minutes by air, but a long and perilous walk. He took off, headed east, and we resumed our patrol, heading west.

Not long after the incident, I was convoked along with other sector commanders of the An Hoa Combat Base, headquarters of the 5th Marines, to a meeting at regiment. As the XO of H Company, most of my duties were in An Hoa. A dozen or more officers were at the meeting, which was chaired by a major I didn't know. "Gentlemen," he said, "there seems to be a problem with the Air Wing. We are getting reports complaining that our rifle companies are calling in med-evacs too close to the enemy and choppers are taking fire. And that isn't all. They say we are calling some missions 'emergencies' only to find out that the wounded weren't hurt that bad." This wasn't exactly news; I had heard of similar complaints before, but never from Hotel Company.

"Why are you telling us this?" asked a captain.

"Because the Air Wing wants to invite some grunts from the 5th Marines to visit them in Da Nang as their guests to sit down informally and air their grievances. It sounds like they invited you to an in-country R&R to discuss their issues over ice cold beer in their air-conditioned officers club. Do I have any volunteers?" All hands were raised.

We were infantry officers on "bush" tours, meaning we were on the front lines in a war that didn't really have front lines. Where the 5th Marines operated, the enemy was all around us. Marines were on 13-month tours in Vietnam, and infantry officers usually had "split" tours, meaning that half their time was spent in the bush and half in the rear on staff positions. That way everyone had a chance to get killed.

It was worse for the enlisted men. No split tours for them. They had 13 months to look forward to (12 months for U.S. Army enlisted men). All of it on the line. There was a policy that if a Marine was wounded three times, his tour would be curtailed and he would be sent out of country. There was an informal policy in play calling for men with two Purple Hearts, the oldest American military decoration, to be moved out of the bush to a job in the rear, such as a mail clerk or driver. Anything to get them out of the bush and keep them in-country.

Many H Company men in An Hoa had two "hearts." We had one E-5 sergeant, 20 years old, who had three "hearts" from his first tour in Vietnam and two on his current tour. Five times wounded and not old enough to drink. We had him assigned to embarkation school in Okinawa. He was an outstanding Marine, and due to his performance under fire was given a battlefield commission.

The meeting in An Hoa ended with a half-dozen officers being selected to represent the regiment in Da Nang as guests of the Air Wing. I was one of them.

A few days later, we put on our best camouflage utilities, i.e. the cleanest ones, shaved, and caught a convoy to Da Nang. I won't say we spit shined our combat boots, because after a few months walking the mountains and rice paddies of western Quang Nam our boots had taken on the salty look of buckskin and under no circumstances did we want to shine them. We were bush Marines and wanted to look the part.

I waxed my mustache, which extended beyond my mouth and was therefore not in step with Marine regulations. But so were the mustaches of some other officers. We were all following the orders of our regimental commander, Colonel Ord, who wanted officers in Ord's Horde to have non-regulation mustaches. No one ever called me on my 'stash, which identified me to REMFs (rear echelon motherfuckers) as an officer of the 5th Marines, the most highly decorated regiment in the Corps. I was sorry that I was never able to wear the green fourragère, a cord awarded to the regiment by a grateful French Army after the battle of Belleau Wood in France in 1918, where Marines helped blunt a German attack on Paris. I never wore any uniform but cammies in the seven months I was in the regiment. My "pogey rope," as the Marines called it, has never been worn.

The two nights spent with the Air Wing at the Da Nang Air Base were indeed a treat. In "officer country," we were given beds, real beds with sheets and pillows in air-conditioned barracks. In An Hoa, we had cots and poncho liners. Of course, that was better than the troops in the field had it. We often slept on the ground with a helmet for a pillow, an M-16 at hand, and a poncho in case it rained. Some Marines slept with their boots on in case of a night attack and to deny scorpions a hiding place.

The prime attraction at Da Nang was the Air Wing Club. It was air-conditioned, with a variety of food available, and a wide selection of alcoholic beverages on hand served by young Vietnamese ladies in fetching *ao dai* traditional dress of white pants and a turquoise blue tunics. All drinks were 25 cents each, from dry martinis to an array of cold beers. The Air Wing lived in clover and we were their guests. We didn't get a chance to spend our military scrip that passed for money.

As we were being fêted by pilots who succeeded in building rapport with their counterparts on the ground, a pilot at a nearby table gave a shout when he saw me. It was the gunship pilot we had assisted in the Arizona. "Next round's on me," he exclaimed. He wasn't aware that we were already drinking for free, and didn't care. "This is the guy who saved my ass," he asserted, not quite truthfully, but I didn't want to rain on his parade. He had his trusty camera with him and snapped a few photos.

The next day was devoted to serious discussions on the rules of calling in medevacs and the need to keep pilots and crews safe from ground fire. At no time did we object or argue. The Airedales made good points and we agreed to pass the word to the boys in the bush. Thus ended an all-too-brief peek at how the Air Wing lived. I'm sorry we could not return the favor, but An Hoa didn't have a club or air conditioning. What we did have was plenty of casualties. We always appreciated the risks the airmen took in getting them out safely.

CHAPTER 8

Near Death in Da Nang

Part of the combat lore of the Vietnam War for the Marines held that the two most dangerous times in the bush were soon after arriving and just before returning to "the world" after a 13-month tour.

I witnessed the first part while serving as a platoon commander in Company H, 2nd Battalion of the 5th Marine regiment in 1969. When I was moved up to be Hotel Company's XO, second in command of the company, I was replaced by a young second lieutenant fresh from Annapolis. Before he had a chance to get his bearings in combat against an elusive and deadly enemy, he was killed in action. He won the Silver Star for his heroism but he also lost his life.

The second half of the belief was brought home to me vividly late in my tour when I had been shifted to a staff position at 1st Marine Division headquarters near Da Nang after completing seven months "on the line." I was assigned to G-5, Civic Affairs, and I liked the work so much I extended my tour in Vietnam by six months.

One day, an old friend from Marine officer Basic School, First Lieutenant Mike Kudalis, appeared at my office. Mike had served with the 7th Marines south of Da Nang. Now he was going home and wanted to say goodbye. Mike was a "short timer." He had one day and a wake up before heading home. "I'm not short, I'm next. I'm so short I don't have to open doors to walk through them. I'm so short I don't start long conversations." You get the idea. The next day he was getting on "the freedom bird" taking him home.

I was delighted to see Mike, alive and heading home. I had not seen him since Quantico. He was a NESEP, an enlisted Marine selected to attend college paid for by the government and commissioned an officer upon graduation. Mike was one of the best of the best. We both went to the University of Washington and were infantry officers.

My favorite story of Mike's from his enlisted days was inspection of his unit on Okinawa by Lieutenant General Victor Krulak, a hero of World War II and the Korean War. As Mike told the story, the general was inspecting Marines when he abruptly stopped, turned and faced a young Marine. Before the general could say anything, the Marine private spoke.

"Are you a general, sir?" the Marine asked.

Krulak calmly replied: "I am, son. I'm your commanding officer."

Then the private said: "You've got it made, if you don't fuck up."

The general hesitated, as Marines all around him waited for the general to explode; his nickname was "Brute." Krulak simply said, "You got that right, Marine," and continued his inspection.

Mike never told me what happened to the private, but I suspect his gunnery sergeant had a few choice words for him.

I invited Mike to a farewell dinner in Da Nang, the largest city between Hanoi in the north and Saigon (now Ho Chi Minh City to some). Da Nang was important to the U.S. military and a prime target of the North Vietnamese. It was a major port and was bustling with U.S. Navy personnel. The U.S. Air Force ran the airport, the busiest airfield in the world in 1969. The Navy operated a large and modern hospital near China Beach. The Army had an airfield for helicopters near Marble Mountain. But there were few Marines because Da Nang was off limits to Marines. The Marines' mission was to keep the North Vietnamese Army out of Da Nang, not to enjoy the city themselves.

Mike appreciated the invitation but pointed out that Da Nang was off limits. Also, he didn't want to stray too far away from division headquarters while waiting for his flight the next day. My close friend and G-5 colleague, First Lieutenant Jim Jones from Buffalo, NY, told Mike not to worry. As G-5 officers, we had "Jesus passes," which authorized us to go anywhere in Quang Nam province, and we could arrange temporary credentials for Mike. Jim knew the city well, thanks in large part to his beautiful Vietnamese girlfriend, Le Thanh, who worked for the Marines and lived in the city. Among my duties at G-5 was running a culture tour of Da Nang to show combat Marines the side of Vietnam they didn't see fighting the North Vietnamese. The tour included the Catholic cathedral, the great Cham museum dating from 1919 and one of the best souvenirs of the French, and the Buddhist temple inside a cave at Marble Mountain. Da Nang also had excellent Vietnamese restaurants, and Mike, despite his 13 months in-country, had never tasted Vietnamese cuisine.

So after a few drinks in our spartan officers' club, where all drinks were 25 cents each, we drove into Da Nang, about five miles away, passing various checkpoints until we arrived at a quiet Vietnamese bar/restaurant that Jonesy

The Bromans with Jim Jones, left, at a dinner party in Phnom Penh, 1974.

knew well. Jim had an IQ of 152 and was fluent in Vietnamese and German. He was an artillery officer, and the first half of his tour was commanding a battery of 4.2-inch mortars. But he was a born civil affairs officer, one of the few Marines that I knew who genuinely like the Vietnamese, and they liked him.

The restaurant was quiet, the only other customers being a table of elderly Vietnamese men, whom Jim greeted in Vietnamese and chatted briefly with them, as was his custom. An attractive young woman with long black hair and wearing a white *ao dai*, the traditional women's garment of a long tunic, which she wore over her pants, asked what we wanted to drink. We ordered bottles of ice-cold 333 Beer, a relic of the French colonial past.

Mike regaled us with some war stories of his time with the 7th Marines and Jim ordered four or five dishes of high-quality Vietnamese fare, starting with spring rolls and Vietnamese sausage, *nem*. We were having a great time. Mike loved the food, vastly superior to the C-rations that he was used to.

Then, suddenly, the mood of the room changed. In walked a young ARVN sergeant in his camouflage uniform and red beret. He was drunk and he was not a happy drunk. He spotted us and made a comment in Vietnamese. Jonesy understood what was said; it was an insult aimed at us. Normally a man of good will, especially around Vietnamese, Jonesy was now upset. He could not let it pass. He spoke to the man calmly in Vietnamese, informing him that we were allied officers and he was out of line.

This did not have the desired effect. I had never seen an ARVN serviceman so rude and put it down to his inebriation. It got worse. The sergeant drew a gun and pointed it at us. Jim and I were both armed, but he had the drop on us. My first thought was of Mike. He was a short timer with one more night to go in his tour. He had left the safety and moderately good food of the officers' mess at division HQ to foray off limits into a nasty encounter with a gun-waving "ally".

Jonesy was the focus of the ARVN sergeant's attention and tried to calm the man down. One of the old fellows at the nest table quietly got up and left the room. Within a minute he was back, and with him was an ARVN parachute captain. He was clearly the sergeant's superior officer and was equally clearly not happy. While the sergeant railed at Jonesy and waved his .45 pistol around, the captain moved swiftly forward, carrying only a swagger stick—a short cane, an archaic symbol of authority resembling a riding crop. The Marine Corps has done away with them. Parachute officers in the army of South Vietnam apparently had not.

Striking like a serpent, the officer stuck the drunk sergeant's hand, the one carrying the pistol. It dropped to the floor and the possibility of impending death passed. The officer picked up the .45 and said something harsh to the sergeant, who gripped his injured wrist while sobering up fast. The sergeant said something to Jones, apparently an apology, and left.

We all breathed a sigh of relief, including our Vietnamese neighbors at the next table. Jim thanked the one who had gone for help and ordered a round of drinks. That included one for the parachute captain, who was apologetic over the incident. He declined the offer with thanks, saying that he needed to see to the sergeant, and left.

The crisis over, we found solace in more beer. Mike, well aware of the myth of short timers dying in the last hours of their Vietnam tours, suggested we return to the secure confines of the 1st MarDiv Hq, where more drinks were downed to Mike's health and safe trip home. Mike made it home, went to law school and made a rare inter-service transfer to the Coast Guard, from which he retired as a commander.

Jim also survived his tour in Vietnam. He went home, but when his hitch with the Marine Corps was up, he promptly returned to Vietnam as a civilian and married the love of his life, Le Thanh. He worked for years in Saigon, where his fluent Vietnamese language skills were in high demand. I used to visit him regularly when I was posted to Cambodia, and he came over to Phnom Penh for my birthday in 1974.

Jim helped many Vietnamese resettle in the United States after the fall of South Vietnam in 1975. We kept in touch over the years and the Joneses were frequent guests as we traveled around the world at various postings. He passed away in Texas from cancer in 1997.

CHAPTER 9

The Skipper and the Chief

It was a lucky Marine infantry company in Vietnam that had Native Americans with hunting and scouting skills. Hotel Company 2/5 was one such lucky unit.

For openers we had Captain Robert Poolaw, a Kiowa from Anadarko, Oklahoma, as our company commander, or "skipper" in the parlance of Marines. We also had Lance Corporal Cletus "Charlie" Foote, a Hidatsa Native American from the Fort Berthold reservation of western North Dakota. He was widely known as the "Chief," a term of respect and affection.

Captain Poolaw disdains the term "Native American." He likes to be called an Indian. Charlie Foote is more comfortable with Native American. Both men were excellent Marines in combat. Both were wounded in Vietnam and survived the war.

Poolaw's father was a renowned photographer. His son is a gifted artist and his wife, Marty, taught the Kiowa language at university level. I once asked the skipper if he was a "full-blooded" Kiowa.

"Not really," he said in his soft voice. "My great grandfather was part of a raiding party into Mexico in the 19th century. He returned with two Mexican girls and married both of them. One was my great grandmother."

The skipper was soft-spoken but tough. Ex-enlisted, he knew the ways and wiles of Marines and would brook no malingering or insubordination. He once got into a tussle with a difficult Marine who outweighed him by 50 lb. They ended up in a bomb crater half filled with water. When the skipper's head went under water, our agile and aggressive Gunnery Sergeant, Anthony Marengo, jumped into the crater to break up the melee. The incident was handled in-company.

Charlie Foote is from the Low Cap clan of the Hidatsa. His tribal name is Black Bear, passed on from his father. The Hidatsa were also familiar with the ancient custom of kidnapping girls from rival tribes. Around the year 1800, a Hidatsa band captured a 12-year-old Shoshone girl and brought her to their traditional home on the rivers of the upper Missouri. Her name was Sacagawea.

She was later sold to a French-Canadian trapper, Toussaint Charbonneau, and in 1804 the Hidatsa introduced Sacagawea to Lewis and Clark, who were wintering with the Hidatsa and Mandan Indians. She and her husband joined the Corps of Discovery as interpreters and guides. She was 16 years old and the only woman on the expedition. She gave birth to a son en route to the Pacific

Marine Lance Corporal Cletus "Charlie" Foote in Vietnam, 1969.

and distinguished herself in many ways. Sacagawea was memorialized on a one-dollar coin in 2000.

I met the Chief soon after I arrived in Vietnam. After a week in country, the newest platoon commander in H 2/5, I choppered into the mountains along the South Vietnam–Laos border on Operation *Taylor Common*. I commanded the 2nd Platoon of Company H and the Chief was a rifleman in the 3rd Platoon. The battalion established a base camp on a hilltop not far from Laos and we spread out looking for the enemy. At night we would send out ambushes and listening posts to counter NVA reconnaissance units creeping up our lines in the jungle-clad, malaria-infested hills. Typically, an ambush would consist of a squad (13 men) led by a sergeant. But the Chief had his own ideas of how to ambush the enemy: alone. I asked why. "Other people make too much noise. I like to work alone."

This went against Marine Corps doctrine, but the Chief was persuasive. He was given permission to conduct his one-man ambushes. His main weapon was the M18 Claymore mine, the fiendish invention of Norman MacLeod and named after a medieval Scottish sword. The mine is directional and command detonated. Normally, the mines would be set up astride trails and covered with foliage to prevent the enemy seeing them and turning them around. Inside a claymore are seven hundred small steel balls and C4 explosives, making the weapon lethal up to one hundred meters.

The Chief liked to keep his mines uncovered and a short distance away so he could fire them in poor light. He would wait until an enemy would creep along the trail, locate the Claymore, and move to turn it around. The Chief never let that happen. As soon as the mine was touched, he would fire it.

Unlike many Marines, especially snipers—who liked to keep a "head count" of men they had killed in action—the Chief did not have a head count. He would "count coup."

Counting coup was an engrained tradition among the plains Indians of the United States. The Hidatsa followed this tradition, in which personal bravery is deemed of greater honor than actually killing the enemy. An Indian, going into battle on horseback, would carry a coup stick. These were long sticks, often of willow with a feather at the end. In battle, the aim was to tap an enemy brave with the coup stick and thereby "count coup." Notches could be carved in the coup stick after the battle to acknowledge the brave's achievement.

The Chief told me he counted coup 10 times in Vietnam. "I counted coup three times in one day," he noted. I never asked if the death of the enemy was associated with his counting coup, but due to the fact that his weapon of choice was a Claymore mine and not a long stick, I am inclined to conclude that deaths often resulted when Charlie Foote "counted coup." It may have had an educational effect on the North Vietnamese Army who surrounded us in the mountains, where it was downright cold at night in February. Perhaps the Chief's unorthodox manner of waging war in the dark prevented a large-scale attack. I certainly felt safer with the Chief around.

After the war, Charlie left the Corps and returned to North Dakota, where he ran a successful surveying business. When shale oil was discovered on the Fort Berthold reservation, right in the middle of the Bakkan Shale field, the lives of the Indians living on the reservation took a turn for the better. Today, the reservation is home to the Three Affiliated Tribes: the Hidatsa, Mandan, and Arikara. In 2008, Charlie was asked to return to his people and help manage the new wealth of the Hidatsa. He agreed and has become one of the respected elders of his tribe. He may not be the Chief, but the name still fits.

CHAPTER 10

My Favorite Posting

I was extremely fortunate to have been posted only to places where I wanted to serve. That includes five stations in Asia, one in Europe, and another in North America. The last came as a happy surprise in that it was not on my list and was my first time as a chief of station (COS). Finally I was in a post where I could not be declared *persona non grata* by an unhappy host government.

Each posting offered challenges and opportunities. Two or more were world-class destinations. Others fitted my skills and interests and were off the beaten track. One was a country at war in which wives were not allowed at post. I was not declared as a CIA officer to the host government and had to live my State Department cover 24/7. But on the positive side, I was assigned to handle the most productive and sensitive agents, recruited my share of new talent, and met the most congenial, competent, and interesting group of people anywhere. Some became friends for life. That's what made this my favorite assignment: the people.

I am speaking of Cambodia.

It is a country with a long and tortured history. When I first visited Cambodia in 1963 on assignment for the Associate Press, the country was led by the mercurial Prince Norodom Sihanouk, who was ousted in a coup in 1970 and joined the communist Khmer Rouge (KR) against the Government of the Khmer Republic (GKR). The royal family was divided into two factions: one Norodom and the other Sisowath. Prince Sisowath Sirik Matak was a leader of the coup and a long-time foe of Sihanouk. The infighting of the royal family was overshadowed by the invasion of the North Vietnamese Army into Cambodia and Vietnamese support of the KR. U.S. support for the GKR was limited, as the administration in Washington, D.C. was trying simultaneously to withdraw from Vietnam.

My mentor, Serge Taube, was instrumental in getting me a coveted slot in Phnom Penh, where I was officially the Commercial/Econ Officer in the U.S. embassy. I was in the pipeline for an assignment in Thailand, my first choice, but Serge persuaded me that Cambodia was a vastly more important posting. As usual, he was correct. I agreed to the change in plan, and so did the Far East (now East Asia) Division. I quickly appreciated what a difference this made in my career and in my life. Later, Serge engineered my plum assignment to a European station. I wisely turned down an offer to be a chief of station in Africa, and followed Serge to Europe just as I followed him to Asia.

Arriving in Phnom Penh on May 1, 1973, I quickly became friends with an embassy political officer (later ambassador), Tim Carney, who showed me the ropes and introduced me to the local social scene. Another embassy officer who helped me fit in to the fast-moving military and political scene was the embassy's Consul, John "Black Jack" McCarthy. Jack was an army infantry veteran of Vietnam and handled a complex and difficult job with consummate professional skill, especially at the end in 1975 when he saved American and Cambodian lives by rapidly approving visas and getting people out of the country as the Khmer Rouge moved in.

The assignment had its challenges. The embassy was limited by Congress to no more than two hundred "official" Americans on the ground at one time.

Political Officer Timothy Carney in a bar without electricity just before the evacuation of the embassy in Cambodia, April 1975.

A head count was made daily and it turned out that if the number was exceeded by temporary visitors, people had to be flown to Saigon to keep the figures correct. Air support to the Khmer Republic was halted by Congressional mandate in August 1973. The international press gathered for a "death watch" on Cambodia, but they were premature. The Khmer fought on with dwindling support. No American military personnel were permitted to "advise" their Cambodian counterparts, unlike Vietnam, where there were thousands of advisors. It seemed like someone didn't want our Cambodian allies to win.

The caliber of U.S. military personnel was high, with the exception of a naval attaché who was an embarrassment to his service and the embassy. He was eventually court-martialed. One of the best was army Major Alan Armstrong, a seventh-generation graduate of West Point. Alan was a fluent French speaker with two tours under his belt in Cambodia. He stayed until the end and was on the last helicopter out when the U.S. Marines evacuated the embassy staff in April 1975. He sat next to Ambassador Dean, who grimly gripped the U.S. flag that had flown over the embassy. On the short ride to the helicopter landing zone, Alan was ashamed when a Cambodian policeman snapped to attention and saluted the motorcade of Americans who were bugging out.

The last fixed-wing plane out of Cambodia, with a baby being lifted on board, April 1975.

In keeping with my cover role, it was only natural that I would become good friends with the leading American businessman in Cambodia, Frederick Kroll, the Esso director. Freddie was a gregarious, French-speaking Yalie and former Marine Corps recon officer. His missionary grandfather was once a religious advisor to Queen Liliuokalani of Hawaii. Freddie's winsome Thai wife, Dao, was "safe-havened" in Bangkok, as was BJ, and we remain in close touch with the Krolls, who now split their time between Seattle and Hua Hin in Thailand.

Freddie was famed for his Sunday water skiing parties at his houseboat on the Bassac River in Phnom Penh, which featured a hearty lunch of spicy Cambodian curry washed down with high-end Chateau Pavie wine from St. Emilion, thanks to Freddie's partner on the boat, USAID officer Pierre Elisabede, whose family owned the famous Bordeaux winery and sent cases to Pierre annually. It seemed almost criminal to be swilling such a great wine with curry at a temperature in excess of 80 degrees; almost.

Kroll was also a founder of a small private club for businessmen in Phnom Penh, the Chamber of Commerce of Kampuchea, or the COCK Club for short. This included the cream of expatriate commercial people from Australia, Switzerland, Holland, and the United States, as well as a few Cambodians. Tim and I were both members. There were French businessmen in town, mostly rubber growers. They kept a very low profile, probably because they were working and paying off the Khmer Rouge who controlled the plantations. None joined the COCK Club. Darts was the only sport played at our charming little French colonial clubhouse in the tree-lined neighborhood in Phnom Penh behind the Hotel Phnom. We were as serious fans of the blue-collar sport as any pub crawlers I knew. It was there that I had the rare privilege to meet the writer John le Carré and defeat him in a game of 301.

With a background in the Associated Press, it was no surprise that I became good friends with Matt Franjola, the AP bureau chief in Phnom Penh. Matt was an outgoing, larger-than-life lacrosse player from Cortland State

Matt Franjola, left, with Dao Kroll and Fred Kroll on a Khmer navy gunboat at their houseboat in Phnom Penh, 1974.

University in New York. He had worked in Thailand, Laos, and Vietnam before coming to Cambodia, and was unique among the foreign press corps in that he conducted his interviews in Cambodian and eschewed French as a colonial language. He was something of a ladies' man and was often known as "Captain America."

Matt went to the front to report on the progress of the war more than any correspondent I knew. Some didn't go at all, preferring to cover the war from the Café de Paris, a tolerable watering hole, or Madame Chantal's opium den. He filed his reports from the AP suite of rooms at the Hotel Phnom, the best of a bad lot of hotels. Thanks to his competent staff—which included Denis Gray, later a long-serving AP bureau chief in Bangkok, and Chhay Born Lay, the best Cambodian newsman I ever met—the AP outshone the competition in the daily coverage of the war. Matt also had a bevy of brave young Khmer photographers who risked their lives for less than $2 per day documenting the war. Phnom Penh was virtually surrounded for much of my two years in Cambodia, so fighting could quickly be found down any road leading out of the city. With the data from his "shooters," Matt maintained a very accurate battle map of the county which filled a wall in his office. I suggested he keep it covered when people like the Polish military attaché, "Ziggy," dropped by looking for information and a peek at Matt's map.

I traveled to the front regularly with Matt, rarely more than an hour's drive in his jeep, a purchase he made from a Vietnamese army officer. One of our trips was to Oudong, a former royal capitol of Cambodia thirty-five miles from Phnom Penh and heavily damaged when the Khmer Rouge temporarily captured the town in 1974. Matt took a photo of me in a Peugeot 404 automobile destroyed in the battle. It is on the cover of this book. Most CIA officers avoid talking to the press, which usually is a wise decision. Some journalists, including some in Phnom Penh, would have been delighted to "out" a CIA officer. Matt probably suspected I worked for the Agency, but he never asked.

The war attracted a wide spectrum of journalists, from the pro-communist Italian Tiziano Terzani, who worked for the German magazine *Der Spiegel*, to the erudite and articulate William Shawcross from London's *Sunday Times*. Agence France Press (AFP), the French wire service, was ably represented by Count Charles Antoine Marie de Nerciat, a Cambridge-educated aristocrat with an English mother. He spoke with a posh English accent and would not have been suspected of being a French nobleman. He was widely and affectionately known as Count Charlie.

A poet/writer, James Fenton, filed for *The Guardian* and became one of the best war poets of his time. I have fond memories of sitting alone with

Barry Broman in Khmer army fighting hole near Phnom Penh, 1973. (Image courtesy of Tim Carney)

BJ, left, with two Cambodian friends, Sophya Heumann and Kim McDevitt. Both the ladies lost their fathers and much of their family to the Khmer Rouge when they took power in 1975.

James on my veranda at night by candlelight, sipping malt Scotch whisky and hearing ingoing and outgoing artillery in the distance. We traded highlights from memory of a 1950s BBC radio program, *The Goon Show*, starring Spike Milligan and Peter Sellers. It was a zany program of comedic genius that we enjoyed from our days as English prep schoolboys. A quiet fellow, James was an island of calm in an ocean of chaos.

One fellow who made a great impression on me was the American Warren Hoffecker, who worked for Catholic Relief Services (CRS). Warren was a Princeton graduate and a decorated officer of the U.S. Army's Special Forces in Vietnam. His father was a Marine pilot killed in action in the Korean War. Warren was witty, lived simply on low pay, never complained, and was a complete pleasure to know. He became obsessed with Cambodia, and after the war ended in 1975 he would take annual leave from his well-paid job in Saudi Arabia to visit the war of resistance waged against the Vietnamese puppets in Phnom Penh to assist his old friends.

Despite the war that raged all around, life went on in Phnom Penh. The city suffered from a lack of electricity and an influx of more than a million refugees displaced by the war. Social life for the diplomatic corps and Khmer elite was much reduced, but parties, usually dinners that ended with dancing, went on. A key figure in this scene was Mme. Kim Dupree, the Cambodian wife of a French coffee planter whose plantation was in the mountains on the Thai border and rarely visited Phnom Penh. Kim was the English-educated

Barry cooling off in water-filled jar on the verandah of his villa in Phnom Penh, 1973.

daughter of a Cambodian ambassador to France and close to both factions of the royal family. No party was complete without the vivacious Kim, who was fluent in Khmer, French, and English. She survived the war, but many of her family and friends did not.

In October 1974, I celebrated my 31st birthday with a small party at my villa while BJ was visiting from Bangkok. The theme of the party was "Where were you in '62," and Matt Franjola came dressed like a teenage character from the film *American Graffiti*. For a couple of hours we put the war aside and danced to rock and roll music from our youth.

Cambodia is best summed for me by the words of Charles Dickens: "It was the best of times. It was the worst of times."

CHAPTER 11

John Gunther Dean

In my 25 years in the CIA, I had the honor of knowing and serving with a number of distinguished ambassadors, both career Foreign Service Officers and political appointees. One of the best of the former was John Gunther Dean, under whom I served in Cambodia from March 1974 until the country fell to the communist Khmer Rouge in April 1975.

Dean was born Gunther Dienstfertig in Breslau, Germany, into a Jewish family. They escaped Germany in 1938 and came to the United States, where the family name was changed to Dean. He attended Harvard University, became an American citizen, and dropped out in 1944 to join the U.S. Army, where he served in military intelligence.

In 1947, Dean returned to Harvard and received a BS Magna Cum Laude. He then studied in Paris and received a doctorate in law from the Sorbonne in 1949. He returned to Harvard again, where he earned an MA in international relations. He passed the Foreign Service Examination in 1954 and had a distinguished career as a diplomat, serving as ambassador five times. He spoke German, English, and French, and taught himself Danish when he was named ambassador to Denmark.

I was serving as the embassy Econ/Commercial officer in Phnom Penh when Dean arrived in 1974. I was not "declared" to the Cambodian government. Dean was very helpful in preserving my cover. When the USAID director refused to give me an office in the Econ section of the embassy, Dean gave me an office next to his and refused the USAID director's request to let USAID have the space.

During a friendly game of tennis at the residence of the Australian ambassador, I was partnered with Dean. In an embarrassing moment, I served a ball straight into the back of the ambassador's head. Dean turned slowly and said in a loud voice: "Fitness reports are coming soon, Broman." The game

American Ambassador to Cambodia John Gunther Dean, middle, at Armed Forces Day parade in Phnom Penh, 1974.

continued and Dean never mentioned my *faux pas* again. My cover was enhanced by his remark.

When American civilian photographer Al Rockoff was hit near the heart by enemy shrapnel during a firefight near Kompong Chhnang, Ambassador Dean authorized a rescue mission by the CIA airline Air America. Al was flown for medical treatment in Saigon, where his life was saved. After emergency surgery at the American hospital at Clark Air Force Base in the Philippines, Al returned to Cambodia. He was known affectionately as "Al the Head" (Al was an unabashed fan of cannabis). A story was told of the time Ambassador Dean invited Al to an embassy function. According to the tale, Al offered the ambassador a marijuana "joint," perhaps by way of thanking him for helping save his life. Dean is reported to have said: "No thanks Al, I'm trying to quit."

Dean told me a story about his service as a political officer at the American embassy in Paris in the 1960s. In 1967, Robert F. Kennedy, serving as a senator for New York, came to Paris in an effort to help end the war in Vietnam. He stayed at the posh Crillon Hotel at Place de la Concorde, next door to the American embassy. Dean was his point of contact while Kennedy met with Vietnamese officials. One morning, Dean told me, he knocked on the door of Kennedy's suite to discuss the meeting planned later in the day. It was fairly early in the morning and a woman, well known as an actress on American television, answered the door clad in a bathrobe. She quickly disappeared into a bedroom when Kennedy, also in a bathrobe, came out. "Got to stay in shape for Ethel," was Kennedy's only comment to Dean about his guest. Dean was later credited for having played a major role in arranging the U.S.–North Vietnamese peace talks.

The only assignment Dean gave me in my role as an Econ officer was to accompany political officer Timothy Carney to look into ruby and sapphire operations in the remote and malarial town of Pailin on the Thai–Cambodian border to the west. I arranged for Air America to drop us at an airstrip used by a French coffee planter, where the governor, an army colonel, was waiting to greet us. He put us up in Prince Sihanouk's old villa, where the swimming pool was used for military wives to do their washing. The governor and his staff briefed us on the gem trade that thrived along the border. Most of the gems went straight to Thailand through the jungle and unmarked border. We visited open pit sapphire mines that were worked by hundreds of men, women, and children using only hand tools. When Air America failed to pick us up, I hopped on a military convoy readying to make a resupply run through Khmer Rouge-controlled country to Battambang. By good luck, at the last minute, a Cambodian Air Force helicopter arrived. The pilot was looking for Tim, who was needed in Battambang to translate at a high-level meeting. I jumped off a truck and tagged along on the chopper.

When Cambodia fell in 1975, most of the embassy personnel were evacuated to Bangkok. The embassy had a small commissary in Phnom Penh that was not government supported. There were considerable funds left on hand when the country fell, and it was decided to spend the money on a final gathering of those who had served together in Cambodia, including press and other civilians. The event was held on the *Oriental Princess*, a large boat owned by the Oriental Hotel in Bangkok.

It was a sad affair. We were all in mourning, not only for the loss of Cambodia but many Cambodian friends, who were immediately murdered by the victorious Khmer Rouge. Ambassador Dean presided over the wake for Cambodia, and by the end of the evening most of the guests were completely drunk and many were in tears.

Dean was bitter over the way the American government had abandoned the Khmer people after encouraging them to resist the Khmer Rouge and their North Vietnamese supporters. He was particularly unhappy with the role of Secretary of State Henry Kissinger, and said so in front of me and several journalists. One of them was Matthew Franjola, the Associated Press bureau chief in Phnom Penh. Knowing that Dean's critical comments about his boss would get him in trouble, Matt said: "I'll treat your comments as off-the-record, Mr. Ambassador." Dean looked him in the eye and replied: "Print every word." Matt did so. I was told that Dean's undiplomatic comments cost him his next embassy, although it did not end his career.

When serving as ambassador to Lebanon in 1980, Dean was the target of an assassination attempt. Dean suspected Israel was behind the attempt due to him opening talks with the Palestine Liberation Organization (PLO). Always his own man, Dean could be demanding at times. During his watch in Lebanon, a Soviet official defected to the CIA. Dean insisted on knowing details of the defection. The chief of station, a highly regarded senior officer decorated for bravery, declined to tell Dean how the Soviet man had been spirited out of Lebanon. Dean, according to the officer who told me the story, did not have a "need to know."

"You know I could have you sent home for refusing to tell me," Dean told the COS.

"My bags are packed," the officer said. "You probably would be doing me a favor."

Then Dean backed down. "Just kidding," he said. "You know I would never do that."

The officer then told me: "I didn't want to have bad feelings between Dean and the station. I raised my hands as if I was looking through the periscope of a submarine but didn't say a word. The ambassador got the impression that we exfiltrated the defector by submarine."

"Did you?" I asked.

"No, but it made him feel better."

In 1984, I was serving in Europe when my first book, *Old Homes of Bangkok: Fragile Link*, was published by the Siam Society in Bangkok. Dean was serving as ambassador to Thailand at the time. I later found out that Ambassador Dean and his French-born wife, Martine, had thrown a book launch party for my book.

Dean retired from government service in 1989 and made Paris his home. He visited Bangkok in 1992 on a *pro bono* UNESCO mission, and invited BJ and me to dinner. It was great to see the old gentleman again and we relived some of the stories from Cambodia. Despite his outstanding service as a diplomat, including service in Thailand, he was ignored by the embassy on his visit. That probably led to his inviting us to dinner. "Remember this," he told me. "When you are named ambassador to Thailand, whenever a former ambassador visits Thailand you will put him up at the residence's guest house. Understood?" I understood. Of course, I was never named ambassador to Thailand or anywhere else, but the message was clear.

CHAPTER 12

An Awkward Turnover

When the command of a CIA station changes hands, the event is called a "turnover." This is usually a quiet, bittersweet occasion for the departing chief and the arrival of a new chief who will put his or her own brand of leadership on the station. The turnover also has an important official function: all station property and responsibility is transferred with the signing of a document and the torch of leadership is formally passed.

The first station turnover that I witnessed was in Cambodia in 1974. It was also the strangest. Cambodia was at war and rockets were falling daily. The station was small and included a number of "upcountry" officers whose mission was to keep an eye on events in the provinces, some of which were surrounded by the KR. All station officers spoke either French or Cambodian; some spoke both. Life was tough, but I enjoyed it very much after living rough in Vietnam in a Marine rifle company. We all received "danger pay."

The outgoing chief was a soft-spoken South Carolinian whom I will call Laird. He was in poor health and only received his Phnom Penh assignment through the intercession of the director of central intelligence, who overrode the medics. This was his last posting. He was descended from British rulers of Charleston and was educated in Paris. As one of the few station officers who were not "declared," I worked directly for Laird and "handled" the station's most productive asset. While I was supervised by Laird, a sound ops officer, I was always under the paternal gaze of Serge Taube, the deputy chief of station and my mentor from my earliest days in the Agency on the Cambodia desk.

Laird, a lifelong bachelor, lived in a huge mansion near the embassy. He never entertained. I would drop by at night from time to time with fresh intelligence from agents that could not wait until the next morning. I would write it up, Laird would read it—rarely making changes—sign it, and I would take it to the embassy for transmission to Langley, headquarters of the CIA.

On one of BJ's rare visits to the war zone from Bangkok, where she was teaching English, Laird invited us to a lunch at his residence in honor of BJ's visit. This was a first, as Laird did not entertain. To round out the lunch, Laird invited Agnes Gavin, his world-class secretary, who had served in Moscow with Serge and who later in retirement became secretary to Richard Helms, a former CIA director. We enjoyed a sumptuous meal prepared by one of Phnom Penh's most competent but underworked cooks.

Laird was replaced by Dave, a gruff pipe-smoker who had served in the Gordon Highland Regiment of the British Army in World War II. Dave was a pipe-smoking American who had served in some tough posts, including the Congo at war, and was a confirmed Anglophile. Where Laird was reserved and shy, Dave was outgoing and gregarious. He was in his element, leading a station in the chaotic scene of Cambodia at war. Once, he was beseeched on the phone by an upcountry officer asking to be evacuated when his town was under attack. Dave instructed him to "Hold until dawn." At dawn, the officer had sobered up and agreed there was no need for evacuation.

The problem at the turnover was that Laird and Dave disliked each other, an antipathy dating from their days together in Bangkok in the 1950s. This mutual animosity was not initially known to the station, but signs of it were seen when Laird declined to put Dave up in his large villa and instead put him in a hotel that frequently lacked electricity. Embassy residences all had generators to keep the lights and air conditioning running.

I had a clue of Laird's antipathy toward Dave when he turned two of the station's senior agents over to me instead of to Dave. I was already "running" the station's most prolific reporter and was surprised but delighted that Laird considered me, the station's junior officer, capable of taking on two more important assets. All he said was, "Dave will be too busy to run agents. That's what you are here for and you are doing a good job. Keep it up."

Serge Taube, the deputy chief of station, made arrangements for the change of command event with all Phnom Penh hands on deck, and champagne and canapes served. Like the rest of us, Serge did not know about the bad blood existing between Laird and Dave. The event started well enough, with Laird installed behind his desk making small talk while Serge served the wine.

When the moment came, Agnes presented the document that would turn Phnom Penh station over to Dave, who now spoke up. "When you sign that paper," he said, pointing to the document, "I will be chief of station and that," he added, pointing to Laird's chair, "will be my chair."

A hush came over the room. Serge looked worried. We all felt embarrassed. Laird quietly spoke: "No it won't. This is my station until wheels are up on my aircraft."

Serge, ever the diplomat as well as the consummate intelligence officer, intervened and managed to defuse the situation. Eventually, Laird signed the document but did not yield his chair to Dave, who didn't press his claim. Laird left country a few hours later and Dave claimed the office. Later, Serge told me that the scene of the two squabbling chiefs was the most embarrassing moment of his career.

Dave settled in quickly as chief and became much more social than Laird had been. He did not ask me to turn over the two assets that Laird had given me. He encouraged me to bring intel reports that I deemed of "Immediate" precedence to his residence "after hours" for signing off, and more than once invited me back for a pre-curfew nightcap after getting reports off to Langley.

On one of those quiet, one-on-one moments, which I also regarded a teaching moment from Dave—whom I liked and respected—he made an oblique reference to the change of command moment: "When you are a chief of station someday, and I know you will be, when your replacement comes to post, and you have a residence with a guest room, you will host him at home." I nodded in agreement. He had not forgotten, or forgiven, Laird's slight, and I am sure he never did.

CHAPTER 13

The Foreign Service Institute

Apart from the Marine Corps' Officer Basic School at Quantico and the CIA's Basic Ops Course at "The Farm" in tidewater Virginia, the toughest training I ever experienced was the French language course at the State Department's Foreign Service Institute (FSI) in Rosslyn, Virginia, in 1972.

The CIA has a perfectly good language school, but my supervisors thought it best that for my first posting to Cambodia I go to the FSI. Several hard languages such as Chinese, Japanese, and Arabic are taught outside America, some courses taking two years. My French course took 20 weeks, six hours a day, with no English allowed. The maximum class size was five. Most of the instructors were women, native French speakers. Every four weeks I had a new teacher to hear different accents. One instructor was from the Middle East, another was a Vietnamese *métisse*, and several were French, but no one was from Paris. A Parisian accent was deemed unacceptable.

The objective was to receive a grade of 3:3 at the end of the course out of a possible 5:5. Students are graded on their ability to speak and to understand the language. Reading and writing are not graded. A native French speaker with a university degree is expected to speak and understand the language at a 5:5 level. There was a strong incentive to receive a 3:3 grade. An FSO (Foreign Service Officer) cannot be promoted until they are language qualified.

While most of us endured the tough regimen, the Marine Corps, for a change, had it easy. Marines assigned to protect U.S. embassies had their own four-week course. Their instructor was a Frenchman who had once served as a captain in the French Army during the French Vietnamese war. We had both served in the same dangerous part of Quang Nam province about thirty miles west of Da Nang and sixteen years apart. When I told him about the close air and artillery support we received and medical evacuation helicopters that could deliver wounded Marines to a hospital in Da Nang in 20 minutes, the old captain said: "I was in the wrong war." He taught Marines how to direct visitors to the embassy to the right section, how to survive in bars and restaurants, and equally importantly how to speak to ladies politely, in keeping with the best tradition of the "soldiers of the sea."

A favorite instructor was an attractive, middle-aged woman from a wealthy family in the Levant who was educated at private French-speaking schools. She told our class one day, in rapid French, how she met a young Marine embassy guard while she was in high school and became friends with him. In her free time she would hang out at the Marine House, where the Marines lived under the sharp eyes and tongue of the gunnery sergeant in charge of the Marine detachment.

One day, a Marine asked the girl what she did when she came home from her Lycée. "Every day," she told him, "I make a cup of tea and then I play with my pussy." She had a cat for a pet and didn't know that she had just made a hilarious *double entendre*. The French class was silent and shocked as our teacher told her story. "Pussy," she told us, was the same in French slang as it was in English. She went on to explain that every time she visited the Marine House to wait for her lance corporal to get off duty, someone would ask her about her pussy. And, not understanding what she was saying, she said: "So I always told them I played with my pussy whenever I had a chance. One day my boyfriend walked in and was shocked to hear me. He took me aside and explained the American slang. I was so mortified that I never went back to the Marine House. But I married that Marine."

Midway through my 20-week course, there were only two of us left in class. It is moments like this when you become close to those in the trenches with you. Friendships are forged under the pressure to emerge with a 3:3. My partner at the time was a fairly senior FSO who was heading to sub-Saharan Africa as Deputy Chief of Mission (DCM). I will call him Ned. Following instructions from Serge Taube, I told no one at the FSI that I worked for the Agency. That included Ned.

As time went by and we sought to master the subjunctive verb mood, a requirement for achieving 3:3 status, Ned and I became quite close. One day after class, he asked about my forthcoming assignment to Cambodia. "I hear the war is not going too well," he said, which was an understatement. The Cambodian army—small, poorly equipped, and inexperienced—was soundly defeated in several large engagements with the North Vietnamese Army, which had several infantry divisions in Cambodia in direct violation of Cambodia's professed neutrality.

"It's not too bad," I lied. "I expect that my combat time in Vietnam will put me in good stead for Cambodia." Ned would not be put off: "You might not believe it, but I have some very good connections among senior Africa hands. I think I might be able to arrange a new assignment for you in Africa. I am sure you will get your 3:3 and think Africa will be a safer and better place to launch your diplomatic career than in poor Cambodia." I appreciated his offer of help but stuck to my guns, telling Ned I was an Old Indochina Hand with experience in Thailand and Vietnam, and that I sought the Cambodia posting to launch my career in the State Department. The subject was dropped.

Eventually, we both got our 3:3s, wished each other well, and went our separate ways. I went out to Cambodia and after a few close calls—my house was hit by incoming rocket shrapnel four times—I made it out of Phnom Penh one step ahead of the Khmer Rouge.

A few years later, I was having dinner with a State Department friend who informed me he had recently met Ned at a conference in Switzerland: "Ned heard that I had served in Cambodia and asked if you were there at the end. I said 'yes' and also told him that you are one of my best friends in the Agency."

"What did Ned say to that?" I asked.

"'Son-of-bitch,' was the part I remember best," said my friend. "He said it very loudly. You didn't tell him you were a spook?"

"Need to know," I lamely responded. "I was told to live my cover." The sad fact is that the Russians usually know who we are even if fellow embassy officers don't.

CHAPTER 14

Operational "Ladies of the Night"

It is sometimes said that espionage is the second-oldest profession, the oldest, of course, being prostitution. Sometimes one profession helps the other.

David Cornwell, better known by his *nom de plume* John le Carré, coined, I believe, the term "honey trap," referring to the ploy perfected by the Soviet intelligence service the Komitet Gosudarstvennoy Bezopasnosti, the Committee for State Security, which existed from 1954–91 and was known as the KGB. The Russians made many recruitments through the honey trap, often by blackmailing the man (or woman) involved. "Work for us, or else!" is a common pitch. Senior foreign officials, including Americans, were coerced into cooperating with the KGB or its successor, the Federal Security Service (FSB), some of them for decades.

Unlike the Russians, the CIA does not include the honey trap in its playbook to attract spies. But that does not mean that prostitutes are completely off limits. I know an officer who made the best recruitment of his career with the assistance of a few "ladies of the night." The irony of the story is that the officer was a churchgoing, all-American boy, and an upstanding citizen. I will call him Louis.

Louis, a bachelor at the time, visited me on vacation at a posting in Asia. He was based at a small station where living conditions were rough and operational opportunities few. Over drinks at my house, he told me that he had "gotten lucky" and recruited an official from one of the hardest of the "hard targets." This usually means a communist country.

"How did you get him?" I asked.

"I met him at a national day reception and knew what country he was from. He was standing alone so I approached him and started a conversation."

"What did he say?"

"Nothing."

"How long did you talk to him?"

"About twenty minutes."

"Why did you keep talking?"

"He could have walked away but he didn't. So I kept talking."

I should note here that Louis was easygoing but also tenacious. Somehow, he developed a friendship of sorts with the target, who spoke little but felt increasingly easy and trustful around Louis. Over time, they began meeting one-on-one, something that was forbidden by the target's paranoid government. This was a good sign; the fellow was breaking strict rules. Louis, ever the optimist, thought he had a chance. Little by little, he began getting information from his new friend, who asked for nothing in return.

"What motivated the man to risk everything?" I asked Louis.

"I finally found out what it was that he wanted."

"Which was?"

"Sex. Not with me, of course. He desperately wanted to get laid and hoped that I could help. It turned out that he asked the wrong American. Some of the guys in the station had local girlfriends but prostitution was illegal and bad girls were hard to find."

"What did you do?"

"My COS encouraged me to find a girl for the target, which I did somewhat unwillingly. Eventually I found a woman, not very attractive and not very friendly but willing to do whatever he wanted. For money."

"What did your agent think of her?"

"He loved her, or rather he loved what she did for him. It seems to be working OK but there is danger at every step. He is breaking his country's law and could be shot. She is breaking her country's law and could go to jail. I am the guy that made it happen and I pay the girl and could get thrown out of country. We could get rolled up at any time."

"What you need," I suggested, "is a girl from this country. Prostitution is an accepted way of life here and beautiful girls can be rented from virtually any bar in town."

"That would be a lot more secure," Louis conceded. "Could it be arranged?"

"Let's ask my chief of station," I said. My chief was a tough taskmaster of few words. He would convoke officers by writing on their reports, in red ink, "PSM" (Please see me). This was an invitation to see the chief, and rarely to be congratulated. More urgent was the notation "PSM ASAP" (Please see me as soon as possible), which invariably caused heartburn in the reader. The notation everyone dreaded seeing was simply "SM" (See me). Hell, it was assumed, might follow; and sometimes it did.

The next morning, I made an appointment to see the COS, a senior officer and not someone I was on a first-name basis with. That came later. But we had a good relationship and made a couple of important recruitments on his watch. Moreover, and probably germane, we both had been Marines in combat.

I explained Louis's situation to the chief and noted that Louis had also been a Marine. "Bring him in," was all the chief said.

The next morning I introduced Louis to the COS, who was welcoming and cordial and asked where and when Louis had been in the Corps. "Wounded in Vietnam" was part of the answer. Then the chief asked what he could do to help Louis's operation.

"It would be great if you could identify and recruit appropriate women who could travel to my country periodically to service our agent," Louis said. "It would be best if they could speak English, were good-looking, and could be trusted to be discreet."

The chief replied: "If you have a bona fide operational requirement for the services of prostitutes, have your chief of station put it in writing and we will support the operation. Does that sound reasonable?"

"Yes sir. Will do."

I took the opportunity to speak up: "Would you like me to handle the operation from this end, chief?"

The old Marine smiled; something I had rarely seen him do. "No thank you, Mr. Broman. This, I think, is a requirement that can best be handled by our liaison branch." That effectively ended my involvement with the case. I do know that my station did provide the ladies requested by Louis's station and their service was satisfactory, possibly outstanding. I also know that Louis received the Intelligence Star for this recruitment.

CHAPTER 15

Spy vs Spy

Most of my career at the CIA (1971–96) was spent during the Cold War, which is considered to have ended with the demise of the USSR on December 31, 1996. Over the decades, many of the best Russian agents that the CIA "ran" were walk-ins, men or women who volunteered their services. They were often motivated by a hatred of the Soviet system and a desire for revenge. Many of these people had lived in the West and saw how much better life was there than at home.

The challenge for CIA stations was to make direct contact with Soviet targets and to build a relationship based on trust that would lead to recruitment. This required the ability to meet, develop, and assess these hard targets. Soviet counterintelligence kept a close eye on their officials at home and abroad, and finding opportunities to meet and mix with targets was often difficult.

I worked the Soviet target in a large Asian city in the 1970s. The local Foreign Correspondents Club (FCC) hosted a Saturday lunch at the bar of the best hotel in town. Most of the attendees were not working journalists. They were "associate" members of the club, mainly local expatriate businessmen with an interest in political matters. Local diplomats could also join the club, and many did. Chief among these were intelligence officers of the United States and the USSR. The venue was a rare spot where the CIA could meet, mingle, and hopefully recruit members of our main enemies, the KGB and Soviet military intelligence, the GRU.

It was easy to become a member of the club and a regular attendee of the buffet lunches at the sumptuous riverside hotel's main bar. The Soviets had a few working journalists from TASS, their news agency and often a cover for the KGB. A few other working journalists and more local businessmen and diplomats were working as "access agents" of the CIA. Their job was to befriend Soviet targets and develop personal data that would show vulnerabilities that could assist in their recruitment. The Saturday gatherings were very popular and "clubby." Many of those present were not affiliated with the dark world of espionage and did not understand the undercurrent of spies at work in the plush convivial setting. Beer, Scotch, and especially vodka flowed freely.

I recall sending a cable home after a Saturday lunch and identifying all the persons sitting at the bar. They all had cryptonyms (names assigned to targets or assets) or pseudonyms (names assigned to CIA officers so their true name never appears in print). This was an intense venue.

Two club members—one a Soviet official and the other a West German— could be found every week at a small table for two. The Soviet apparatchik was an elderly KGB officer and the German was equally old, a dour correspondent for a German magazine. Both were veterans of the Great Patriotic War, known in the West as World War II. The German had been a POW who learned his Russian in a prison camp. This odd couple spoke in Russian, sat alone, and drank to excess. No one was allowed to sit with them. The Soviet never tried to recruit the old German, who passed along anything of value to friends in the intelligence community. But mainly they were just old enemies and now firm drinking buddies.

The person I selected to target was a young and personable Russian diplomat, not an intelligence officer, but a target in his own right as a member of the Russian *nomenklatura*, well-connected members of the Soviet elite. Their privileged and often spoiled offspring were known to us as "Golden Youth." I will call my target Igor. He was tall, athletic, and outgoing. In his late twenties, Igor spoke fluent English and was a graduate of Moscow State University, widely known as the "Harvard of Russia."

Igor was never left alone. There was always a KGB "minder" with him to make sure that he didn't make contact with Westerners, especially intelligence officers like me. The Foreign Correspondents Club was one of the few places he was permitted to visit. Igor was eager to make new friends, but it was not easy. I sat next to him at the bar one Saturday while his minder was occupied by a friend of mine. I struck up a conversation with Igor, who was not visibly upset to learn he was talking to an American official. On the contrary, he quickly made it clear that he was a big fan of American pop music: a good sign.

"My favorite band is the Beach Boys," he told me, and proceeded to tell me the names of their singers and give a detailed history of the band.

"I am also a big fan," I responded, "and loved surfing from my days living in southern California." A slight exaggeration. I didn't mention that my time in southern Cal was at the Camp Pendleton Marine Corps base, where surfing was not one of the pastimes of most infantry officers.

To end this story on a happy note, I will cite another Soviet case in Asia that occurred in the last years of the Cold War. I was only tangentially involved in the case, which was run by a young, tenacious friend who was a loner and a perfect case officer. I will call him Pat. A bachelor and a drinker, Pat struck up a relationship with a young KGB officer, Ivan, who had an unhappy marriage and an abiding love of vodka. They became drinking buddies and then friends.

Ivan knew that Pat was a CIA officer but did not report the friendship he developed with his American friend. In the end, Ivan accepted recruitment and even passed a polygraph examination. He reported critical intelligence on the events in the Kremlin that led up to the resignation of Mikhail Gorbachev as General Secretary of the Communist Party in late December 1991. Ivan outlived the Soviet Union and Pat was decorated for his extraordinary recruitment. Somewhat ironically, Pat was regarded by some of his peers in the station as a malingering alcoholic. None of them knew that Pat was running one of the best hard-target cases in the world. They had no "need to know." That's how it should be.

CHAPTER 16

Lady Bump

A wise old case officer, whom I will call Stuart, told me he always "hung out his CIA shingle" when he arrived at post, most of which were backwater, Third World cities in Africa and Asia. These were places where few Americans could name the capital and even fewer would ever want to go. Not speaking Russian, he frequented national day celebrations looking for disgruntled Soviets, especially intelligence officers from the KGB (civilian) or GRU (military).

Stuart told me:

> They will know you are CIA before your host government does, so that solves one problem. You need to identify people with the access to the information we are looking for. They also need to have the guile to survive as an agent. They need to trust you more than they like you; they are putting their lives in your hands. There are about 10 percent who would jump if they had the chance and maybe 40 percent who already know that they are working for a bad system and could do much better in the West.

Stuart was known for his wit. I regret never working with or for him in the field. He once engineered a situation that got him declared *persona non grata* by the host government in a perfectly horrible country in Africa, and came away looking stalwart and willing to "take one for the team." He so impressed his career State Department ambassador in another African country that was deficient in everything but poverty and brutality, that the ambassador named Stuart *chargé d'affaires*, the person in charge of the embassy while the ambassador was away. The act of putting a CIA officer in charge rather than the DCM, a State Department Foreign Service Officer, is unheard of. It probably says a lot more about the bad blood between the two men from Foggy Bottom (home of the State Department) than Stuart's fitness for the job.

It was, therefore, with a clear vision that I went looking for Soviets when I was assigned to a large station in a country with a large number of Soviet targets in a few embassies and several international organizations. Although Soviets were not on my list of things to do or people to recruit, I figured one would make a good "target of opportunity," and looked for the opportunity.

Among my circle of contacts in the city was a senior Asian official in a large international organization. Although not a target himself, he knew some people who were. Over drinks, I asked if he knew any presentable Soviets who I might like to meet. He thought it over and remarked there was one fellow, not a Russian but fairly senior from an important Soviet republic who I should meet. He offered to invite both of us to a social event and I accepted with thanks. I put the fellow in the category of "semi-willing collaborator." These are people who want to help but might balk at becoming a spy.

BJ and I attended the soirée hosted by my friend, a member of a royal family in a neighboring country and widely regarded as a serious bon vivant. The introduction to the target was effortless and effective. I will call him Oleg and his vivacious, blonde, Rubenesque wife, Tanya. I experienced none of the grim, defensive reaction that often accompanies introductions to Russians. They are always wary, sometimes hostile. We are the enemy and always represent danger.

Oleg was in his mid-thirties, outgoing, and spoke excellent English. He was an economist by training and it quickly became apparent that he was one of the "Golden Youth." Oleg was interested in all things Western. Tanya was even more effervescent, although her English was not as polished as Oleg's. She was interested in BJ coming from Hawaii and asked non-threatening questions about food, customs, and surfing. It was clear to me that this was a contact I needed to pursue.

I took a little chance when I asked Oleg if he had to report foreign contacts to the embassy. He laughed and said he didn't work for the embassy and had no contact with them. I took that as a "no." Then I asked if he could accept invitations to dinner. Things were looking better. However, it crossed my mind that this could be too easy. Maybe he was being "run into" me. This could be a provocation; he could be under KGB direction as a "dangle." I had read of this ploy but never seen it. I needed to tread carefully. The game was afoot.

Before I could invite Oleg and Tanya to one of our weekly dinner parties, he invited us to his apartment for a traditional dinner. This further raised my suspicion that this might not be as good as it looked, but both the Soviet specialist in the station and headquarters told me to proceed. I was convinced that I was on the right track when my immediate supervisor, a man I did not like or trust, suggested I turn over Oleg to him for further development. I declined and accepted Oleg's dinner invitation.

Oleg and Tanya had two small children, who like most Soviet offspring were not allowed to accompany their parents abroad. They were hostages as a guarantee that their parents would not defect. The separation affected Tanya greatly, and she made extended visits home to see her children while Oleg stayed at post. One of these visits had recently ended, and when Tanya returned she did so with the best food and drink that the Soviet Union could offer. We were treated to these treasured viands from the old country. The feast started with several types of caviar, followed by smoked sturgeon, sausages, and wild mushrooms, along with vodka from Russia and Poland, wines from Moldova, and brandy from Armenia.

There were just the four of us. Again, I thought we were being set up. But we genuinely enjoyed the evening; the food and alcohol, but also the company. As often happens when being entertained by Soviets (or Chinese), drinking is mandatory and enjoyable. Mercifully, BJ is not a drinker, so driving home was not a problem. After dinner, Oleg and Tanya moved the dinner table to one side. "What's next?" I enquired innocently.

"Dancing, of course!" said Oleg, mildly drunk. "Tanya loves to dance; I hope you do too."

"Of course we do," I answered, not too sure where this was going. "BJ used to dance traditional Hawaiian hula." True, but this was not hula night. It was "Lady Bump" night. In 1975, Penn McLean had a pop disco hit called "Lady Bump," Tanya's favorite tune. More than a song, it was also a dance which featured physical contact when one dancer "bumps" his or her partner with a fairly violent hip motion.

I learned this dance the hard way, on the receiving end of Tanya's energetic hips. She bumped me across the room sideways as Oleg watched with amusement and BJ cringed. There was no lasting damage, but it gave me a better understanding of Soviet partying. The dancing led to more drinking, Oleg's forte, and BJ eventually driving me home. I am vague on the details, but everyone said I had a good time.

We reciprocated with a more conventional diplomatic dinner party, to which we invited my friendly Asian prince, partly in thanks for the introduction to Oleg and partly because he was a big fan of BJ's cooking. He accepted our invitation with a request that BJ make her famous cheesecake for dessert. It is made with a graham cracker crust, Philadelphia cream cheese, and on this occasion topped with fresh strawberries. In Asia, BJ frequently used mangos when in season. Tanya was equally smitten by the cheesecake and asked BJ for the recipe.

Other guests included a Belgian nobleman, who was a close friend of the prince, and a Thai diplomat with his elegant Italian wife. For dinner, BJ made French coq au vin served with an American wine *en carafe* to surprise guests with the quality of Willamette Valley pinot noir wine from Oregon. The prince announced at the outset of the evening that BJ was making, after much begging, a cheesecake. As expected, it was a huge hit, served with a chilled sweet Sauternes wine. Oleg and Tanya were quiet all evening; this was a new experience for them and they appreciated it. Oleg, it turned out, was a jazz buff and enjoyed the low background music of Dave Brubeck.

A few weeks later, I called Oleg and invited him to lunch in a small restaurant not too far from his office. "Of course, I accept", he said, "so I must invite you."

"Not this time," I insisted. "It is a favorite restaurant of mine and easy for you to find."

"Will there be other guests?" he asked.

"No. I don't share this restaurant with many people. It is very small. I hope you like Vietnamese food."

"I don't know Vietnamese cuisine and look forward to you introducing me."

Oleg was on time and quickly took off his jacket and tie in the open-air restaurant. We were the only Western customers. The owner waited on us personally, and it was clear to Oleg that we were old friends, although Oleg didn't understand what we were saying. I ordered a simple meal of fresh spring rolls and beef pho soup. Plus beer.

This was our first one-on-one meeting, and I moved the conversation to politics. I told him my father had served in the Great Patriotic War and was one of the first Americans on German soil in 1945 when he crossed the Rhine as a glider pilot. "Was your father in the war?" I asked.

"Yes, he was wounded at Kursk, a big tank battle. Today he is a senior official in the government of our republic."

Oleg then asked, with a little hesitancy: "Did you serve in Vietnam?"

"I did. I was a Marine infantry officer."

"Is that where you learned to eat Vietnamese food?"

"Yes, after I finished my time at the front and was involved in Civil Affairs where I became a fan of Vietnamese food."

I asked Oleg if he had many Russian friends and if coming from a minority Soviet republic hurt his career. His answer shocked me.

"I have few Russian friends. My grandfather died in the Gulag in the 1930s when Stalin killed many of our people. Some day we will be independent."

"Are you a member of the Communist Party?"

"Of course," he laughed. "If not, I could not travel abroad. Everyone with brains and ambition must be in the party."

I was uneasy. Oleg was talking out of school. Normally, Soviets I knew—mostly TASS correspondents or embassy officers—defended the USSR loyally and loudly. Suddenly I was hearing something different. I thought I might have a fish on the hook. My gut told me that Oleg was not a dangle, but I never found out as he was transferred home soon after our lunch. Tanya wanted to be with their children. They enjoyed being out of the USSR, but family came first. He didn't know if he would ever have a foreign posting again. I could see my best Soviet case slipping away. I needed to know much more about him, and especially his access to intelligence. I thought it would be nice to keep in touch, but that was out of the question. It looked like this might be our last chance to meet. I took out a card and on the back I wrote the address of my father, retired in Olympia, Washington.

"If I don't see you again, take this card and if you ever come out again, or need my help, write to my father and say how and where we can meet," I said. "He will reach me."

Oleg took the card but didn't offer a contact for himself. I never heard from him, but hope that he rose to a position of power and influence in his republic, which achieved independence in 1991. I suspect that Tanya today is Babushka Bump and famed for her cheesecake.

CHAPTER 17

Air America: The World's Most Shot-at Airline Gets Revenge

One of the worst films I ever saw was *Air America*, a 1990 production starring Mel Gibson and Robert Downey Jr. It could have been great, as the true story of the airline is better than fiction. But it was an embarrassing farce, full of lies and short on fact.

Air America was a proprietary airline owned by the CIA. The original airline was Civil Air Transport (CAT), founded by Claire Chennault of World War II Flying Tiger fame. He formed it in 1946 as a commercial airline and sold it to the CIA in 1950. The name was changed to Air America in 1959.

I had the pleasure of flying in Air America helicopters and fixed-wing aircraft in Thailand, South Vietnam, and Cambodia. The pilots were mostly a collection of former military pilots with years of experience, extraordinary skill, and unmatched bravery. Their motto was "Anything, Anywhere, Anytime, Professionally." I was what they called "The Customer" and flew in back in comfort and sometimes under considerable stress.

My first ride in an Air America plane came before I was a "customer," in 1970 when I was a Marine first lieutenant assigned as a liaison officer in Bangkok that took up half of my six-month extension in Vietnam. I promised BJ that I would bring her with me when she came out to Bangkok, her first visit to Asia. A U.S. Army colonel, Daniel Lord Baldwin III, insisted that BJ and I stay at his large villa, not wanting me to expose my wife to the low-end Nana Hotel, where I enjoyed a suite for $164 a month. I accepted Dan's kind offer with pleasure. During BJ's visit, I took her to Chiang Mai in the north for a weekend.

In Chiang Mai I contacted my old Thai teacher from the University of Washington, Professor Amnuay Tapingkae, who taught while he was getting his doctorate in education. Amnuay, and his equally brilliant wife, Siti, who also taught me, greeted us warmly. Knowing that I was a photographer, Amnuay asked if I would photograph the campus of the University of Chiang Mai from the air for a university publication.

"Of course," I said. "I would be delighted. How?"

"I have a friend at Air America," he told me. "He can arrange a flight."

And he did. I had little knowledge of Air America, but knew it was connected to the CIA. Amnuay made a phone call, and BJ and I were invited to a short flight on an Air America Pilatus Porter single engine aircraft. My mission was to photograph the campus, which was a mile or so away from the airfield. It was a complete delight. Amnuay came along with a Thai colleague. We climbed rapidly in the Swiss-made aircraft and circled the campus at about five hundred feet while Amnuay gave the pilot instructions. We made several passes while I took photos.

After about ten minutes, I said I had enough photos. The pilot asked if we had ever seen King Bumiphol's Phu Ping Palace in the mountains nearby. I said no. He said, "Hang on," and took the powerful little short takeoff and landing (STOL) plane into a steep climb. Two minutes later, I could see the ornate palace below surrounded by thick jungle and a Hmong hill tribe village. He took the plane into a dive and pulled out as we passed the elegant structure, built in the classic Siamese style of the 19th century. That ended my first ride with Air America. But it was not my last.

The only time I had a problem with an Air America pilot was when I was carrying a bag of fresh durian from Saigon to Phnom Penh in a Pilatus Porter aircraft in 1974. I had been visiting my old Marine Corps buddy Jim Jones and his Vietnamese wife, Thanh, and was returning to Cambodia. Thanh knew I was an aficionado of durian, the fruit that was said to "taste like heaven and smell like hell." Often eschewed by foreigners and forbidden in any hotel in Thailand, the spiny fruit is an acquired taste. As our aircraft entered Cambodian airspace, the pilot turned, looked back at his six "customers" in the back, and asked: "What died back there?" All eyes turned to me and my bag of a dozen durians. As I disembarked at Pochentong Airport 30 minutes later, the pilot looked at me with thinly veiled disgust. "I've got to fly this bird back to Saigon," he said. "I'm going to remember you." It was the first and last time I carried durians on an aircraft.

Air America was much more than an airline ferrying people and freight all around Indochina. Many of the landing zones were in rugged karst topography in the mountains of Laos, through "rock filled clouds" and especially dangerous in the monsoon season, when heavy rains obscured visibility. The planes were unarmed but the cargo ranged from double-bagged rice to "hard rice," the Air American euphemism for ammunition. Hmong children, mountain dwellers whose leaders supported the CIA in their "secret" war against North Vietnamese Army invaders in Laos, thought rice came from the sky. And they called the men of Air America who delivered the rice, men from "Sky."

In addition to supplying outposts in Laos and delivering people and cargo all over Vietnam and Cambodia, Air America had another, even more dangerous mission, Search and Rescue (SAR). This involved rescuing downed American or allied airmen, especially American fliers shot down over Laos. James "Jim" Mullen, an old Marine intelligence officer and later an Air America employee in Laos in the 1960s, disabused me of the notion that Air America was unarmed:

> In order to protect aircraft on SAR missions that the military declined to fly, we armed a few old aircraft for close air support. The Air Force Second Air Division in Saigon would not authorize the use of Navy AD Skyraiders, which were the only prop aircraft available to support rescue missions. The jet aircraft available could not provide the air to ground support we needed. So we came up with Air America-manned T-28s and not Skyraiders. The T-28 was a trainer that was also used for counter insurgency in the Vietnam War to great effect.

"Did you lose any aircraft or pilots?" I asked.

"Not many."

"Did they fly with Air America markings?"

"No. The T-28s flew under the colors of the Royal Lao Air Force with American crews. These were the only armed aircraft piloted by Air American flyers. I was involved with a number of these missions."

Like U.S. Marines anywhere, at any time, we told war stories. Typically, a fairy tale begins, "Once upon a time ..." A Marine war story often begins, "Now this is no shit ..." As an old grunt myself, I had a lot of stories from Vietnam and a few from Cambodia and Burma. But Jim outdid me.

"Have you heard about the Air America shootdown?" he asked coyly. I hadn't.

"It took place at Lima Site 85 in 1967." Each airfield or landing zone in Laos had a designation by the CIA. Lima stood for Laos. LS-85 was at a top-secret mountain-top facility in northeastern Laos manned by USAF personnel on a 5,600-foot mountain called Phou Pha Thi. I knew about this sensitive post, where a paramilitary friend of mine was almost killed A small team of airmen directed American bombers into northern Vietnam nearby. This little outpost was responsible for directly half of the bombing raids into the north, especially targets in and around Hanoi. The North Vietnamese wanted badly to destroy the site. It was mainly guarded by Hmong tribesmen working with the CIA.

Jim explained: "The NVA launched a bizarre air attack against LS-85 using Russian biplanes designated An-2 by the Soviets and 'Colt' by

Painting of an Air America aircraft shooting down a North Vietnamese biplane in Laos.

the Americans. The North Vietnamese modified them into bombers capable of dropping 120mm mortars." I did some research and found that this sturdy little bird was designed as a crop duster and went into production in 1946, three years before the T-28. It was also used in fighting forest fires in the Soviet Union. A small number of aircraft were used for military purposes, including dropping paratroopers. Four An-2s were delivered to the North Vietnamese Army.

The NVA launched their fleet of An-2s against the site on January 12, 1968. The planes had tubes attached to their bellies where large mortar shells could be dropped by hand. They dropped mortar shells that killed four Hmong civilians, and the defending Hmong shot down one of the An-2s. The Vietnamese claimed their crop dusters had destroyed the radar site, but they were wrong. The site was not destroyed, there were no American casualties, and the radar site was untouched.

When the attack started, there was an Air America Bell Huey chopper with former army pilot Ted Moore at the controls in the air above LS-85. Moore had never been in an aerial dual before. Flight mechanic Glen Woods was in back with an AK-47 rifle to use if their chopper was shot down. Moore watched as the Colts made passes at the radar site, dropping their mortar rounds. Moore's Huey was faster than the old biplane, and Moore caught up to a Colt and took position above it. Glen Woods, laying on his belly, fired on the Colt and brought it down. The two surviving Colts decided to call it a day and headed for home.

This was a first. An Air America aircraft had engaged an enemy aircraft in flight and shot it down. Later, the remains of the Colt would be put on display in Vientiane, proof of North Vietnamese aggression against neutral Laos.

CHAPTER 18

At the End in Laos, 1975

During the spring of 1975, I was nearing the end of my posting to Cambodia. When the U.S. Congress cut off assistance to Vietnam and Cambodia the writing was on the wall and we prepared to abandon Cambodia to the communist Khmer Rouge. The embassy in Phnom Penh drew down personnel as they planned for Operation *Eagle Pull* to evacuate the embassy when the end was near. I left on the last Agency fixed-wing aircraft with documents and passengers. On April 12, Marines flew in on *Eagle Pull* and brought out remaining embassy personnel and allied diplomats. The Cambodian cabinet voted to stay, and all were immediately killed by the Khmer Rouge.

A few weeks later, the Republic of Vietnam fell to the North Vietnamese Army amid a wild dash to get as many of our personnel and allies out. It was a chaotic scene in Saigon on April 30 as helicopters, many of them belonging to Air America, lifted off, destined for U.S. Navy craft offshore.

The situation was much different in Laos. The country on the Mekong River between Thailand and North Vietnam had been at war with the North Vietnamese for more than a decade. In 1963, President Kennedy forbade the use of U.S. military forces in Laos, despite the invasion of North Vietnamese troops in support of the communist Pathet Lao and later to transit Laos en route to South Vietnam and Cambodia via the so-called Ho Chi Minh Trail.

To challenge the North Vietnamese, the Central Intelligence Agency was directed to mount their largest ever covert action military operation in a not very covert "secret" war using an assortment of ethnic groups in Laos, most of them Hmong tribesmen numbering around 30,000 men. A similar number of Thai Army "volunteers" were also in Laos, fighting under the direction of the CIA. U.S. Air Force aircraft based in Thailand were used heavily in Laos, including B-52 bombers from U-Tapao air base on the Gulf of Thailand. Some 200 unarmed aircraft of the CIA-owned Air America supported the military programs in Laos, along with Continental Air Service aircraft under contract to the CIA. Unarmed Air America became known as "The world's most shot-at airline."

Commanding these forces in 1975 was Chief of Station Daniel Arnold, no stranger to war. Dan was a veteran of the Marine Corps and saw action in the Pacific during World War II. He was an infantryman carrying a Browning Automatic Rifle on two landings in the Marshall Islands and was in the first wave ashore on Guam in 1944, where he was wounded. Dan was a corporal when he was discharged after the war. His brother, also a Marine, was killed on Iwo Jima.

In Laos, Dan's rank was the equivalent of a three-star general and he was effectively in command of sixty-five thousand CIA-led troops. They harassed and provided intelligence on more than a hundred and ten thousand NVA invaders and their Pathet Lao communist allies. The fate of Laos was determined by the Paris Peace Accords of 1973, the brainchild of Henry Kissinger and others to get America out of Indochina wars "honorably." It was the beginning of the end for our allies in Vietnam and Cambodia.

For years, the fiction was maintained that Laos was "non-aligned," a royal kingdom that was not involved in the wars raging in Vietnam and Cambodia. The Accords required the United States to disband its "secret" army and return the Thai "volunteers" to Thailand. It was only a matter of time until the Pathet Lao (PL) marched into Vientiane and took power. The PL were permitted to station military forces in every Lao city. They were given half of all ministerial positions. The Royal Thai Government was required to provide housing and facilities for the communists. A platoon of PL was billeted three houses away from Dan's residence. Another platoon was placed immediately behind the U.S. embassy compound.

Dan was ready for the PL. As soon as the Accords were signed and it was clear that the PL would soon be arriving in Vientiane and the other Lao cities on the Mekong, he began to prepare for them. Dan made plans for the evacuation of ethnic tribal minorities, mainly Hmong, who had fought for the CIA for many years. He also planned surprises for the Pathet Lao that they did not anticipate and may still not be aware of. That's the kind of leader Dan was: quiet, competent, and crafty. The surprises worked, but I won't say more. The Pathet Lao do not have a "need to know."

Dan drew the station down as the PL moved in. He also helped anti-communist members of the Royal Lao government escape across the Mekong River. In May 1975, the PL began an accelerated squeeze play. One day they seized the Customs posts; another day it was the Immigration offices.

Early one morning, the PL occupied the main U.S. Agency for International Development (USAID) compound in Vientiane. This was serious. Some CIA personnel were under USAID cover, and some USAID buildings were used by the Agency for storage. Dan had already evacuated classified Station files to Udorn Base in Thailand across the Mekong, which was actually a base of Vientiane Station. But after debriefing personnel working in the compound, it was discovered that many classified documents had been left behind.

Stunned but not dismayed, Dan Arnold acted. He wrote:

> I concluded that it might be possible to get into the compound and into the CIA building ... I asked for three volunteers and a team led by a daring Korean American went in. Under cover of darkness, they scaled a high wall and barbed wire and entered the building. They opened every safe, removed every remaining piece of classified material, and then shredded them.

The plan to destroy the documents was the brainchild of the volunteer who led the three-man team into the Pathet Lao-controlled compound. I will call him Richard. The other team members were local Lao employees of the CIA. Richard spent the night opening 15 safes and shredding all classified documents, while his two Lao assistants stayed on the main floor of the building checking all desk drawers for documents. Their work took about two hours. Richard worked all night shredding classified material. His main problem was not having any drinking water. Mindful that shredded documents might be reconstituted, as happened with documents seized and shredded in Iran in 1979, Richard soaked the shredded documents in water that turned the paper into mush.

Other items that the team discovered included cash and bags of mail destined for station personnel. The entry and exit of the team was aided by the presence of local workers who gathered at the compound to demand their wages. This fracas allowed a station vehicle to enter the large USAID compound and pick up the team, who stuffed the mail bags into the trunk and quietly made their departure. The operation was a total success.

Another building in the USAID compound used to store technical equipment in support of Vientiane Station was in danger of falling into PL hands. With the assistance of a senior USAID officer, Dan arranged for a pro-Pathet Lao employee to be given a key to the building and be told that the building contained hobby gear and he wanted USAID employees to enjoy the gear before the PL got their hands on it. Within a day, the building was emptied by USAID employees.

Dan wasn't through. The building was also full of equipment that the COS did not want to fall into PL hands. Through the assistance of a senior USAID official, Dan passed on the name of a pro-Pathet Lao local employee of USAID along with a key to the building. The USAID officer told the employee that the building was full of "hobby" equipment and wanted USAID "good guys" to have the equipment before the PL "bad guys" took it. He passed the man the key and the combination to the inner steel vault door. Within a day, the Lao employees emptied the building.

By the time Vientiane Station folded its flag and shut down operations, several dozen sites through the country were closed down without loss of life, including four installations that were overrun by the PL. No classified documents or equipment were lost. The Thai "volunteers" returned to Thailand where, over the years, more than eighty of them were promoted to general rank in the Royal Thai Army. Many tribal fighters, notably the Hmong, were evacuated to Thailand with their families, and thousands later settled in the United States. With CIA staff safely gone, his mission complete, Dan flew out of Vientiane on May 14, 1975.

Sadly, the citation that Dan proposed for Richard's bravery in successfully destroying the documents and saving the mail was lost in the confusion of the collapse of Indochina in the spring of 1975. This oversight needs correcting.

CHAPTER 19

A Close Call in Haiti

One of the toughest jobs in the Foreign Service is that of Consular Officer. The most prestigious jobs are Political Officer followed by Economic Officer. Consular Officers are responsible for granting visas, often a difficult, thankless job and sometimes dangerous. Enormous pressure is put on Consular Officers in Third World countries, where the majority of visa applications submitted are fraudulent, leaving it up to the overworked officers to make quick and lasting decisions on who gets a visa and who doesn't. A case in point was explained to me by Matt Ward, with whom I served in Southeast Asian in the late 1970s.

On a hot Indochina day, after a strenuous tennis match, Matt and I relaxed over gin and tonics on the sports club's stately, colonial-style verandah looking out at one of the toughest little golf courses anywhere. There were so many water hazards that golfers employed forecaddies to retrieve balls from water, usually shallow ponds.

Matt was a witty Irish American from Maine, and one of my favorite Foreign Service Officer friends. He had served in Vietnam and we had some mutual friends. Matt was also the most fastidious person I ever knew. He wore bespoke white linen suits and expensive shirts that were carefully ironed by his maid, who later worked for the ambassador. When Matt departed post, his FSO wife, Emily, told me: "If she satisfies Matt with her ironing, she can please anyone." Matt wanted his dining room walls to match a yellow tablecloth. It required several tries before the beleaguered painters got the color just right. I was told that Matt once eschewed a suite in the best hotel in town because the wall colors clashed with his red hair. Matt was old school.

We have a photo of Matt in his white suit atop an elephant looking every inch a colonial Raj of an earlier place and time. The photo appeared in a State Department recruiting publication. BJ and I are also in the photo, but all eyes go straight to Matt. What the recruiting brochure *didn't* report was the story that Matt told me as we sipped out G&Ts on the verandah.

"You know some FSOs don't much care for the CIA, but I am not one of them," he stated. I found his remark rather strange and wondered if it was going someplace. It was an open secret that many State Department officials were not happy letting CIA officers pose as one of them. USAID officers were even worse. It was not something one talked about, especially directly to a CIA officer. I sensed there was a story coming, and was not disappointed.

"Have you ever heard of the Ton Ton Macoute?" Matt asked.

Matt Ward, left, on an elephant at the Suring elephant round-up in Thailand with the Bromans, *circa* 1978. (Image courtesy of Tim Carney)

"Papa Doc Duvalier's thugs in Haiti?" I answered.

"Exactly! In 1971 I was assigned as a consul in Port-au-Prince, a difficult job in the days of "Papa Doc." One day a man made an appointment to see me regarding visas to the United States. He said he was an American citizen and a bishop of a Christian church in Ohio. He urgently needed one hundred visas for Haitians to visit the US. They were a choir going to Ohio to perform at a convocation sponsored by his church. Time was very short, he needed the visas immediately. This happened the day before Thanksgiving and nothing was going to happen fast and I told him so."

"What happened next?" I asked.

"The story did not ring true. I suspected fraud at work and told the bishop to come back with proof of who he was, proof that there was a convocation for the choir, and the passports of the choir. I sent him on his way but said I would be willing to meet him the next day, Thanksgiving Day, to help him. The bishop left, not too happy, saying he would be back the next day. That night I reported the meeting to my superiors who agreed that I might be offered a bribe for the visas."

Matt met with several senior officers and got a crash course in how to handle an attempt to bribe him. The ambassador became involved, and also the regional security officer. If a bribe was offered, he was told to take it. This needed to be witnessed. It was arranged for a Marine Security Guard (MSG) to be on hand to act as the witness. A tape recorder was set up discreetly to have a record of the meeting.

The bishop arrived on time, carrying a briefcase and his passport, which Matt copied. The bishop did not have the required documentation that Matt had requested, but he did have his passport. He claimed he could not find proof that there was a religious event to which the Haitian choir was invited. He relied on the briefcase to get Matt's attention. He opened it and showed Matt that it contained $5,000 in American currency, all for Matt. Here was the bribe. The bishop said he would provide another $5,000 the next day. Matt put the money where the MSG could see it through a window. The tape recorder had the bishop on tape.

Matt handed the bishop 100 visa application forms and told him to have all of the choir members come to the embassy the next day for their interviews. He told the bishop that each applicant would have to be interviewed individually the next morning, and the passports would be returned to the applicants in the afternoon. The bishop left happy. The $5,000 stayed with Matt. The Marine was called in and shown the money. Then he and Matt went to see the Deputy Chief of Mission, who was waiting for them. At that point, Matt was temporarily removed from his consular duties.

It was Thanksgiving Day and Matt, a bachelor at the time, had been invited by the CIA chief of station for dinner. Matt briefed the COS on the bribery-in-progress and agreed to spend the night at the COS's residence.

The next morning, Matt met the bishop at 0730 hours and received the promised extra $5,000 in Haitian gourdes, not U.S. dollars. Then the choir arrived and the interviews began. They were told to return to the embassy at 1500 hours to pick up their passports and visas. When they did so, they were informed that they did not qualify for a visa. The plot thickened.

The State Department wanted to know when the bishop was returning to America, and his itinerary. The COS was told he would be notified when the bishop boarded his plane. Matt did not expect to hear from the bishop again, but rather than leave Haiti, the bishop showed up the next morning at the embassy, accompanied by two dangerous-looking men. It was a Saturday and the embassy was closed. The duty officer met the bishop with a Marine guard present.

The bishop's escorts wanted the embassy to verify that Matt had taken the money but did not issue the visas. The thugs accompanying the bishop were clearly members of Papa Doc's paramilitary force, the Ton Ton Macoute. One said: "You took our money, but did not give us the visas. This is not how we do business." The Ton Ton Macoute were notorious for their violent human rights violations, including rape and murder on the orders of the president. They were Papa Doc's gestapo and every bit as dangerous.

The duty officer played his role coolly. He told the Ton Ton Macoute that none of the applicants would be getting visas, and the money had been confiscated and would be sent to Washington, D.C., where an investigation would be conducted. The bishop watched in horror as the Ton Ton Macoute were told they would not be getting their money back. The duty officer also told Papa Doc's goons that they should not interfere with the bishop's return to the United States.

With the Ton Ton Macoute now in the picture, it was decided that Matt should not return to his house. A Marine picked up Matt's clothes and took them to the DCM's residence, where Matt was now a guest.

The next morning, the COS arrived at the DCM's house to report that the Agency had intelligence that the Ton Ton Macoute were "going to teach the red-haired consul a lesson." They put a "hit" on Matt. Things were now getting serious. The bishop flew out that morning to Miami, where he was met and arrested by the FBI for attempting to bribe a public official.

Matt was the man of the hour. He recalled: "I moved into the ambassador's residence, where I was treated like a VIP. I could travel only in the ambassador's limo accompanied by armed Marines. I never saw my little house again." The investigation took about two weeks, after which Matt was driven to the airport in a motorcade of three vehicles. "I exited the ambassador's car on the tarmac, walked up the stairs of the American Airlines plane, with armed Marines around me, was shown to my seat, and the plane took off."

"So you can see," Matt told me, as he ordered another round of gin and tonics, "why I have a soft spot for the CIA."

CHAPTER 20

Bangkok Scavenger Hunt

All work and no play makes Jack a dull spy. In this case, Jack is the name I will use to describe a CIA case officer who was famed for his scavenger hunts. He was a China specialist who many years ago organized a scavenger hunt in Hong Kong, to wide acclaim. In the 1970s he did the same in Bangkok, and I received a first-hand account of that event.

Espionage is a stressful occupation: leading a double life; a diplomat by day, and a spy by night. It is therefore therapeutic to take some time off and have a little fun. That was Jack's idea when he organized his Bangkok hunt. A scavenger hunt is a game in which the participants are formed into teams to gather items on a list. The first team finding all the items wins.

Of course, a CIA scavenger hunt is not all fun and games. At least this one wasn't. At least one of the participants was an active target of the CIA, whether they knew this or not. Jack invited 20 people to participate, not counting himself and his wife, whom we will call Jill. As the organizers and hosts of the event, they did not actively participate.

The guests were divided into five teams of four, with wives and husbands separated. Because Bangkok is a large and at times a difficult place to navigate, each team had at least one Bangkok "hand." There were no Thai guests. After an initial meeting at Jack's large Bangkok residence, the guests were divided into teams, handed their lists of items to scavenge, given a drink and snacks with which to fortify themselves, and sent into the night.

The list was not long; eight items only. But it was difficult, larcenous, dangerous, and led some naïve diplomats and their wives into uncharted territory in Bangkok's seamy underside. There was no set priority for finding the items; it was up to each team to decide in what order they would hunt, being mindful that the goal was to finish first.

The first item was to visit the 7th Day Adventist Hospital and obtain a handout pamphlet on the evils of smoking. It was a straightforward requirement, but only a few people knew where the hospital was located. In the 1950s it was a leading hospital, but 20 years later it was almost forgotten, located in a dingy part of old Bangkok.

The next item required a visit to Klong Toey, the port of Bangkok. This was another part of Bangkok rarely seen by diplomats. They had to find and identify the name of the ship docked nearest to the entry to the port, passing the infamous Mosquito Bar just outside the gate.

Perhaps the easiest item was to obtain the signature of the night guard at the Jim Thompson House, a private museum with several Thai-style residences rented to foreign residents of Bangkok on the property. The house was well known to the diplomatic community and its affable old night guard spoke some English. But getting his autograph was not easy as he was not briefed on the hunt.

An item that warned of danger was the requirement to count the number of columns at the Victory Monument. This was trouble, as the monument was located in the middle of a large and very active roundabout, very much like the Place de l'Étoile in Paris surrounding the Arc de Triomphe. This required a car to enter the roundabout, carefully navigate to the monument itself, and slowly circumnavigate the monument to count the columns while traffic swirled all round. It required skill and daring, plus the ability to find the monument itself. "What Victory?" you may ask. Every time I pass the monument in a taxi, I ask the driver what victory is commemorated. No one has ever provided the correct answer. The "victory" was in 1940, when the Japanese assisted Thailand in recovering some territory lost to the French.

Less dangerous but by no means easier was to visit a liquor store and purchase a bottle of Maekhong whiskey, Thailand's finest. Not just any bottle, but one bottled on a particular day. How do you know when the whiskey was bottled? Easy: each bottling date is printed on the back of the bottle's label—in Thai. This required a knowledge of Thai to tell the store keeper the day needed. It was a boon to be able to read Thai.

A small measure of larceny was needed to obtain, i.e. steal, an ashtray from the Erawan Hotel. At the time, the state-owned Erawan was a leading hotel and its large lobby had a number of ashtrays available for the use of guests or visitors. But they were not for sale, and stealing them was a criminal offense. Good luck hunters, you are fortunate you have diplomatic immunity, but your ambassador would probably not be amused to learn of your arrest.

The final two items could be found in and around Pat Pong Road, the notorious nightlife center of bars, brothels, and live sex shows near Silom Road, not too far from the American embassy. One required item was a book of matches from the Lonely Boy Bar on Pat Pong III. Few diplomats knew, and fewer wanted to know, about the existence, let alone the location, of the Lonely Boy Bar. It was the exclusive venue for homosexual men, including foreigners, who flocked to Bangkok. Once found—not easily done—obtaining the matches was quickly done. The Thai are famed for their courtesy and friendliness. This is especially true of the gay community.

The last item on the list was not too difficult to find, and not too expensive to obtain, but opened a lot of eyes among the hunters and remained a topic of conversations among participants for years. The item required hunters to locate and enter the Bunny House on Pat Pong Road. It was an upstairs bar and live sex show. The door was locked and no Thai were admitted, as they could be police or police informers. The clientele of the Bunny House were foreigners, almost always male. A few of the scavenger hunters may have heard of the Bunny House and may have even visited. But none would admit it.

The item required was to have Daeng, one of the female entertainers, write a message: "WECOME TO BANGKOK (enter your name)." Not a problem. This was Daeng's specialty. It would cost 100 Baht (about $5 in those days). Daeng would strip naked for the "show" and proceed to deftly print the requested message on an 8.5 inch by 11 inch piece of paper with a Magic Marker inserted in her vagina. She wrote with a remarkably clear "hand," was happy to comply with the first hunter's request, and was delighted to learn that four more requests would be following. One of the first hunters advised her: "Charge 200 Baht per person, and take your time."

The team that found Daeng first was also the winner of the scavenger hunt. Eventually, Daeng made 900 Baht from hunters that evening. The Erawan Hotel lost five ashtrays and no arrests were made. Not all teams found the right bottle of Mekhong, located the needed ship berthed at Klong Toey, or counted the columns at the Victory Monument. But every team had matches from the Lonely Boy Bar, an autograph from the Jim Thompson house's night guard, and a pamphlet warning of the evils of smoking. Almost everyone had a good time and everyone learned a little more about Bangkok.

The scavenger hunters enjoyed a late dinner of Thai curry back at Jack and Jill's, accompanied by bottles of Maekhong whiskey provided by several of the teams. The main topic of conversation at dinner, of course, was the hunt and Daeng. The evening was deemed to have been a great success.

Jack went on to high rank at the Central Intelligence Agency.

CHAPTER 21

Incident with a Swedish Ambassador

I have always been proud of my Swedish heritage. On my father's side, both of my grandparents were Swedes. For balance, my mother's side were Canadian French and Irish. My paternal grandfather, Frans (later Frank) Broman, emigrated from Stockholm early in the 20th century to make a better life for himself as a custom tailor, and succeeded.

He met and married Lillian Wallenberg, born in Minnesota in the Great Blizzard of 1888 and a survivor of the San Francisco earthquake and fire of 1906. She once told me: "We were the poor Wallenbergs, not the rich ones." I sometimes wonder if she was aware of the activities of Raoul Wallenberg, a Swedish diplomat credited with saving the lives of thousands of Hungarian Jews from the Germans during World War II. He died in a Soviet prison after the war and is one of the very few people given honorary U.S. citizenship.

It was, therefore, a pleasure when I met a Swedish ambassador during a posting to Southeast Asia. We were both members of the local sports club and both played tennis. On a hot afternoon early in my tour, I bumped into the fellow on the club's expansive verandah enjoying a local draft beer. I will call him Haggar. He introduced himself and we exchanged calling cards.

"Broman. By your name your people must have been bridge men, at least the first one was," he said, referring to the fact that Broman means "keeper of the bridge" and acknowledging that we were fellow Swedes. We exchanged ancestral info as we enjoyed local beer.

"My grandfather was a tailor," I explained, "and made suits for Hollywood figures of the silent screen. My father is an architect and was a glider pilot in Europe during the war."

"My father," he said, "was poor and emigrated to France. He helped smuggle Jews out of France during the war. I was educated in Sweden and became a diplomat." Haggar was exuberant, self-assured, and a socialist. He wanted mainly to talk about Vietnam and his affection for the North Vietnamese. He had served in Vietnam and had high-ranking friends in Hanoi, which made him of interest to me. But Haggar was openly, and it seemed proudly, anti-American and I often received the brunt of his ire after a few glasses of beer.

I knew my association with Haggar would be tortuous when I learned that he was a protégé of Swedish Prime Minister Olaf Palme, an unabashed supporter of "national liberation" movements, especially North Vietnam and Cuba. He accused the United States of war crimes in bombing North Vietnam. Nonetheless, I would see Haggar regularly at the sports club, usually on the verandah after lawn tennis. Invariably the talk centered on politics and Indochina. We maintained a cordial diplomatic relationship, possibly fostered on his part by our shared Viking heritage and probably motivated by my expertise in the history of the area. At no time did we ever agree on any subject. I would describe the discourse as lively, if not friendly.

It was, therefore, something of a surprise when I received an invitation to dinner from Haggar. Of course I accepted, and hoped he would be serving Scandinavian fare. I was not disappointed. It was an outside affair, around the swimming pool, complete with a live band and a dance floor. I knew a few of the guests from the diplomatic circuit and was looking to meet some North Vietnamese. There were two on hand, and one seemed interested in talking to me when he learned I had served in Cambodia when it fell in 1975. His French was better than his English, so we spoke French. He was reticent talking about the Khmer Rouge but agreed to a follow-up lunch, which made the whole evening worthwhile.

It seemed the entire staff of the Swedish embassy was on hand, all of them professional and pleasant, in stark contrast to their ambassador, who seemed to take pleasure in being belligerent. BJ and I took full advantage of the smorgasbord buffet of Swedish cuisine, starting with gravlax, a national icon of cured salmon. There was also a selection of local Asian dishes, which gave the long table a healthy East–West mix.

The evening was very relaxed and the company convivial. Haggar, our host, seemed to be enjoying himself, although I only talked to him when he greeted us on arrival. He was busy with more senior, and politically sympathetic, guests such as the austere Vietnamese ambassador, who Haggar fawned over. I thought it should be the reverse. Haggar was responsible for Sweden's enormous aid program for Vietnam, much of it wasted through corruption and poor planning.

Working the crowd with glass in hand, Haggar bantered in a semi-friendly manner with the tall and urbane Danish ambassador, a conservative.

They seemed to have a running feud going. Finally, the band went into action and guests stepped out on the dance floor. It was a warm tropical night and the Filipino band was excellent. BJ and I were enjoying ourselves and the evening was a cut above your standard diplomatic bun fight. BJ is a good dancer and dance parties were rare.

Suddenly, while on the dance floor and enjoying a little rock and roll, I was grabbed from behind and spun around. BJ was in shock and the dance floor cleared as the music stopped. It was Haggar, and he had my full attention. I didn't know what was going on, but it looked like he might hit me. I made a quick assessment of the situation and decided that if Haggar struck me, I would take one for the team and not get involved in a violent encounter. I should here note that Haggar was bigger, older, and intoxicated. But he didn't hit me. He wasn't even angry, at least not at me.

"You always argue with me Broman, maybe that's why I like you," he said. The guests watched silently. With a hand still on my shoulder, Haggar gestured toward his appalled staff and added: "They always agree with me. You never do." He made it sound like agreeing with him was a bad thing. He then walked away; the crisis passed. The band started again and people returned to the dance floor.

If Haggar really liked me, it can only be my Swedish heritage that made it so. Frankly, I doubt he liked me any more than I liked him. I never met a less diplomatic diplomat.

CHAPTER 22

CODELS

A bane in the life of American embassies everywhere is the Congressional Delegation (CODEL). These delegations from the U.S. Senate or House of Representatives range from small, fact-finding visits to large boondoggles complete with wives with shopping lists, expensive U.S. military aircraft, and a drain on the staff of the embassy. During my time in Cambodia at war, from 1973–75, we were not troubled by visits by congressmen or even their staffs. In Europe, on the other hand, a day hardly went by without someone from Congress needing to visit one of the world's great cities at American taxpayer expense.

Usually, CODELs do not spend much, if any, time with the CIA or its station personnel. But very often, Agency officers, under State Department cover, will be tasked with assisting in the care and feeding of visiting Congressional groups. Such a group of both senators and congressmen from both political parties, accompanied by wives, visited Bangkok *circa* 1977. Because of the high rank of several of the visitors, there were dinners arranged, with calls on senior Thai officials, sometimes involving the palace. While the American officials were busy with matters of state, their wives were often shown the many sites of the city and taken on shopping expeditions.

The visitors stayed at the Dusit Thani Hotel, not far from the embassy, and a "hospitality suite" was booked for the CODEL to relax between meetings and dinners. Embassy officers were assigned to be on hand to assist the visitors. Late one evening, after a formal dinner with senior Thai officials, a number of the delegation were relaxing in the suite, where a Bangkok station officer was on hand to assist.

A senior senator from the Deep South, well known and well liked by most people who knew him from both sides of the aisle, approached the station officer in his guise as an embassy political officer. "Son," he said in his pronounced Southern drawl, "I know what your duties are and I don't want to intrude on a personal matter, but I could use a little help."

Appreciating the senator's polite appeal for help, unlike the more frequent demands from visitors or even their staffers, the officer replied: "I am here to help you in any way I can senator. How may I assist?"

"Son, my wife is a great consumer of Drambuie, a liqueur from Scotland based on Scotch whisky, honey, and spices."

"I am familiar with the liqueur, senator, in fact I have a bottle at home," said our officer.

"That's good, son. The problem is that the hotel doesn't have any."

"I find that hard to believe, sir. The hotel has several bars; perhaps if I checked for you."

"Thank you, son, but she has drunk all they had. I need a bottle now and would appreciate your help finding one."

"As I mentioned, sir, I have a bottle at home. We could send the duty car to pick it up. It might take a little while, with traffic an' all. Or I could phone a friend who owns a bar which is very close. I am sure he could help."

"Whichever is quicker, son, I would appreciate it."

The officer then phoned Rick Menard, owner of the Gran Prix Bar on Pat Pong Road.

"Rick," the officer said, "I am in the presidential suite of the Dusit Thani and have an urgent need for a bottle of Drambuie. Could you help me out? I will repay you tomorrow."

"Ten minutes," was all that Rick said.

About 10 minutes later, there was a knock at the door of the presidential suite. The station officer opened the door. Standing there was a tall, statuesque, beautiful Thai woman dressed in an evening gown. The officer recognized her as one of Rick's finest hostesses. The woman handed the CIA man a package with the words, "*Khun Rick hai*" (a gift from Mr. Rick). The duty officer accepted the gift and thanked her in Thai. She then gave a polite Thai "*wai*" with hands clasped before her face, bowed slightly, and departed.

The officer handed the parcel to the senator, who said: "Who *are* you, son?"

CHAPTER 23

Home Leave

Espionage is never easy, especially if you are undeclared to the host government that you work for the CIA. At any moment, an agent can be arrested or a recruitment target could refuse a "pitch" to spy for the Agency and report you to his or her government. When that happens, the officer and his family could be declared *persona non grata* and be on the next plane out. All of this for a sometimes 70 hours a week job, much of it at night, and no overtime.

It is worse if the officer works in a "denied area," usually a country hostile to the United States, where an officer should expect to be followed wherever he goes, have his phone and house tapped or bugged, and his local staff co-opted by the host government to report on the officer. This is an environment where an agent caught spying for America could expect torture and a death sentence.

Hence, an annual trip back to the States for families is a welcome relief to relax, visit friends and family, recharge batteries, and, in the case of officers assigned in Asia, travel home business class on American-flagged airlines across the Pacific. We had two venues for home leave. The first was Hawaii, to visit BJ's parents and her brother, Ken. Apu and Tutu, grandparents to Seth and Brendan, lived in the sleepy village of Pepeekeo, an old sugar plantation near Hilo on the Big Island. The second venue was Seattle, where we visited my parents, Booge and Grandpappy to the boys.

During the years when I was posted in Southeast Asia, home leaves were greeted with anticipation, especially by our two sons, both seasoned international travelers. Seth was born in Asia five years before Brendan, who was born in Europe. They especially liked flying Tokyo to Honolulu on Northwest Orient Airlines which offered high-quality sushi platters in business class. The boys helped themselves liberally when the carts rolled by.

The boys kept their boogie boards—starter surf boards—at their Uncle Ken's house in Kona and loved to hit the surf. The only downside was arrival at the international airport in Honolulu, where the lines were long and slow-moving. After clearing customs and immigration, we had to walk to the domestic terminal. All of this after 15 hours in the air and a layover in Tokyo.

Often, on the same trip that took us to Hawaii, we would fly on to Seattle, my home town. It was always good to be back in the Pacific Northwest. A frequent

Seth gets a ukulele lesson from his grandfather, Simplicio Apilado, in Pepeekeo, Hawaii.

stop on summer home leaves was to see our oldest family friends, Dr. Harold Pebbles and kin, at their summer home on Puget Sound, where we could fish for salmon, dig Manila clams, and pick oysters off the beach. Fresh steamed Dungeness crab, arguably the best crab in the world, available just offshore, rounded out a locavore banquet that only needed fresh ears of corn on the cob and a bottle or two of white Washington State wine.

One year, before the boys were born, BJ and I were in Seattle on home leave and were invited to dinner by my close friend, Bob Peterson. He was a college roommate, a fellow photographer on the University of Washington's daily newspaper, and my best man when BJ and I were married in 1968. Bob was also a photographer for *LIFE* magazine in New York for years, and returned to Seattle to direct television commercials when *LIFE* folded.

Bob was an accomplished chef, with the figure of Falstaff, and was the life of every party. He prepared our meal while his wife, Lynn, BJ, and I sat around the kitchen "island" sipping wine or Perrier. Over the course of three hours, we ate multiple delicacies, including sautéed geoducks, large clams native to Puget Sound. Then came grilled hanger steaks with an aged bottle of Chateau Lynch Bages from Bordeaux, from Bob's impressive cave. At least four bottles of wine were consumed that evening, plus a bottle of vintage Croft port that I picked up for Bob at a Tokyo airport duty free shop.

Around midnight, Lynn excused herself and went to bed. Bob produced a bottle of Cognac and some cigars as we talked into the early hours of

Bob Peterson photo of Clint Eastwood during filming of *Dirty Harry*.

the morning. Finally, it was time to go home. Bob walked us out to the car to say goodbye. BJ, a teetotaler, took the wheel and drove us home. Late the next morning, I called Bob to thank him for a memorable evening. Lynn answered the phone and was unusually brusque. I asked if something was wrong.

"I was awakened by the paper boy this morning around 6am," she said. "He found Bob on the lawn and thought he was dead. Bob had curled up and gone to sleep on the lawn after he said goodbye to you and BJ. The front door was open wide." That was the last night of wretched excess dinner parties that I remember at Bob's house—at least for several years.

CHAPTER 24

Close and Continuing Contacts

A vexing and insoluble problem that has faced American military and civilians posted abroad is the matter of men and women developing close personal relationships with persons in the countries to which they are assigned. This is an issue that mainly involves bachelors seeking companionship that morphs into long-term relationships. For the Agency, such a practice was frowned upon. These days it is forbidden.

As a young Marine officer in Vietnam, I was told stories of old Marines posted to Asia, usually "China Marines" who would have mistresses or even families in Asia that their wives in America were unaware of. Even after World War II, when the Corps had a division of infantry assigned to Okinawa, a Marine could expect to spend one-year unaccompanied tours in Japan on a regular basis in the Fleet Marine Force (FMF). This led to the custom known as "ranching," where the Marine had two families—one on each side of the Pacific Ocean. This led to the quip, "It's time I left my family and returned to my loved ones."

Even during my posting to Vietnam during the war, I knew a Marine lieutenant colonel on the staff of the 1st Marine Division in Da Nang who had an American girlfriend who was a stewardess and a frequent visitor to Da Nang. When she was in town, the colonel would arrange for a friend at the American consulate to invite her to stay at his large colonial residence where the colonel would be invited to dinner, and to spend the night.

Similarly, in Bangkok I knew a senior U.S. Army officer whose wife declined to accompany him to Thailand. He found solace in the arms of a German stewardess on the Bangkok run. When she was in town, she served as the officer's hostess at dinner parties to which no American wives were invited. The arrangement worked quite well.

There was even the case of a senior State Department officer whom I knew in Asia. He was married, with a wife and family in the States. He was also a Vietnamese linguist, with numerous postings to Vietnam during the war. In Vietnam, he started another family with a local lady and kept both families for years without the American family learning about his Vietnamese counterpart.

In the CIA, the issue of local liaisons becomes a security issue in addition to one of morality and common sense. Hostile intelligence services, notably the Soviet KGB, have, as we have seen, made a fine art of luring Americans with secrets to share by using attractive ladies in the ploy coined by the late novelist and former British intelligence officer John le Carré as the honey trap. The Russians were not alone in their use of women to gain access to American secrets. A female CIA secretary in Africa was seduced in Ghana by a local fellow and gave up the identities of the station's assets there. She went to jail.

To reduce the counterintelligence dangers, the CIA introduced strict guidelines on what was termed "close and continued contact with foreign nationals." Naturally, this disrupted a number of intimate relationships, involving both married and single employees of both genders. I recall the case of a female non-official cover (NOC) officer in a large station in Europe who entered into an illicit relationship with a male national from the country to which she was assigned. She kept the relationship secret from the Agency and her colleagues for a long time. She was so certain of the fidelity of her paramour that she told him that she worked for the CIA. That was another mistake. He reported her to the local counterintelligence service. She was declared *persona non grata* and immediately sent home. Her career as a spy was over. Relations with the country to which she was posted were damaged.

In Asia, I knew an Agency officer who had a close relationship with a local girl whom he installed in his large and luxurious apartment. He was single and knew what he was doing. As an officer trained in running clandestine operations, he ran one to protect his secret relationship. For starters, no one was invited to his apartment and he never entertained at home. He was discreet, and so was his girlfriend. I knew of only one friend, stationed in a country nearby, who was invited to stay with his "family" when they were in town. When the officer's tour ended, he retired and immediately married the girl.

Perhaps the most bizarre yet successful story of a philandering case officer with a local girlfriend took place in Saigon. The officer's wife was "safe havened" in Taipei, Taiwan, with other wives for their security. With the wife away, the officer, whom I will call Ted, developed an attachment to a pretty, young Vietnamese girl and installed her in his house. It went well until the wife announced she was coming for a short visit. Ted arranged for his girlfriend, whom I will call Mai Lee, to take a vacation in Vung Tao at the beach while his wife was in town. He moved all of Mai Lee's clothing and personal effects out of the house and into boxes in the garage. He also arranged for a number of war-maimed beggars to be placed in front of his house, at his expense, to make the place look undesirable. Finally, one night he arranged for his Nung guard to throw a concussion grenade in the garden late at night. It made a loud noise but no harm was done. Calling this an attempted attack, Ted convinced his wife that she would be safer in Taipei. She finished his tour safe on Taiwan. Mai Lee came back from the beach to find the house as it was before she left. The beggars were gone and there were no more grenade attacks. Mai Lee never knew of the wife's visit.

CHAPTER 25

Covert Communications Training

While serving at an Asian station, my deputy chief of station (DCOS), an outstanding officer with a wry sense of humor, called me in one morning and announced: "Broman, this is your lucky day. I am sending you off on an all-expense paid vacation. Congratulations."

I was wary, immediately remembering the ancient advice, "Beware Greeks bearing gifts."

"To what do I owe this stroke of luck?" I asked.

"Relax," he smiled. "No catch here. I would be happy to go myself but you need some down time and the experience this trip will bring."

"Where will I be going?" I asked. "And what will I be doing?"

He named a large and attractive city in the region:

"You will pick up an agent that was recruited there and will participate in his communications training. He will be posted home soon but not for long. He will be assigned to a denied area which is why he will be trained in a new and secure satellite commo system. This will obviate the need for face-to-face meetings and the use of dead drops in the future. He will be getting the cutting edge of clandestine communications. And you will be in charge."

"When do I go?"

"Soon. Two commo officers will handle the training. Training will be done in the presidential suite of a five-star hotel. That's where the trainers will stay. You will be nearby in a lesser hotel but all your meetings will be in the presidential suite. When the time comes you will go shopping with the asset to purchase a concealment device in which he will hide his commo gear and any other spy gear we give him. Plan to be gone for more than a week."

It all sounded good to me. I was chuffed. A new case to be run and a sexy new commo system to be used: a new adventure. The DCOS handed me a thin file to read on the agent. I'll call him Bruno. A few days after the meeting, I was told to pack my bags. The agent's training had started. Two days later, I was in the city, my first time there. I checked into a modest hotel near the tall, elegant site where my new agent was being trained on the top floor. At the appointed hour, I knocked on the double doors of the presidential suite. A middle-aged man answered, inviting me in. He was the senior communications officer. He introduced me to Bruno. Bruno's handler had departed post, so this was the "turn over" meeting.

Bruno was old enough to be my father. He was tall, well dressed and spoke good English. He was more relaxed in French, so we communicated easily in a mix of both languages. I was a little worried that being so much younger would worry him, but he seemed happy to have me as his case officer. That did not seem to be an issue. He had high praise for his recruiting officer, as well as his commo teachers. We chatted for a while, getting to know each other. He described his career as a government functionary, his education, and his two children, who were the light of his life. I mentioned my own background, which included service in the Marine Corps in Vietnam. This seemed to interest him. He had never been in the military and had a number of intelligent questions about my time in Vietnam. He didn't ask any questions about my time in the Agency.

The two trainers were in tech heaven. The senior officer clearly knew his business. The junior tech was there to learn as much as teach. They were both very professional and were delighted at their venue and with Bruno. They worked about a four-hour day, depending on Bruno's schedule. They had an elaborate cover story to explain their extended vacation in the presidential suite. The host government was not aware of this clandestine activity taking place in their capital; while friendly with the United States, they would have been upset to know what we were doing on the top floor of one of their best hotels.

The communicators were beer drinkers and stocked the fridge with local beer. They never drank during working hours, whether Bruno was there or not. They told me privately that Bruno was a quick learner and had mastered the operation of his satellite system. Bruno drank moderately, mostly European wine or vodka, in our one-on-one meetings. I contributed a bottle of Johnnie Walker (Black) scotch and a six-pack of Perrier.

When it came time for shopping for a concealment device (CD), an officer from the Technical Services Division (TSD) of the CIA arrived to go shopping with us. He was posted to a nearby station and was the man tasked with modifying the desk with a hidden space that would hide the commo gear. He was an outgoing middle-aged fellow with lots of experience modifying furniture for the Agency. He had a list of local furniture makers and stores where we would seek the perfect work desk for Bruno. After a couple of days shopping, we found a desk that pleased both Bruno and the tech. I was appalled at the weight of the impressive, carved teak desk that would fit nicely with Bruno's needs and space. It would take a few hefty men to move it. This was not an item that could be easily stolen; another selling point. After a little bargaining, Bruno struck a deal. He arranged for the desk to be shipped to an address, from where the tech could move it to his workshop for necessary modification. Ultimately, the desk was delivered to Bruno's home when he returned from his current posting.

Finally, the training was finished and Bruno passed with honors. He had small gifts for the trainers, which I thought was a nice touch. The desk arrived safely at the tech's address, and I returned to my station to await Bruno's arrival. The elaborate and sophisticated commo system, which Bruno was delighted to be given, was not for use in his home city but in his next assignment, where it would be essential for his security.

It was a chore to move the desk from the plane delivering it to Bruno's home town to the truck that he rented to transport it home in the dark. Bruno had friends and staff standing by to shift the carved teak desk, which weighed over 200lb, to his home office. He told me later that while moving the desk upstairs, he and his grown daughter noticed that the door of the concealment device had been triggered by someone unwittingly pressing the release button and the door opened up. Bruno was aghast. Fortunately, he was a quick thinker and slammed it shut, commenting to his daughter about the shoddy workmanship of the manufacturer. No harm was done, and in the privacy of his den he later opened and closed the secret opening of the CD without problem.

Later, I passed the commo equipment to Bruno at a brief late-night meeting. He took his new and very expensive commo system home and successfully set it up, much to the relief and delight of headquarters and the boffins in the commo shop. Bruno reported via satellite throughout the remainder of my tour. We had a few administrative meetings before my tour ended. I was later informed that he continued to report from a denied area. As I was no longer involved in the operation, I had "no need to know." But if he had been compromised or arrested, I think that I would have been told either by friends involved with the operation or, in the worst case, from press reporting of an American spy captured. That never happened, so I was confident that Bruno succeeded in his mission.

I sometimes ponder about Bruno's motivation in risking his life in the clandestine service of the United States. He was a quiet man with the air of an academic, with the respect of his peers and certainly of the case officers who met him. I doubt he was motivated by greed or politics. He held an important position with his government, but was not a wealthy man. I perceived that he wanted the best for his children, especially in terms of education. They attended private schools and universities in the West, all of which were expensive. I am certain that a large part of the money he received from the Agency went to the education of his children. After all, the Clandestine Service is in the business of making dreams come true. And in this case they did.

CHAPTER 26

A Small World Occurrence

This is a true story. A discerning reader will ask: "Aren't they all true?" The answer is "Yes," and although this one seems improbable, it is nonetheless true.

In 1975, after the fall of Cambodia, BJ and I went around the world to unwind from the war, see old friends and new places, and gear up for my next Asian assignment. We began our journey with a stop in Kathmandu, Nepal, to see "Jason," a former Marine buddy who invited us to forget the war zone and see the Himalayas.

It was a good place to start, even though our host was not there to greet us. Jason, an embassy officer, was driving up from India and arrived on our second night as we were sitting down to dinner at the famous Yak & Yeti Restaurant run by the irascible Ukrainian Boris Lisanevich. Just as we were starting to eat, Jason walked in, saw us, and shouted across the room: "Don't eat the salad!" A hush filled the restaurant. Everyone with salads put their forks down. Boris was not happy. Apparently, proper cleaning of lettuce was not up to international standards at the Yak & Yeti. Without salads, we loved the borscht dinner, Boris's signature offering. It was good seeing Jason again. He had been badly wounded in Vietnam and enjoyed his posting to Nepal. We spent a couple of days exploring Kathmandu, a quiet town with amazing lapis lazuli jewelry.

Our next stop was Paris, where we had another friend, "Edward," waiting to show us the bright lights and cuisine. We flew to New Delhi and a long layover waiting for the Pan Am flight to Paris. While waiting, I struck up a conversation with an American. Wearing a tan Palm Beach suit, white button-down shirt, and a Princeton tie, I suspected he was a Foreign Service Officer posted to the American consulate in Madras. I will call him Joel. He was heading for Beirut. I wanted to see if he might be a colleague of mine.

I mentioned to Joel that we had just visited Jason in Kathmandu, and asked if he knew him.

"Not personally," he said, "but I have heard of him. I think he was in the Marines. Is that where you knew him?"

"No," I said. "Jason was in Vietnam before I was. I met him at the Farm." By mentioning "the Farm," the CIA's main training facility in Virginia, I was essentially telling Joel that I worked for the CIA, and waited for his response.

"I was at the Farm before Jason," he said, "but have heard good things about him." That cleared the air and we had a long chat about mutual friends and current events.

Our Pan Am flight left New Delhi on time, bound for Karachi, Pakistan, where we had engine trouble. We sat in the aircraft with the engines shut down and the doors open for seven hours. The heat in the cabin exceeded 100 degrees Fahrenheit. To dissuade people from getting off, the aircraft was surrounded by armed guards in jeeps.

Eventually, we took off. I made a mental note never to return to Pakistan. Several hours later we landed in Beirut, where we would spend the night. Our bags were put on the connecting flight to Paris the next morning. Since we had missed the connection and the next plane was full, we were booked on a flight to Frankfurt that connected with one to Paris.

We had a problem. Our bags were on the Pan Am flight going to Charles de Gaulle Airport (CDG), but we were going into Orly Airport on the other side of Paris. Worse, I could not reach Edward, who would be meeting the CDG flight, to warn him that we were now going to Orly.

We spent the night in Beirut, the "playground" of the Mediterranean. Bone tired, we booked into a top-rated hotel on the Corniche. BJ went straight to bed, exhausted from our tedious delays. Joel told me he had a friend in Beirut, "Oscar," whom he called and arranged dinner at a fashionable Italian restaurant.

I had not met Oscar before, but knew his name. He had served in Phnom Penh station before I arrived there in 1973. We spent much of the evening briefing Oscar on the last days of Cambodia before the Khmer Rouge took power. About halfway through our delightful meal, the convivial mood changed abruptly to the sound of a Kalashnikov AK-47 rifle firing a burst of bullets not far away. It was all I could do to stop myself diving for cover. Oscar and other diners ignored the gunfire.

"It's just somebody letting off steam," Oscar explained. "Pay it no attention. Beirut is the safest place in the Middle East. Everyone keeps their money here. We are in no danger." Oscar was wrong. Some months later, our fancy hotel was a burned-out shell and Beirut was in ruins. When I returned to the hotel, BJ was in deep sleep. I pondered our next move.

Our flight to Frankfurt was uneventful. Still unable to reach Edward, I decided to have a drink. BJ waited in the transit lounge. I found solace at a stand-up bar nearby. While enjoying my libation, I noticed a man drinking nearby with another man and recognized him as a senior Agency officer whom I knew from Headquarters. I'll call him Tom. With drink in hand, I walked over and said hello. He remembered me, greeted me warmly, and introduced me to his companion, another Agency officer. Tom was also waiting for a flight to Paris. It turned out to be the Pan Am flight that we couldn't get seats on.

Tom knew Edward, who would be meeting the flight in Paris. So I gave Tom our baggage stubs, and asked him to give them to Edward, and told him our flight number and time we would be landing at Orly later in the day.

We caught our flight to Orly to find Edward waiting for us. Our luggage was in the trunk of his car. Tom had surprised him at Charles de Gaulle when he handed him our baggage tags. Tom hosted us for a few days, showed us Paris, and took us down to the Loire Valley for a weekend visiting chateaux and eating at our first of many Michelin-starred restaurants.

Our next stop was London, where my father was waiting. He had flown from Seattle to show us around the city he knew well. After a few days sightseeing, attending a West End theater and eating at Pappy's favorite restaurant, Simpsons, we took a train to Canterbury. The city still showed the scars of relentless German bombing during the Battle of Britain in 1940. I rented a car and we visited our old home, Deepdene, 7 miles away in Herne Bay. We spent a few days visiting old British friends and made a pilgrimage to RAF Manston, now closed as a military airfield but still boasting the longest runway in Britain. I photographed Pappy next to a Spitfire aircraft on display. The sign in front of the fighter aircraft read: "Treat me Gently, I am old." It could also have been describing Pappy.

Our around-the-world trip ended with a lengthy visit home in Seattle and another on the idyllic Big Island of Hawaii, visiting BJ's family at the Pepeekeo Sugar Plantation, before returning to Asia and my next posting. Our batteries were fully recharged. The highlight of the trip had to be the chance encounter with Tom in Frankfurt. What are the odds of that happening? It is good to have friends everywhere. And it's always good to be lucky.

CHAPTER 27

A CIA "Dirty Trick" in the Cold War

In 1962, one of CIA's best Soviet agents, GRU Colonel Oleg Penkovsky, was arrested, tried, and executed. The Military Intelligence officer had provided vital intel to the West, including vital information on Soviet missile installations in Cuba that allowed President Kennedy to face down Soviet leader Khrushchev and avert a nuclear war. Penkovsky was credited with altering the course of the Cold War.

Senior officers of the CIA's Directorate of Operations (DO) sought to salvage something out of Penkovsky's loss. An elaborate, carefully scripted disinformation operation directed at selected KGB and GRU officers worldwide was developed. The idea was to discredit and bring suspicion against otherwise guiltless and often very capable adversaries in the Cold War. A large station in a Southeast Asia country was included in this operation, and the station's deputy chief was enlisted to participate. I will call him Clay.

Clay was no novice in the arcane world of anti-Soviet covert action. Earlier in the year, he had caused great heartburn to the Soviet embassy when he surfaced in a Soviet radio broadcast in the language of a neighboring country, blatantly insulting the revered and much-respected king in the country where Clay was posted. The Soviet ambassador was brought to tears when he was called in to explain the broadcast, and Soviet relations with the country suffered.

Perhaps that was why Clay was tapped to cause greater harm to the Soviet Union and its intelligence services.

The plan called for senior CIA officers, probably known to the Soviet intelligence services as being with the Agency, to select a non-threatening venue where a brief conversation could be held. Clay selected an event taking place at the country's premiere sports club, where he already had an invitation. He arranged for three more invitations to be sent to senior KGB and GRU officers and their wives. Clay already knew that two of the couples would be unable to attend, but hoped that the third couple—an effective GRU lieutenant colonel and his wife, a GRU major—would view the invitation as an opportunity to meet possible targets of their own.

The plan worked. The couple attended the event and seemed delighted to be able to meet senior officials of the host government. Clay had also arranged for selected American embassy officers and wives to attend to unobtrusively separate the GRU wife from her husband, the target of the operation. The ploy went as planned and Clay made his move:

> I introduced myself to the target by my true name and identified myself as a CIA officer. The colonel looked at me with a mildly surprised smile and said he wondered why he and his wife had been invited to the reception. We proceeded to engage in a bit of small talk, during which he said the Soviet Embassy would soon be hosting a visit of the Bolshoi Ballet. I replied that I had always admired the Bolshoi from afar and would love to see the ballet. He responded by promising to send me tickets to the ballet and in return I thanked him for his generosity.

Then Clay went for the jugular:

> I abruptly changed the conversation to say that we knew that he was a GRU colonel and that his wife was a GRU major. I continued by saying that while we had monitored their clandestine operations, we had never done anything to interfere or embarrass him or his wife in any way. Because of our respect for them we wanted to give him and his wife the opportunity to work for us for a period of time after which we would arrange for them to go the United States and to begin a new life with great promise. I explained that Penkovsky had given us his name as someone who might want to collaborate with the CIA and that a number of his colleagues had been similarly approached.

Of course, Clay was lying: Penkovsky never gave the names of GRU or KGB officers who were likely to work for the CIA. But the Soviet colonel didn't know that. That's why I call this a "dirty trick." But all's fair in love and war, and this was war—a cold war.

The colonel listened quietly while Clay made his pitch. Then he lunged for his wife, who was nearby chatting with American embassy wives. He grabbed her by the arm and bolted for the exit. In his haste to get away, the colonel hit two parked cars as he sped from the sports club. Clay had arranged with a friendly host country liaison service to monitor the colonel and his dented getaway car. Their report was most interesting. It is standing Soviet procedure after any approach by a hostile intelligence service for the officer to immediately report the incident. The GRU colonel did not do that. Instead, the couple drove around the city for hours, clearly discussing their options. Eventually, they drove to the home of the KGB "resident," the senior Soviet intelligence officer in country. Clay knew that the couple were about to go on home leave and return to the Asian country for a new tour. After reporting Clay's approach, the couple did not return to their apartment but were sequestered inside the Soviet embassy compound. Soviet embassy personnel visited the couple's landlord and cancelled the lease on their residence. They also fired their servants. The hapless GRU couple were escorted on the next Aeroflot flight to Moscow. They were never allowed to serve abroad again.

This scenario was repeated in a number of major cities in Asia and Europe with equally unlucky KGB and GRU officers, all of them deemed by the CIA to be hardworking, efficient enemy intelligence officers whom we needed to put out of action. Each CIA officer who made an approach had a legend or story that included one or more names of a KGB or GRU officer at another location, so it was a carefully embroidered script that must have done enormous damage to both Soviet services. Clay was not told what happened in the other cases—he had "no need to know"—but he was confident that his own case would have an uneventful, possibly truncated career ahead.

The Soviet system was paranoid and had been since the days of Josef Stalin's reign of terror before World War II. Millions of innocent Soviet citizens were murdered and millions more disappeared into the Gulags, a vast system of forced labor camps. Everyone feared the "midnight knock" on their doors, usually conducted by the KGB, the Soviet Union's vast and unforgiving intelligence service with internal as well as external duties. Anyone who may have had his name passed to the Americans by the late Colonel Penkovsky as a potential spy willing to work for the CIA would never be trusted again, even if the information was false, as was the case here. Their careers would take a new arc, and not a happy one. I like to think that Penkovsky would have welcomed this creative ploy by the Agency. Even in death, we would be able to confound and damage his former employer.

The story is not quite over. Headquarters was effusive in their kudos to Clay and asked that he attempt to contact the colonel one last time. Clay called the Soviet embassy, asked for the colonel's extension, and was somewhat surprised when the GRU officer came on the line. Clay made no mention of his recent bold attempt to ask the colonel to spy against the USSR. Instead, he said in a pleasant tone: "I hope you are sending me my tickets for the Bolshoi Ballet that you promised."

The Russian was not amused. If fact, he was livid: "You son of a bitch! You have a hell of a nerve calling me." He did not mention that he was being recalled to Moscow, his career in tatters. He slammed the phone down. Soon he was gone, never to be seen outside the Soviet Union again. And Clay never got his tickets.

CHAPTER 28

A Favorite Agent

I have liked and respected most of the agents I recruited and ran, but a few stand out. One was a senior diplomat from a non-aligned nation that was friendly to the United States. My target, whom I will call Max, was pro-American, well connected, and totally amoral. That is the kind of guy I was looking for.

Max spoke good English, was well educated and well traveled, and devoted every spare moment looking for (and usually finding) young ladies to bed. He was more-or-less happily married to a woman who was also from the elite of their country, who had her own career and several children. When I met Max, she had no idea that her husband was a serial philanderer. That came later.

Max and I worked the diplomatic circuit and quickly became friends. He was witty, urbane, and reveled in keeping me informed of his success with the ladies. He was also candid in his remarks regarding sensitive and even secret matters concerning his own government. This information was of interest to the U.S. Government and I disseminated several reports from Max, who may or may not have suspected that I worked for the CIA.

In short order, Max became a target for recruitment. He had the necessary access to the intelligence we wanted and he showed no reticence in sharing this information with me, knowing I would report it. I quickly became aware that although Max was well paid, his womanizing was costly. He needed a new source of income. Enter the CIA.

I broached the idea of my underwriting his extra-marital hobby and he immediately agreed to provide secret information in exchange for money. My relationship with Max changed, but not by much. If anything, he was more eager to fulfill my requirements because now he had an obligation to earn his newfound income. I asked questions that were provided by the analysts in Langley and he did his best to answer them.

There was only one problem: Max had little interest in what went on in meetings he attended or in documents that he read. He was happy to be debriefed, but admitted that paying attention, especially to boring government issues, was not his forte. But he had a solution: "Why don't I just give you the documents?"

This was espionage gold. Accuracy in reporting is essential, and mental recall, even among people who pay attention, is not infallible. Getting documents is always the best solution, but often a dangerous one. If caught taking classified documents out of the office or, worse, caught copying or photographing them, Max would be in very serious trouble. Neither his charm nor connections would save him.

But while lazy, Max was also gutsy and was able to securely copy secret documents that needed only to be translated. The problem was solved. Running Max suddenly became easier and more efficient. Ninety percent of his reporting was via documents, and the other 10 percent came from meetings or conversations he had with colleagues.

I ran Max for a couple of years until I was posted elsewhere. The turnover went smoothly, and from time to time I saw reporting from Max, who juggled two secret lives successfully until he retired.

A Handling Challenge

A mid-level case officer, I'll call him Jerome, in a large European station was surprised and a little concerned when he was convoked by his chief of station. He was a competent and well-liked officer, who had never had a one-on-one conversation with his COS, an Ivy League alum and mandarin of the Clandestine Service.

Jerome was ushered into the plush but tasteful office of the chief, who greeted him warmly and asked him to sit. The greying but robust tennis-playing chief offered Jerome his choice of coffee or tea and seemed to be in a good mood. Jerome opted for black coffee and quickly sensed that he was not in any trouble. That thought was challenged when the chief, whom we will call Kinloch, opened the meeting with the words, "You are my best case officer."

Jerome was savvy enough to know this was trouble-on-the-hoof. First of all, he was probably not the station's best case officer. He smiled appreciatively, while simultaneously dreading what was coming. Kinloch poured them both cups of coffee and let the other shoe drop.

"I am considering letting you handle the station's most sensitive and one of our most productive assets," Kinloch announced quietly while sipping his coffee.

Jerome quickly replied: "I would be honored, sir. May I ask why I have been chosen?"

"As I said, I think you are the station's best case officer and I am giving you the chance to prove it. Having said that, I should warn you that headquarters thinks the case may have come to the attention of the host service. I have been asked to consider termination but don't want to do that. The man has been a valuable asset for years and I would hate to let him go just because some nervous Nellies in Langley feel he has been compromised."

Jerome quickly understood the situation. He was expendable. If the agent was compromised and under investigation by the counterintelligence organization, there was a good chance that Jerome could be rounded up and declared *persona non grata*. This is the fear of every case officer, who would be sent home immediately, while the agent could be arrested and be sent to prison for espionage.

Kinloch, sensing that Jerome was hesitant to welcome this career-enhancing opportunity, continued: "Of course I am not directing you to handle the case but would ask you to review the file for yourself and determine if I am correct in putting this important case in your hands." Jerome knew he was trapped. To refuse the offer would mark him as being cautious, or worse. Deciding that he wanted to do the right thing, Jerome said: "I would be happy to review the file and give you my answer."

At that, Kinloch returned to his desk and picked up three thick files. "You can see that his agent has been with us a long time. Here is his file, read it carefully and give me your answer tomorrow." That ended the interview and Jerome departed with the files. He noticed a look that may have been pity on the face of the chief's secretary as he departed the front office. He suspected she knew what had transpired with the chief, and his suspicion was confirmed when she quietly said "Good luck" on his way out.

For the next four hours, Jerome poured through the file. The agent's history immediately drew Jerome to him. Let's call his code name STARFISH. He was a senior intelligence officer from the host country and nearing retirement. He ran a network of two other, younger officers, who would continue working for the Agency after STARFISH retired. He was fervidly anti-communist and strongly pro-American. He was prolific and provided documents. STARFISH accepted no salary, but his escrow account held by the Agency was in excess of $300,000 and growing monthly. Over the years, he had been handled by a long line of case officers, all of whom were delighted to work with STARFISH.

In recent years, there was growing concern from Langley that the government was aware of STARFISH's connection with the CIA, but nothing was proven. Jerome could see why Kinloch might want to protect the senior station officer who was currently handling STARFISH, and put the onus instead on a more junior officer who was not one of the chief's inner circle. Despite the risk, Jerome was determined to take the case. But he had conditions, which he explained to the COS the following morning.

"Chief", he began, "I will be happy to run STARFISH and can see why headquarters may have some concerns. But I won't meet him in country and will need a safehouse where we can meet securely."

"Agreed, whatever you want," replied a relieved Kinloch, who concurred that not meeting STARFISH in country would add a needed layer of security to the case. Jerome met with the officer handling the case, who also seemed relieved to be getting off the hot seat. A coded message was sent to STARFISH announcing the change of handler and setting up a meeting in a nearby country.

The "cold" turnover meeting went well. Jerome booked a small suite in a fashionable inn a quick train ride away in west-central Europe. The initial meeting was a quiet dinner to set up a lengthy debriefing the next day. STARFISH had little English, but Jerome was fluent in STARFISH's native tongue. Recent contact reports in the file noted that business was handled first, and a follow-up meeting was scheduled. Then the case officer broke out a bottle of STARFISH's favorite drink, a Scotch malt whisky, and the next few hours was spent killing the bottle while STARFISH regaled his new case officer with stories of his past close cooperation with the CIA. STARFISH took his whisky neat and showed no effects of the alcohol. Jerome, a moderate drinker, watered his drinks down.

STARFISH turned out to be everything the record indicated and his latest case officer described. Once business was concluded, documents were passed over by STARFISH and fresh requirements levied by Jerome. At length, Jerome brought up the security issue that vexed Langley and asked STARFISH if he suspected he was compromised. The elderly gentleman laughed. "Don't worry about me," he said. "If the counterintelligence staff was interested in me, I would know about it. Also, if arrested, I would never talk." That set the tone for a mutually productive continuation of the old agent's career as a spy for the United States.

Back in the station on Monday morning, Jerome met with Kinloch to report on the meeting. The chief of station was visibly delighted with Jerome's success and said he had some good news. "We are looking for a secure meeting site," he said, "and it so happens that the station is friendly with a veteran of the Office of Strategic Service [OSS], who has a little-used vacation home in a nearby country. It could make a good safehouse for meeting STARFISH and I would like you to meet the fellow." Jerome agreed and thanked the COS for his swift action.

The meeting took place in an upscale tearoom and the introduction was made by a senior station officer with decades of experience in Europe. The OSS veteran was an investment banker, wealthy, and eager to assist the Agency. It quickly became apparent that the banker was taking a measure of Jerome and not vice versa. In the end, Jerome passed and a set of keys were given to him, along with the history of his new safehouse. The remote, elegant cottage proved ideal.

The case ran successfully for more than a year at the height of the Cold War, until one day, without warning or explanation, headquarters decided it was time to end the secret relationship with STARFISH. Either they knew something the station did not, or someone was afraid to continue running an operation that was fraught with unspeakable blowback if the agent was "rolled up." Jerome was called in by Kinloch, who informed him it was time to pull the plug on STARFISH. No more wet meetings in a bucolic setting, with the passage of sensitive intelligence.

An emergency "brush pass" (a brief encounter between case officer and agent where something is passed between them) was arranged late at night in the capital city, where Jerome handed the accrued funds that the Agency had kept for STARFISH over the years. The old spy seemed to be expecting termination and signed a receipt for the money, saying it improved the quality of the retirement home he was purchasing. He added: "Here is a phone number that will reach me. If you ever need me, call. Thank you for everything. It has been my pleasure to help the United States."

Jerome always remembered the gentle STARFISH, who risked his life and freedom to assist the United States. Several years after the termination of STARFISH, Jerome was at the headquarters building on a short visit. In a hallway, he was greeted by the case officer who had turned over STARFISH to him years earlier in Europe. "Remember our old friend?" he asked Jerome, who nodded. "He's back. They couldn't live without him." Jerome was delighted, and later that evening lifted a glass of malt scotch to his agent, back on board.

CHAPTER 30

A Hard Target Recruitment

It is the goal of every case officer to make a "hard target" recruitment. Usually that means one of our main adversaries: China, Russia, or North Korea. Few officers achieve this goal, and a small number get lucky by attracting a "walk-in," someone who volunteers his or her services. Over the decades, some of our best agents started as walk-ins. My *modus operandi* was to look for hard targets with access to useful intelligence and then look for what they most wanted, their dream. Critical in any operation is to gain the trust of the target. Without trust, you cannot expect a spy to put his life in your hands.

Toward the end of my career, I met a young officer who was unique in my experience with the ability to spot, develop, and recruit targets with seeming ease. One of these was a Soviet KGB officer. Our officer, I will call him Keith, spotted a Russian who seemed simpatico but troubled. Like Keith and most Russians, the target, whom we will call Boris, liked to drink. Keith's first efforts were to build rapport without tipping his hand or scaring Boris away. Trust would come later. Boris was a loner, and being a Soviet intelligence officer had more time to himself than the average apparatchik.

Keith was also a loner, and many of his colleagues saw him as a party boy who drank too much and worked too little. None of them knew he was working on a Soviet and that the relationship had advanced to serious bouts of convivial drinking, during which Boris unburdened himself on his new American friend. Only a few people in the station knew of Keith's late-night project, and none objected. While Keith labored quietly with Boris, he was also successful with other targets and became the center of attention, and jealousy, among his less successful peers.

Over time, Keith and Boris established a firm friendship. There was no cat-and-mouse spy banter, each seeking to recruit the other. Keith sensed that Boris wanted to be recruited and felt no threat coming from the Russian, who had personal problems in a troubled, arranged marriage. Keith was a sympathetic listener, and a patient one. He never pressed Boris for details as the sad facts of his unhappy life emerged one by one. At no point did Boris ask for help or suggest that he was interested in defecting. Defection was the last thing on Keith's mind. He viewed Boris as a potential recruited agent, willing to return and work as a spy from inside his own headquarters, the ultimate goal of every hard target recruitment. Work-in-place is the most dangerous challenge of all.

I was one of the few station officers who knew of Keith's close and continuing contact with Boris, but never mentioned it to him. I watched the case unfold from afar. Keith knew of the disdain of his peers, and it propelled him to further success. He was happy to be known as an alcoholic wastrel. But while the relationship progressed admirably, no intelligence was obtained. Even some of the people "read in" on the operation were skeptical—until the night, after an evening of heavy drinking and little else, that Boris made his move. "I am KGB," he whispered in Keith's ear above the bar music, "but I think you know that."

"I do," said Keith in return. "And I am a CIA officer, but I think you know that too."

"I didn't," Boris answered, "but I hoped you were."

"Why do you say that?" Keith asked, trying his best to stay calm. His months of damaging his liver in the service of his country were finally paying off.

"Because I don't want to waste my time and future drinking with a State Department officer. I want to help the CIA and I want the CIA to help me."

"What is it you want? And what can you give us?"

Boris unbuttoned his shirt. Next to his skin was a large manila envelope stuffed with documents. He passed the envelope to Keith. "Inside, you will find a list of all my KGB classmates and where they are posted, as much as I can find. I also am giving you a list of all KGB agents in this country. Please hold this information inside the CIA."

"Thank you," responded Keith, unbuttoning his own shirt and placing the envelope next to his T-shirt, still warm from Boris's body heat. "What do you want from us?"

"Eventually I want resettlement in the United States, but I am willing to work for you inside Russia while I build up a retirement nest egg. I will only work with you but am willing to be debriefed. Does that sound fair?"

"It sounds good to me. Let me see if my masters concur. And thank you. I know you are taking a great risk."

This watershed evening moved the case dramatically forward, with increased risk to Boris. His information was of considerable value, especially the identification and location of his KGB classmates and the identification of all KGB and GRU officers in country. The list of KGB assets in the country where Boris was serving was laughable, given the paucity of both quantity and quality of agents listed. Some were outright fabrications, intended to make the KGB *residentura* look good at KGB headquarters in Moscow.

Requirements arrived for Boris to respond to. He was offered and accepted a substantial salary that would be held in escrow until he could collect it, presumably in the United States at a date to be determined. The timing of the recruitment was of particular importance as it was a time of great upheaval in the Soviet Union, and the CIA was suddenly presented with a new agent who could fill in many of the gaps in intelligence. To assist in the vetting as a new and sensitive source, he was afforded a polygraph, a rare event for a new KGB asset. And he passed.

Some folks on the seventh floor in Langley were delighted to learn that Boris was willing to go back and report from inside. Others were not so sure this was a good idea. Sensitive agents in Moscow had been "rolled up," captured, tried, and executed, and no one knew if this was due to poor handling, better counterintelligence, or plain bad luck. It was, in fact, due to Aldrich Ames, a CIA officer with access to the names of agents in Moscow and a traitor to his country. Ames was finally caught, but not before a number of agents were executed.

I know that Boris was a rare and important find at a critical moment in the history of the USSR. I know that Keith continued to be thought of as a drunk in the eyes of his colleagues in the station. I also know that he was a hero to a very few people with a "need to know." But I don't know what became of Boris, whether his dream to make it to America ever happened. I hope it did, and I like to think of Boris and Keith in old age sitting together in a convivial bar somewhere, telling stories of the last days of the Cold War.

Africa Beckons

One of the strengths of the Clandestine Service was its organization into area divisions, where an officer would be "home-based" for much or all of his or her career. This specialization in languages, area knowledge, and repeated tours in the same country afforded the opportunity to meet people whose careers would rise along with that of the case officers. In my case, I saw myself as a Far East Division (later East Asia Division) officer, with no intereste in the rest of the world. After all, one of the reasons I chose a career with the CIA was the opportunity to return to Asia after my experiences as a newsman and Marine officer.

I was not disappointed. With past experience, Thai language skills, and a master's degree in Southeast Asian Studies, I was slated to be sent back to Asia. As a fresh Career Trainee in 1971 working on the Cambodia desk, I developed a friendship with Gordon Martin, the head of the Thai desk. Gordie and I quickly became friends. He had been a Marine in World War II and had a jaw shot off on Iwo Jima in 1945. He saw me as Indochina material and helped me to be invited to join FE Division. He also arranged for a slot to Bangkok station once I finished my clandestine training at The Farm, the CIA's tidewater Virginia facility.

Despite my status as an FE officer, I was twice approached for assignments to Africa Division, known as AF. In FE, an officer could count on many years, perhaps a decade or more, before being tapped as a chief of station in one of FE's large stations such as Tokyo or Bangkok. One of the selling points for AF Division was its small and numerous stations, often located in countries most people could not find on a map, where an officer could be a chief of station after one or two tours. These stations were in places like Nouakchott in Mauritania, N'djamena in Chad, or Bangui in the Central African Republic. These places had few things to offer except the one thing the CIA was looking for: hard targets.

In 1980, I was serving my first tour (a tour is two years) at headquarters in Langley, Virginia, across the Potomac River and upstream from Washington, D.C. I had completed three tours in Southeast Asia and it was my turn to see how things worked at the head shed and do some networking in preparation for my next assignment in the field. I wasn't much worried as my mentor, Serge Taube, the man responsible for my Cambodia posting, was now busy arranging my next assignment in Europe, another plum posting.

While at headquarters, I was tapped to work with the British Secret Intelligence Service (SIS), also known as MI-6, on a joint operation that went very well. It helped me land a promotion early and brought me to the attention of senior management. One of these men was Hugh "Ted" Price, a Yale graduate and a former Marine Corps officer. Without knowing Serge's efforts to get me to Europe, Ted offered me a posting to Africa. He was headed to a large station as chief and wanted me to go with him. There was a slot opening up that demanded a French-speaking officer, and Ted thought I would be suitable.

He gave me the "Africa brief," the benefits in store for a junior officer with operational skills as a recruiter and ambition. He pointed out that success at the post would open the door to a chief of station posting in Africa Division. I told Ted, a first-rate officer who I would be delighted to serve under, that I was already tapped for Europe and thanked him for considering me for Africa.

My second brush with Africa came one day when I was told to present myself to Clair George, Chief of Africa Division and a veteran of the "night soil circuit," undesirable places where life was difficult and often dangerous. He served as chief of station in Beirut, and the man who replaced him was assassinated. He then volunteered to replace the chief in Athens, who had been assassinated. He was a street man, a headhunter, and a man of action.

I wondered why he wanted to see me. "I want to make you a chief of station," he said, almost the first words out of his mouth. "I hear you did good things in Cambodia and that you are a recruiter." I thanked him and asked what post he had in mind for me. "Antananarivo," he said, and added "Madagascar" in case I did not recognize the city. All I knew about the country was that it was the lemur capital of the world and had a North Korean military presence. Under other circumstances, I might have been interested, but I politely declined the offer and told George that I was headed for Europe. His reply was memorable: "Then get the fuck out of my office."

I never saw Clair George again, and thought that I may have made a mistake in refusing his offer. So I went to the officer whom I had replaced in Cambodia in 1973. I will call him Leon. He was a Southerner, with an accent that suggested an aristocratic background. He also held degrees from Yale, Harvard, and Princeton, and was on the fast track to senior rank. Serge Taube assured me that one day we both would be working for Leon.

I dropped by his office and explained what had just happened at my interview with Clair George. "Now Barry," he began in his patrician drawl, "don't worry about Clair, his bark is worse than his bite. But he doesn't like being told 'no,' especially when he thinks he is doing you a favor. I know Serge wants you with him in Europe and that assignment is much better for you than anything in Africa." I thanked Leon for his counsel and went back to work confident that I had made the right decision.

Leon immediately went to Clair George's office and said he had heard that there was an opening for chief of station Antananarivo. He got the job, but the assignment did not go well. Neither Serge nor I ever served under Leon.

As for Ted Price and Clair George, they both went on to be Deputy Director for Operations (DDO), the job responsible for running global espionage operations for the Clandestine Service.

CHAPTER 32

Communicators in Cambodia

It was April 17, 1975, and a CIA communicator in Phnom Penh, Cambodia, was the last man out of the U.S. embassy. The Khmer Rouge was about to enter the city and the Marine Corps was sending in helicopters to rescue Americans and allies before the city fell. It was the end of the Cambodian war. The last message from the embassy was sent. All sensitive communications gear was safe. As a parting gesture, the young commo man left wires exposed when he shut the vault door for the last time. They led to nothing, but the Khmer Rouge didn't know that. Years later, when the Americans returned to Cambodia after the Khmer Rouge had been expelled, the door was still intact, wires in place.

The communicators—men and women who send classified information from posts around the world—are the unsung heroes of the Central Intelligence Agency. They work long hours, often in dangerous situations, and cannot talk about their work. For security reasons, they are forbidden to marry foreign nationals. All of America's enemies, and a few of its friends, would love to recruit a commo officer and learn our secrets.

I got to know a few commo men in Phnom Penh, and all impressed me. Often I would have intel reports that needed to reach Langley immediately. The chief of station had signed off on my reports, sometimes in his bedroom late at night, and I carried them to the commo room, where I was never invited in but my messages were soon winging their way to Langley. The commo room was open 24/7. I was told there was a picture on the wall of the commo room of an old, beaten-up cowboy. The caption read: "There were a lot of things they didn't tell me about this outfit when I signed on." It was a cautionary note, and most would agree with the sentiment. But communicators still loved their work.

Two communicators rented a house in Phnom Penh and installed a 4-foot-deep swimming pool in the room. To support the added weight to the roof, a friendly Cambodian army engineer provided timbers to shore up the rooms below. They had one of the few swimming pools in the country, and certainly the only one on a rooftop.

The same pair had a deal with colleagues at CIA commo headquarters in the States, who sent weekly video tapes of Washington Redskins football games to Phnom Penh during the football season. They were shown to a restricted number of guests. The football viewing parties in Phnom Penh were videotaped, and among the guests were usually a few young and attractive Cambodian female guests who were either topless or nude. The tapes were sent to communicators in Virginia to inspire them to keep up the flow of football game videos.

At the time, Phnom Penh was completely surrounded by the Khmer Rouge. Almost all classified documents had either been removed or were destroyed, leaving only a few minutes' "burn time" until everything classified was gone. At times more than a hundred enemy 107mm rockets rained on Phnom Penh daily. Near the end, the Khmer Rouge was within 60mm mortar range of Pochentong Airport, less than 2 miles. The city was crowded with refugees, and tons of rice was flown in daily. The aircraft never shut down. Rice bags on pallets were pulled off aircraft, which were offloaded in a few minutes, and the empty planes took off, often under fire and with shrapnel on the runway. No aircraft were lost.

To get away from the war for a few days, two intrepid communicators took annual leave together. No one knew where they were going until they returned. They were not headed for the bright lights of Bangkok. Their mission was to set up a ham radio station on an uninhabited island in the South China Sea, and communicate via short wave radio with other amateur ham radio operators around the world. I don't know what the island is called, but it may have been one of the Spratly Islands that were claimed by both Vietnam and China. They organized their operation with great skill and in secret. They flew to a place where they could rent a boat, which they outfitted for a beach vacation with tents, food, liquid refreshment, and, of course, radio equipment. As far as I know, they did not seek permission for this risky and possibly dangerous holiday. They follow the time-honored tradition of seeking forgiveness rather than permission.

A key element to the enterprise was the creation of QSL cards. This is written confirmation of two-way radio communications from their lonely little island (which they identified as a new country). Such a QSL card would be a rare treat, and the commo men sought to make as many contacts as they could while on the island and then send QSL cards, the size of postcards, around the world wherever they made contact. The operation worked like a charm.

The communicators got in without incident, made contact with the world by ham radio, and got away before being discovered. They quietly returned to Phnom Penh, where they told their story.

There is a story told among CIA communicators that I believe is accurate. It revolves around a senior communicator who served in Bangkok. He was an old bachelor and an avid golfer. I will call him Hank. He was also a bit of a ladies' man, and was well and favorably known at some of the city's leading watering holes. One Sunday, after an early morning round of golf, the men ended up on Soi Cowboy, a short street filled with several dozen bars off Sukhumvit Road. It was early afternoon and nothing was open. Hank assured the guys that they would be welcome at the Toy Bar. The door was unlocked and there were about 20 girls inside. It was hot, the girls were in their street clothes, and the air conditioning had not been turned on. Work didn't start for hours. As soon as the girls saw Hank, three things happened: the air conditioning went on; the door was locked; and the girls took off their clothes.

Hank was well known at the Toy Bar, and the golfers settled down for an *apres-golf* Sunday afternoon.

In 2003, I found myself in Bangkok accompanied by my British friend and editor, John Stevenson. John and I had just been in Burma working on our book *Irrawaddy: Benevolent River of Burma*, which was published the next year. The journey on the Irrawaddy had been great fun, but also tiring. I promised John a memorable Vietnamese dinner in Bangkok and made good on the offer when I took him to Le Dalat, a high-class restaurant owned by an old friend on Soi 23, Sukhumvit Road, in a stately old mansion away from the noise of the city. It was a short walk to Soi Cowboy, which cuts between Soi 23 and Soi 21. I remembered the story from the commo man about the Toy Bar, and to my surprise the place still existed. The street was crowded that night and the Toy Bar was packed with girls in varying degrees of undress dancing on a small stage. John and I found standing room at the bar. I ordered two Mekhong whiskey and soda drinks and I related the story of Hank and his golf buddies to John.

Next to us at the bar was the *mama-san* who ran the place. She overheard my story and turned to John: "He tell truth."

"And how do you know that?" asked John quietly in his erudite Oxford English.

"I know because I was one of the girls," she laughed. "You guys commo guys?"

I said that sadly we were not. But she bought us a drink anyway. We drank to Hank.

CHAPTER 33

BJ and the CIA

James Bond, Ian Fleming's over-the-top fictional intelligence officer for Britain's Secret Intelligence Service, had Q. He was the chap who led a group of boffins in the arcane art of making gadgets in support of secret operations, sometimes with great lethality. The CIA has its own Q; actually, many of them. The CIA has the men and women of the Office of Technical Services (OTS) and the Technical Services Division. The TSD, for a time, employed the services of Betty Jane Broman, my wife.

Wikipedia has very little to say about the OTS, which is good because it is a secret office of a secret organization, the CIA's Clandestine Service in my day. It merely says the OTS supports "clandestine operations with gadgets, disguises, forgeries, secret writings, and weapons." The OTS does not belong to the DO. It is part of the Directorate of Science and Technology (DDS&T) and makes gadgets that MI-6's Q could only dream about. That's about all I know of the OTS's activities, because they don't talk about their toys and ops, and BJ does not talk about them either. She, like the Agency we worked for, operates on the principle of "need to know."

BJ's main career, and the one which she found the most fulfilling, was as an educator. She taught at schools around the world, including the International School of Bangkok and the International School of Yangon, a city also known as Rangoon. She co-wrote teaching materials and the text for a series teaching English for Thai television.

During an Indonesia posting, BJ worked for the U.S. Department of State as the embassy Community Liaison Officer (CLO), sort of an ombudsman position but also sort of a chaplain. If you had a problem, you went to the CLO, and what you said went no further. BJ got to know many people in the embassy, far more than I did, and she helped many of them. I don't know exactly what she did because CLOs also operate on the principle of "need to know." I not only didn't need to know, I didn't *want* to know. The job carried a lot of weight with the Department and there were a few perks. For one, when Vice President Dan Quayle and his wife made a state visit to Indonesia, BJ was the official greeter. She also conducted cultural events and organized shopping excursions for embassy staff and spouses.

On occasion she even took VIPs visiting Indonesia shopping. One memorable shopper was the wife of a senior senator from Pennsylvania with presidential aspirations. The woman wanted to buy the finest Indonesian textiles. BJ knew just the place to take her, and the woman made a large purchase. The problem came when the owner of the shop called the embassy to say the woman had cancelled her credit card charge and the Indonesian woman was out hundreds of dollars.

BJ with an orangutan at the Surabaya Zoo in Indonesia.

The State Department is loath to do anything likely to upset Congress or anyone connected to Congress, especially the wife of an important senator. They draw the line at theft, however, and politely asked the senator's spouse to either pay for her purchases or return them. Eventually she returned the textiles.

The Agency also had needs for BJ's talents, and working for the TSD was one of them. She worked for the TSD in Asia and in Europe, receiving training at a secret facility in Washington, D.C. She liked her work, but didn't like working in a vault where the sun was never seen and the complex combination lock caused her fits. She worked with secret cameras and their special films that required developing and printing, and also with secret writing systems.

At one Asian station, the chief of station enjoyed a close relationship with the most respected man in the country, a relationship that was special and known to only a few. BJ was one of the few. She didn't know the content of the messages the COS passed, but she did prepare the envelopes carrying the messages. They were sealed in the ancient style of keeping the messages private for centuries, with a wax seal on the envelope. In this case, the seal carried the chief's initial, a large "A."

The TSD must have had even more special trust and confidence when they hired BJ because she was never afforded a polygraph that everyone I ever knew who worked for the Agency was given, usually numerous times. The only setback among the operations she worked on was when a requirement was levied to kill a tree. The tree obstructed the line-of-sight between an observation/listening post and its target. Poison was administered to the tree surreptitiously, but in vain. It thrived, and in the end another OP/LP had to be acquired. Looking back on her brief but noteworthy career with the TSD, which BJ enjoyed immensely, her only regret was not being able to take the Locks and Picks course offered to would-be burglars on government service.

CHAPTER 34

Across the Pecos

Never in my wildest dreams would I ever think I would cross the Pecos River of New Mexico on a zip line. But it happened, and at government expense.

In 1993, I was chief of the Thai/Burma branch of the East Asia Division in Langley, Virginia. The division's budget for training had received a large infusion and our leaders sought ways to spend the money. Training was not a large part of my time at the CIA, apart from the Farm and a language refresher.

Now a large group of mid-level management officers were selected to attend a two-week course in "team building." It sounded like, and pretty much was, a paid vacation to bond with people we had worked with in a remote, picturesque desert setting astride the Pecos River, not too far from Santa Fe, New Mexico.

The course was run by a private company that help major American corporations to achieve greater efficiency and effectiveness in their management cadre. I have no idea how the CIA got involved with such a classy venue, but applaud those who made it happen. The course had nothing to do with intelligence and focused on putting colleagues together in a non-work environment to better get to know each other, and in many cases to meet new people. Since case officers are essentially "people"-oriented people, it should have been an easy assignment. And it was.

There were essentially three elements to the program. The first filled our mornings and was right out of the playbook of the Marine Corps. A series of outdoor challenges were constructed that looked somewhat like the obstacle course I remembered from the Officers Basic School at Quantico, but with several twists. First of all, great care and expense had gone into making our tasks completely safe from physical harm or injury. In the Marines, it was every man for himself and look out below.

Secondly, the course was designed for three-person teams, often connected together by rope, to work together to obtain team success. This was the core of team building, and was fun as well as challenging. There were about 60 of us drawn from all over the East Asia Division, the largest area division in the CIA at that time. We were mostly of GS-13 to GS-15 grades (major to colonel in the military). Many of the best and brightest men and women in the division were represented.

My first event was with an old friend with whom I had served in the field. He was a branch chief headed for Asia as a chief of station. Our third team member was a petite lady with no field experience but a lot of enthusiasm. We were roped together about 6 feet apart and told to climb a wall about 30 feet high with hand holds in the wall. Such structures are used to train mountaineers or rock climbers. The problem is that no one person can climb the wall alone, as the handholds are too far apart. It could only be climbed as a team. We were lucky that "Janine" was light. She was in the middle, so as we climbed, whenever we came to an open area where she could find a hold, we would lift her up. Slowly, we made our way to the top with complete success. Team building had begun.

I should note that in addition to the ropes that tied the team together, each team member also wore a body harness linked to a safety rope and each rope was in the hands of instructors, all extremely competent, so that if one—or all—fell, they would be saved by the safety ropes. I wonder why the Marine Corps never thought of this.

The highlight or our morning thrills-in-ropes came when a team of three had to walk strapped together along a narrow plank about 20 feet in the air. One of the three was my friend "Dave," who was headed for Manila. He had been a Long Range Army Recon trooper in Vietnam; his father had been a four-star general. He was tough and he was rough. Also in his team was a woman neither of us knew, "Doris." She was small, rather old, but athletic and up for the challenges ahead. A challenge soon presented itself when "Dave" slipped on the 6-inch-wide beam and lost his balance. He was saved from falling by a safety wire over his head, but could not pull himself back on the beam.

I was on the ground photographing the episode for posterity. All eyes were on "Dave." Without waiting for instructions, "Doris" calmly walked out on the plank. She moved to where "Dave" was holding on to the safety wire, leaned out, and grabbed his harness. Then she pulled him back to the plank. The exercise moved on; team building continued. Everyone viewed "Doris" with new appreciation after that, especially "Dave."

The least interesting aspect of our training was group sessions indoors in the afternoons. "Dave" described them as "psycho-babble," and I am in agreement. We were a very diverse group, ethnically and professionally. There was Chinese, Japanese, Korean, and Vietnamese linguists present, and IT mavens who were leading the division new commo technologies. There were reports and support officers, but we were mainly case officers, most with military backgrounds. I knew about 15 percent of them going in and about 50 percent coming out.

Things really picked up in the evening. We were housed in elegant Spanish-style villas. They were spaced in groups around the desert hillside, each with a hot tub that would accommodate around 12. There was a central building with a restaurant that would rival any in Santa Fe. The cuisine was totally Southwest-Mexican fusion. Our only cost was for alcoholic beverages, of which there was a wide assortment available: exotic beers, sophisticated wines, and prize tequilas.

After dinner we would relax, slip into swimming gear, and gather at the hot tubs for more bonding and a little more tequila. This nightly event evolved into roving groups visiting neighboring hot tubs. All of this led to accelerated team building and friendship making. There was also a lot of storytelling, within the limits of what CIA officers are allowed to say even among friends and colleagues. There was also a little recruiting going on. Senior officers are always looking for good people to staff their stations. Valuable networking was conducted, something that the CIA knows all about, and some deals were cut. There was no rank here. Even the division chief who arranged the event was on a first-name basis with everyone. The course was therapeutic as well as professionally useful.

For our final athletic piece of daring, we were led up a trail on our last morning to a lookout point perhaps 100 feet above the languid and meandering Pecos River, which begins in central New Mexico and flows into Texas, emptying into the Rio Grande. We found above us a zip line which was soon to be our final challenge and treat: a quick ride downhill across the river. The experience was optional, and a couple of our group opted for a slow walk back down the trail rather than the zip line.

People pay big money for thrills like this. One by one we advanced out on the ledge over the river to the zip line. Wearing harnesses, we were clipped into the zip line and it was time to jump. I have never parachuted, and thought this might be similar. "Dave," a paratrooper with the 101st Division, said it wasn't as scary or as dangerous as jumping, but was still a lot of fun. The first 10 feet of falling, facing the river before the zip line engaged, was sufficient thrill for me. Then it was all downhill, not too fast, but quite spectacular as I zipped across the river.

For me, the Pecos training was money well spent. I am still in contact with some of the people I met there. I know the trip was successful for me. A decision was made at the Pecos that resulted in my assignment to Southeast Asia the following year as a chief of station. I don't say the training interlude helped, but it certainly didn't hurt, and everyone came away with new friends and contacts, always a plus in the CIA.

CHAPTER 35

Chief of Station Conferences

One of the great pleasures of being a CIA chief of station in the 1980s and '90s, when I was active, was attending annual gatherings of chiefs in Langley, regardless of where you were posted. I attended five chief of station conferences, three of them when assigned to a station in North America with the Foreign Resources Division and two when assigned to a station in Southeast Asia under East Asia Division. We had about 1,000 case officers worldwide. That's about the size of a Marine infantry battalion and less than the number of FBI officers in New York City. We were small but we were well trained, well led, and pleased to be the sharp point of the spear aimed at the Soviet Union.

The Agency in the '70s was moving into its own. It had profited from the early leadership of former OSS officers, many of them Ivy League alumni. It broadened its reach into academic and area specialists throughout the country, and recruited more women and ethnic minorities. Diversity was slow but growing. EA Division always had a number of Asian Americans and foreign-born officers with special language skills. One of my friends was an African American with extraordinary people skills who made two "hard target" recruitments.

Being small was good. The Agency was blessed with excellent recruiters and there was no dearth of applicants. I was told that for every officer who was accepted into the Career Trainee program, the A-Team of the Clandestine Service, 300 were rejected. The area divisions were insular and filled with officers with area, language, and leadership skills. In those days, most recruits had a military background and were imbued with a sense of mission, discipline, patriotism, and adventure.

The conferences were opportunities for senior officers to gather at head-quarters, where a full schedule of meetings and briefings were arranged, from senior Agency officers as well as officers from the State Department, FBI, NSA, and other agencies working on our area. Most of these meetings took place in Langley, but probably the more productive ones were held at the Agency's training facility in tidewater Virginia known as The Farm, where facilities resembling rural lodges were available in a secure and convivial setting. It was in these informal settings, often around evening poker games, that we got to meet new colleagues and counterparts. I recall a convivial evening of poker with senior FBI officers that went late into the night. Some of us were looking to build rapport with a sister service; others were there to make a little money.

Even more useful was the opportunity during the conferences for chiefs of station to horse trade with their peers in seeking lucrative positions for their best officers, and in return looking for officers who had demonstrated an ability to recruit. "Headhunters" are always in demand at CIA. Less than 15 percent of case officers made meaningful recruitments and everyone is looking for those who can recruit. I knew of a female officer whose spouse was also a case officer, but not as sharp or effective as his wife. She was in high demand, her only problem being finding a station that would take her husband before she would sign on.

One speaker I remember vividly was in charge of the CIA's polygraph office, a group that tested our officers as well as our recruited agents. We were always told that the polygraph was merely a tool and the final decision on whether or not an asset should be retained about a questionable lie-detection test rested with the case officer. The "box," as we called it, was more an art than a science and polygraphers are, in my humble opinion, artists.

After hearing the "box" man's spiel on how effective his officers were, one chief of station raised his hand and said: "My station recently had a visit by one of your officers who told us that it is better to terminate nine good agents rather than let one bad one pass." I knew who he was talking about. The polygrapher in question had upset Europe Division, to the extent that the officer was not welcomed in several stations.

The "box" man sighed. "Let me assure you," he said, "that lady has been reassigned and is no longer conducting polygraphs." We all breathed easier. I had seen the aggressive young officer in action, and she almost cost the Agency the services of an important and sensitive agent assisting the CIA in an important operation. In the end, the asset stayed and the polygrapher didn't.

When I was chief of station in Asia, the highlight of our chiefs' conference at headquarters was an unexpected visit by a former Secretary of State who happened to be in the building. He learned that EA chiefs of station were meeting and asked to say a few words. Our schedule was quickly changed. When the old gentleman entered the room, he greeted several of us by name and went on to say how much he enjoyed working with the Agency over his years of government service. He then gave us a 20-minute overview of the state of the world, the kind of talk for which he would get six figures on the lecture circuit.

His visit brought to mind the time he was Secretary of State. The COS of my station in Southeast Asia had an asset who was very senior in the local government and the chief thought that the ambassador should be apprised that the man he was talking to was a CIA asset. The Secretary of State said not to tell the ambassador, so the chief didn't.

After the talk, our guest opened the floor for questions. One COS said he was posted to a country where relations with the United States were poor due to human rights issues, but that cooperation was close on counter-narcotics operations. Our speaker said: "Fuck human rights. American foreign policy should be determined by our interests." That concluded his comments.

While serving as a senior officer, the COS conference coincided with a major political upheaval in the country. The COS and DCOS, who had been slotted to take over a station, were away at the conference and the fickle finger of fate thrust me into the acting COS position for the duration of the crisis. Apart from a death threat, which I didn't report, I appreciated the opportunity the conference afforded by putting me at the helm, if only briefly.

On another occasion, when I was COS in a North American station, I arrived at the headquarters building in my rental car, showed by credentials, and requested a visitor's parking pass. I was expecting to be assigned a spot in a remote parking lot a long walk to the main building. Instead, the security officer at the main gate said: "You will be in the VIP lot, Major Broman." I was surprised and amazed. Why put me in the most coveted parking lot of all? How did he know I was a major in the Marine Corps reserves? "Do I know you?" I asked. "You used to, sir," he replied. "I was a Marine Security Guard in Europe where you were assigned. You wrote me a recommendation for a job at CIA security and here I am. Enjoy your visit, major." My fellow conference attendees were equally surprised, but didn't turn down lifts to West Lot to their cars after work.

CHAPTER 36

China-born Officers

Since the communists took over in 1949, the People's Republic of China (PRC) has been one of the CIA's hardest targets. With the end of the Soviet Union and decline of Russia, China has emerged as America's most serious threat.

In the 1950s, a small group of well-educated Chinese men, many from Shanghai, were recruited by the CIA as translators of Chinese documents and transcribers of Chinese audio recordings. They were not staff CIA officers, but worked on contracts in a building far from the CIA headquarters building in Langley. In fact, most never set foot in the headquarters building in the early years of their employment.

Over time, the CIA slowly came to the conclusion that these officers could make a larger contribution to the men and women of China Operations as case officers working in the field and at headquarters as staff officers of the Agency. The program that was established for this small cadre of men was called STBREA, pronounced "S.T. Bray." No longer were these valuable human resources considered second-class contract officers; they were given clandestine ops training and many turned out to be outstanding recruiters and handlers of "hard" target Chinese.

It was my pleasure to work on a number of cases with STBREA officers. They possessed the critical language and cultural skills that allowed them to develop close personal relationships with targets and persuade them to become spies. These officers had varied backgrounds. One officer's father was a warlord in the early 20th century in a remote part of China, wielding great power and influence. A number of officers were graduates of St. John's University of Shanghai, widely respected as China's Harvard. They often married well among China's elite. One STBREA spouse was a member of the New York Stock Exchange. They were a colorful but cliquish bunch who were involved in many sensitive and dangerous operations into China.

I served with one of these officers in Southeast Asia in the late 1970s. He suffered from a speech impediment which, combined with a very strong accent, made his English difficult to understand. He was affable, well liked, and well connected in the local Chinese community. But he incurred the wrath of the America ambassador one day after the officer accepted a speaking engagement sponsored by a local Chinese chamber of commerce. Without first getting permission to give his talk from the station or embassy, the fiery anti-communist speech was widely reported locally and met with the approval of the host government—but not the U.S. Government. The STBREA officer survived the gaffe and a certain notoriety around town

I ran one operation with a STBREA officer whom I will call Roland. We were in pursuit of a young PRC target who had been "spotted" by an access agent of mine whom I will call "Bob," an American. Bob volunteered his time and energy *pro bono* to assist the CIA in recruiting hard targets. Bob, a successful businessman, was no threat to the target. Over time, Bob determined that the target was ambitious, well-connected by family to the Chinese Communist Party, and motivated by money. And he didn't seem to care how he made it. He was my kind of target.

We arranged for me, posing as a businessman friend of Bob, to meet the target, "Mr. Wong." The story was that I was passing through and Bob included me in a dinner that he had earlier arranged with Mr. Wong. I arrived at the appointed hour and was introduced to Wong as Mr. "Allison," an old and trusted friend of Bob. During the course of the evening, I pretty much ignored Wong while catching up with my buddy, Bob.

Wong was very presentable, self-confident, and spoke excellent English. He listened intently while I explained to Bob that I had just finished a successful business trip to the Philippines, where I recruited a number of consultants for my U.S.-based company.

"What sort of business are you in, Mr. Allison?" Wong asked.

"I am a headhunter," I replied. "My firm is looking for experts in many fields to assist businesses looking to expand abroad. My own expertise is Southeast Asia. I just hired a city planner, a computer programmer, and an economist."

"How much do your consultants make?" asked Wong, who, happily, went straight to the point.

I replied:

"It all depends on the experience of the consultant and the needs of the company. I normally would start a consultant off with a small amount. But that could grow upward fast if they did top work. Every case is different. We are looking for people who already have jobs and their work for us should be considered confidential and part-time. They do not need to declare their extra income to anyone."

Wong mulled that over while I continued my conversation with Bob, who ordered another bottle of wine. At length, Wong interrupted my conversation with Bob and asked: "Do you hire Chinese consultants?"

I smiled and said: "Not personally. I just cover Southeast Asia, but my company does. China is a growth area for us and competition to find the right consultants is fierce. Do you know anyone who might be interested?"

"I might be interested," he said. "I think Bob would vouch for me and my credentials."

Bob nodded and told me: "Mr. Wong is the kind of guy you are looking for. He has good credentials back home, knows the right people, and I see him as a potential valued consultant."

Mr. Wong beamed.

"Well there could be interest," I said. I asked Wong, "Could you provide me with a copy of your CV and an idea of where you think you could be of help?"

"I can give Bob my CV tomorrow," he said. "I would appreciate it very much if you could see if I can help your company."

"Excellent," I said to both Bob and Wong. "I will talk to my boss and put in a good word."

Bob received the CV the next day, and it provided all the needed information for us to proceed. Two weeks later, Bob informed Wong that my company was indeed interested in talking to him and that a colleague of mine would be passing through their city en route to China. That was cue for our STBREA officer, a Shanghai-born fellow with 30 years in the game, to meet Mr. Wong.

The case officer, "Roland," contacted Wong directly, thereby cutting Bob out of the operation. Roland set up a meeting. He enjoyed his meeting with the eager Wong, who wanted to augment his income. Roland levied a list of requirements that he hoped Wong could fulfill and was very satisfied that this was someone who could provide useful information without ever knowing he was dealing with the U.S. Government. When I departed the scene for another assignment overseas, the case was progressing smoothly.

My favorite STBREA story involves an officer I will call "Andre." I never met Andre, and wish I had. He was something of a legend among his close-knit crew. I was told the story by officers familiar with Andre and his accomplishments.

According to the tale, Andre was serving in an Asian country in the 1970s and contrived to meet a Chinese-speaking secretary of a very senior official in the local government, a valid target for the CIA. The woman was single, had never been married, and had access to very serious decisions of the local government. She was intelligent, middle-aged, and rather homely. Let's call her "Anna." She had no life outside work and seemed delighted to have a charming fellow like Andre interested in her.

The objective of the operation was to get her to provide sensitive information about the intentions of the government. Andre's development of Anna included determining what would induce her to betray her boss and her country. In a short period of time, Andre reluctantly but correctly identified what Anna wanted and what she needed.

Anna needed sex.

Andre was faced with the opportunity for what former British MI-6 officer David Cornwell (better known to readers of spy fiction as John le Carré) coined a "honey trap," a well-known ploy of the Soviets. It involves information in exchange for sex. It is not normally a page in the CIA playbook, but fortune favors the bold and Andre was bold. He was also rather good-looking and debonair. Andre thus pursued and wooed Anna.

Soon, their friendship morphed into a romantic tryst, and eventually into a recruitment.

Over the years that the operation ran, Anna provided hundreds of reports from her unique vantage point, seeing every document that crossed her desk and having countless daily conversations—most banal, some important—all duly reported to Andre, who culled the chaff from the good stuff, resulting in a goldmine of intelligence reporting.

I don't know how the story ends. I wish I did. But I know it ended happily for the CIA. I hope it ended happily for Anna as well.

CHAPTER 37

Brendan's Friend, the General

In the early years of my CIA career, I was "undeclared," meaning that the host government was not told I was an Agency officer. I got a hint of the good life that "declared" officers enjoyed when we were invited to stay with, on vacation, the deputy chief of station of a large station in Southeast Asia. As we disembarked from the aircraft to waiting buses, a young man holding a sign marked "BROMAN" was waiting at the bottom of the stairs. I identified myself to him. He was the teenage son of the DCOS and asked for our passports and luggage tags. I handed them to him and he gave them to a local employee of the station. Then he said, "Hop in," and opened the door for BJ and thee boys to get into a waiting van. "Your bags and passports will be delivered to the house in an hour," he added. Just one of the many perks of being "declared."

Six years later, I was posted to the same city and was housed in the same house. I was now "declared" to the local army and police, who pretty much ran the country. I was mainly involved with the army, but also had the opportunity to work with a very senior police officer, whom I will call the General. He had long experience working with the CIA, mostly fighting the narcotics traffickers who were smuggling large amounts of heroin to America. In a country where corruption is a way of life for many civil servants, the General stood out, almost alone, as a beacon of honesty and—as I learned later—bravery. He was once a member of the national rugby team, a sign of his athletic ability and toughness. He was also a scratch golfer and played at some of the great courses in the world, starting with St. Andrews in Scotland.

The General succeeded at everything he set his mind to. All but one thing: he wanted to teach me to play good golf and did not succeed. I don't blame the General. He was not working with good material. I will always remember the day I dropped a ball 8 feet from the pin on a 167-yard par three hole.

The General was giddy with anticipation. He had never seen such a fine shot from me. He was quiet as we approached the hole. His ball was 30 feet from the cup; he missed his putt and made par. Now he focused on me and getting my ball in the hole. He didn't want to overplay his hand, and quietly read the putt for me. "Looks like it will break an inch to the right," he said. I agreed. The tension was mounting, more for him than me. I sank the putt, my first birdie. I was delighted. I thought the General would cry. Moments like that were few and far between for me on a golf course. But I always wanted to please the General and I credit him for my making the putt.

The General's wife was a soft-spoken lady who had a thriving business. They had two sons, each with a PhD from Harvard and Florida. Their daughter did her medical studies at Johns Hopkins in Maryland. The General had a great wife, over-achieving children, and was one of the most respected and admired men in the country. But, as he told me, he only wanted one thing: a grandchild. The problem was, none of his children was married yet.

Enter Brendan Broman, our youngest son. Brendan was born in Europe and was 7 when we arrived at post. He was a happy, smart little guy who took pride in his pigtail, a long thin length of hair that hung down a foot beyond the hair on his head. He called it a "rat tail." No one remembers where he got the idea from, but it suited him. The General liked it too, and he liked little Brendan. It time, it transpired that Brendan became something akin to a willing surrogate grandson for the General, at least until a real one came along. The General hosted dinners in top-quality Chinese restaurants. It always took him time to reach our table, as he would see people he knew having dinner and would stop to say hello. More frequently, people he didn't know at all would come up to him and thank him for his service. They never asked for favors, just paid their respects. The General could have been a very successful politician, but in his country he was better serving being in the police force.

Brendan was always given the place of honor on the right side of the General. Invariably, the General would ask Brendan what he wanted to eat. Brendan paused, as if thinking about it. Then he would invariably answer: "Peking duck, General." Peking duck it was, one of the great delights of Chinese cuisine. There were other dishes, of course, and the General's wife would quietly order more after consultation with BJ.

A short digression. A few years later I was assigned to headquarters, and the General and a few other police officers visited Langley. As part of this high-level liaison visit, I arranged golfing out in the Shenandoah Valley, a cruise along the Potomac River, and a private dinner of Chinese food with the Bromans. I selected the restaurant which the sitting U.S. president, George Bush Senior, had declared his favorite spot for Peking duck. Naturally, I ordered duck. Sadly, it was not up to the standard of the duck in the General's country. I was very embarrassed, but the General, in his offhand, casual way, laughed and said: "All the more reason for you to come back for the real thing, right Brendan?"

"Right, General."

Back in the General's country, we became involved in a number of high-profile counter-narcotics operations. This was outside his purview, but given his senior rank he could do anything he wanted to do. In this case, he set up a special "go-team" of hand-picked men to focus on major narcotics traffickers. When a major bust was about to be made, he called me: "I will lead the team tonight to make sure there are no slipups." There were none. Over 1,100lb of high-quality heroin was seized. The next bust led personally by him yielded more than 120lb of heroin. These were the largest seizures in the history of joint drug operations, and were just the tip of the iceberg of his daring operations.

At our last dinner with the General, the usual protocol was followed. The General asked Brendan what he wanted for dinner. Everyone was surprised when the little follow said: "I don't feel like Peking duck tonight General."

"Not a problem, Brendan," said the General. "What would you like tonight?"

"Abalone, General." That was the only item on the menu that cost more than Peking duck. Abalone it was.

Postscript: the General, retired from the police and ran for a seat in the Senate. He received 80 percent of the vote. It turned out he *was* a good politician after all.

CHAPTER 38

Diversity in the Clandestine Service

In 1971, there were two Career Trainee classes per year. My class had around 28 officers, including two women, two Latinos, and one African American. We were not all destined for the Clandestine Service. A few of my classmates were interested in working for the Directorate of Intelligence (DI) and became analysts. One of them, for example, was a young man fresh from the Navy who became an expert on the Soviet navy. After a quick orientation, we were sent off on two interim assignments of three months each. One was to the DP (Directorate of Plans, though later Directorate of Operations) and the other to the DI. I was lucky to be assigned to the Cambodia desk of each directorate, where I could see how raw intelligence was generated from the DP and turned into "finished" intelligence in the DI before being disseminated into the intel community, notably to the White House, the State Department, and the Defense Department.

In its early years, the Clandestine Service was dominated by male Ivy League graduates, many of them veterans of the wartime Office of Strategic Services, who conducted sabotage and intelligence gathering behind enemy lines. Because of the elite educational background of the officers, the organization was known to wags as "Oh So Social." One of these officers, Hugh Tovar, was a Columbia-born Harvard graduate who served in the OSS in Asia. As a young captain in the U.S. Army, he parachuted into Laos to take the Japanese surrender in 1945. I served under Hugh in Asia and learned a lot from him.

I will describe a cross-section of a few of the other officers I worked with to give readers an idea of the wide diversity in the backgrounds of the people in the Clandestine Service. Some of these men and women became close friends. I will use true names where I can and aliases where necessary.

First is a fellow I will call "Robbie." He was an African American from Washington, D.C. who worked his way up in the Agency to become a much-respected and widely liked officer. Robbie had street smarts, an infectious smile, and liked to refer to whoever he was talking to as "Squire." Robbie had the magic touch that separates the best operational officers from the pack. He had the ability to make people like him, and more importantly, to trust him. He had incredible people skills, and I know that he recruited two hard targets from our main adversaries, the Soviets and mainland Chinese. He may have made more recruitments; I would not be surprised if he did. Robbie was a pleasure to know and work with.

At the other end of the spectrum was Katherine Stark Bull, one of the first female case officers. Her husband was Dick Bull, a distinguished officer from the 1954 class of Princeton. Katherine was a Vassar graduate and the couple were from old St. Louis money—her father had been governor of Missouri. When the Bulls were posted abroad, Secretary of State Henry Kissinger rented their spacious Georgetown house. I worked with Katherine in the early 1990s when I was chief of the Thailand–Burma branch at headquarters and she was a senior officer responsible for counter-narcotics in the East Asia Division. Katherine was old school. She wore pancake makeup, pearls and white gloves, and spoke with a patrician's accent that must have served well in postings to Europe which included Vienna, Belgium, and London. She was extremely polite, well spoken, and knowledgeable about the arcane and sleezy world of drug lords and narco traffickers. She was a class act.

Johnnie was a classmate and paramilitary officer who performed so well as a contract officer that he was made a staff employee and sent to The Farm, our training base, to qualify as a case officer. He had worked for the legendary Anthony "Tony Poe" Poshepny in the jungles of northern Laos, and we quickly became fast friends. Upon graduation, Johnnie, a Texas boy, was sent back to Laos to work with a Royal Thai Army battalion of "volunteers." While I was preparing for my assignment to Cambodia, Johnnie was killed in action. One of the 139 stars (as of this writing) on the CIA Memorial Wall at the entrance to the headquarters building belongs to him. The Director of the Agency (DCI) asked Johnnie's widow what she would like to do and she asked to join the Clandestine Service. The DCI made it happen.

My two Latin American classmates both had interesting backgrounds that helped them get the coveted assignment to the Basic Ops course, a six-month adventure taught at The Farm and surrounding cities. The first was a Cuban I will call "Paco," who had been captured by Fidel Castro's army during the abortive invasion of Cuba at the Bay of Pigs in 1961. Paco had debated Castro in Havana while a university student in the 1950s. He was ransomed with other freedom fighters and served in the Marine Corps in Vietnam before joining the CIA. The second officer, "Diego," had been a contract CIA officer in South America and was a member of the Bolivian Army patrol that captured the Marxist guerilla Che Guevara, a close friend of Castro, in 1967. The CIA wanted Che taken alive, but the Bolivians decided otherwise and summarily executed him.

During the war in Cambodia, I was impressed with the cool performance under her baptism of fire of a young American woman I will call "Kathy." She worked in another Asian country and was in Cambodia on business. Later, I was informed that Kathy was a non-official cover (NOC) officer of the CIA. She only knew me as the embassy's commercial/economic officer. A few weeks after Kathy's visit to Cambodia, I was told that she had been murdered in a neighboring country. The crime was never solved. I believe that one of the stars on the Memorial Wall belongs to Kathy.

One of the first Asian-born officers in the Clandestine Service was a Shanghai-born ethnic Korean officer who followed his brothers into the U.S. Army and later into the CIA. He came on board in 1956 and was one of the first Asian staff officers in the CS. He is mentioned elsewhere in this book as "Richard" regarding when he distinguished himself in an act of heroism in the last days of the war in Laos in 1975. Now in his 90s, Richard is still active and was very helpful in the preparation of this book.

I would be remiss if I did not mention two Mongolian brothers who did yeomen service in the Clandestine Service targeting mainly Soviet officials who, in turn, tried to recruit them. I knew one of the brothers during an Asia posting and found him amusing, intelligent, and dedicated to recruiting Russian-speaking targets. I was told he retired to an elegant Mongolian yurt-style house in northern Virginia.

And then there was the Irish American, David "The Bear" Spillane, who was very large, hence the nickname. But he was a gentle bear, and everyone liked him. He had served in the U.S. Army as an enlisted man in the Army Security Agency, where he was a Vietnamese linguist eavesdropping on North Vietnamese Army traffic. He eventually graduated from the University of Pennsylvania and acquired fluency in Cambodian and Thai in addition to Vietnamese. We served together in Cambodia and elsewhere in Southeast Asia, and were close friends. He was at his best working with liaison services, where everyone was impressed by his linguistic skills. He once taught me a Thai expression that dealt with the beauty of a woman. The phrase, *by wat dai*, translated as "she is pretty enough to take to a village Buddhist temple fair." I was having lunch with a Thai army general, later prime minister, when a pretty woman walked by and I used the phrase.

"What does that mean?" the general asked, perplexed. I explained. He laughed.

"I never heard that expression. It is delightful, and that woman who just walked by is indeed pretty enough to be taken and shown off at a *wat* [temple] fair. Where did you learn it?" he asked.

"From The Bear."

"That figures," said the general. "He speaks Thai better than many Thai people, and far more slang than I do."

The Bear ultimately married a beautiful Thai businesswoman and passed away some years ago after retiring in Chiang Mai. She puts flowers on his grave every week.

When I joined the Agency in 1971, it was comprised of mostly white males. There were minorities and women, but the "glass ceiling" was clearly in place. Over the years, I saw the Agency make strides to correct the imbalance. In the East Asia Division, where I spent my entire career, there was more ethnic diversity, due in large part to the linguistic skills that these officers brought. In recent years, I am told that there are growing numbers of men and women with Asian origins in the Agency, many of them legacies of parents and even grandparents who served before them. There are also many more officers with blue collar family backgrounds than the OSS gentry who led the Agency in its early years.

CHAPTER 39

FLASH

The highest precedence on cable traffic to and from Langley, Virginia, is FLASH. In descending order, it is followed by IMMEDIATE, PRIORITY, and ROUTINE. On May 17, 1992, Thailand was in the grip of a serious political crisis as more than 200,000 peaceful demonstrators took to the streets protesting against a military coup d'état that overturned a democratically elected government. The mood of the crowd was almost festive as speakers addressed them on the Pramane Ground near the Grand Palace in Bangkok. Eventually, the crowd started to march on Government House, not far away. The CIA's Bangkok station was used to political upheaval in Thailand and kept a close watch on the situation.

The police were waiting on the Phan Fa Bridge, which blocked the route to the seat of government, as the throng moved slowly along Ratchadamnoen Avenue, the Champs Elysees of Bangkok, past the Independence Monument. The CIA acting chief of station (ACOS) was on hand personally and moved with the protesters. He spotted a senior army officer, a friend he had worked closely with in the past. He asked the general if he expected trouble. "I have ordered my men not to fire under any circumstances," the general replied. "But army troops are being brought into Bangkok from the West and I am worried about them."

After dark, protesters tried to force their way past police and casualties were taken on both sides. A battalion of Royal Thai Army armed with automatic weapons was brought in. Firing broke out, and in the ensuing one-sided fight dozens of protesters were killed and hundreds disappeared. The venerable Royal Hotel became a triage center where the dead and wounded were brought in, the floor awash with blood. The crisis was resolved when King Bumiphol stepped in on May 20. Four days later, Genera Suchinda Kraprayoon resigned as prime minister. No station personnel or assets were injured in the fighting.

The ACOS received one death threat by phone and believed that it came from the right-wing generals who were responsible for the violence. He never reported that call to headquarters, feeling that he might be recalled and his tour terminated.

One senior station agent took refuge in an embassy residence, but the ACOS assured him he would be safe. Three days later, he returned home and resumed his duties as the danger passed.

When the fighting broke out, the ACOS moved directly to the embassy and sent a FLASH, the highest-priority message, to Langley reporting the violence.

In my career, I have been involved with several FLASH messages. The most were generated by CIA headquarters informing the chief of station in Europe where I was posted of possible imminent war involving the host country and urgently requesting the answer to a question regarding the country's planning. I knew nothing about the FLASH message until I was convoked by the COS. It transpired that no station agents and assets could answer the question. In a state of anxiety bordering on desperation, he asked if I could help.

I told the chief that while none of my agents had the answer, I did have a friend in the host government who might know. The man was a long-time friend whom I had never considered agent material, as he had no vulnerability. He was unaware of my Agency affiliation, was pro-American, and had been useful in making introductions to me in the past. I put him in the "cooperative unwitting contact" category and told the COS I was willing to pose the question to him and foresaw little blowback if he declined to talk.

"Do it," he ordered. "Do you need to break cover?"

"No," I replied. "He might suspect I'm Agency but he has access to this kind of information and might help, but because of his work load it usually takes me a week or more to get a meeting."

"I need it *today*," the chief said. "Do what you can."

A few minutes later, I was speaking to my friend on a pay phone.

"It has been while," I opened with. "Could we meet for a very quick chat?"

He laughed and said: "I think I know why you are calling. Can we make it tomorrow?"

"Today would be much better," I replied. "I only need five minutes."

"I can give you two," he said, and told where and when we could meet.

I was there early and he was right on time. He did indeed know the question I had in mind.

"You must be looking for a scoop," he said by way of greeting, and proceeded to take up one of my two minutes with a clear and detailed answer to the FLASH question.

I thanked him profusely and began to make my exit. My two minutes were up.

"This will cost you a dinner," he said smiling.

"My pleasure."

"Wives included."

"Done."

Then he said something strange: "Since we are here and time is short, I have something else for you. For free." He proceeded to give me sensitive intelligence on a terrorism matter that was sure to get Langley's attention.

"Many thanks. How about a lunch down the road?"

"Done," he said.

Back at the embassy a few minutes later, I went directly to the chief of station's office, where he was waiting for me.

"Got it, chief!" I exclaimed, and proceeded to hand him the response to the FLASH message. I had drafted it in the taxi back to the embassy.

"Excellent work!" he said, and called his secretary in. "Send it," he ordered, handing her the one-paragraph message. "FLASH precedence."

In those days, field intelligence reports were graded. Reports that were not disseminated to the intelligence community were graded "0." These were to be avoided at all costs. I never had a grade 0 in my career. Only slightly better were reports graded "1." These were also to be avoided. I sought to get my reports graded "5," which was considered "good."

The answer to the FLASH message received a grade of "20," the first and only one I ever received. The terrorist-related report was graded "10."

CHAPTER 40

Having Staff

In 1943, the British Ambassador to Turkey, Sir Hughe Knatchbull-Hugessen, hired as his valet a Turk, Elyesa Bazna. He was an experienced servant and spoke several languages. He was also a trained locksmith and a German spy. Using his locksmithing skills, Bazna repeatedly broke into the ambassador's safe and stole top secret British documents, including clues to the Allied D-Day landings in Normandy. This is an example of the kind of servant *not* to employ, an object lesson for young (or old) embassy officers and spouses sent overseas where they are expected to employ local staff.

The CIA offer excellent training to prepare their officers for living abroad, but little or no effort is taken to teach officers how to handle servants. A century ago, most American diplomats were white males from Ivy League schools. They were usually affluent and had experience dealing with domestic servants at home, which provided good training for hiring staff abroad.

Times have changed, and so have the challenges facing diplomats and intelligence officers working under diplomatic cover. These officers are especially at risk when assigned to countries that are hostile to the United States, where it must be assumed that all staff have been co-opted by the local counterintelligence service to spy on their employers. They can also plant listening or video cameras and create general havoc for the unsuspecting American.

Even in friendly countries, one must be aware that otherwise loyal and honest staff can be recruited by police or intelligence services converting servants into spies. It is not their fault, but nevertheless, great care must be taken in hiring, supervising, and being ever watchful.

Of course, there is also the matter of honesty, hygiene, and competence, all of which are vital to assuring a happy household in which both the Americans and their foreign employees are content. I hesitate to say that staff should be treated like family. They should not. They should be treated like staff, but always with respect and fairness.

The best staff we had in our decades overseas were my first servants in Cambodia, from 1973–75. I was alone in Cambodia. Because of the war raging in and around Phnom Penh, no spouses were at post. My wife, BJ, was "safe havened" in Bangkok, where she taught English and had a small apartment near the embassy. I would travel every month for four days, and on occasion BJ would visit Cambodia, one hour away by Air Cambodge ("Lose Your Clothes, Fly Air Cambodge"!) and spend a few days of R&R trying to differentiate the sound of incoming Khmer Rouge rockets (incoming) and Cambodian Army artillery protecting the city (outgoing).

I inherited a charming art deco villa in a fashionable part of town from the departing Political Counsellor, who gave me three things before he left: (1) a large hammock from his service in the Yucatan in Mexico, which was very comfortable on our large upstairs verandah; (2) an antique but very serviceable M-3 American .45 caliber submachine gun and ammunition (handy if the Khmer Rouge were in the compound); and (3) my cook, Jeannot Martin.

Jeannot was a French citizen, the product of a French military father and a Vietnamese mother. He had served as a pastry chef in the French Army when Vietnam was still a colony, and was widely regarded as one of the best cooks in Phnom Penh and the finest pastry chef in Cambodia. He was married to a Vietnamese woman, Ba, and they had approximately 18 children, six of whom lived with us. Ba did the washing, and on occasion cooked Vietnamese dishes. Two of the oldest girls, Loan and Nga, served drinks and food. I spoke only French with Jeannot and my poor Vietnamese with Ba. I tried to teach a little English to the girls.

Jeannot showed BJ his notebook of expenses for food on one of her visits from Bangkok. He had every item: eggs, ducks, cooking oil, etc., all meticulously noted. I paid him for the food, but because of the low cost I never checked his books. He wanted BJ to know where the money went. He was extremely conscientious and honest. BJ asked where the costs were of the pedicabs (cycle rickshaws) that Jeannot took to and from the market. He was paying that out of his rather meager salary. (I will note here that I covered all their food and medical costs.) BJ informed him that these were reimbursable expenses and gave him back pay. He probably put some of that back pay into buying us a white tablecloth, something I lacked and rarely used due to the limited entertaining I did while rockets rained into the city.

While I hired Jeannot in Phnom Penh, BJ hired a Thai maid, Sri, in Bangkok. She was a middle-aged, extremely competent, and pleasant woman, divorced with two grown children. After I left Cambodia in 1975, Sri stayed with us

Our cook, Jeannot Martin, and half of his family on the verandah in Phnom Penh, 1974.

for a total of 17 years. After two years working as our maid, Sri informed me one day that she was not really a maid.

"What are you?" I asked.

"I am a baby *amah*," she said, a nanny. "But you don't have any children," she added, putting the onus on me.

"I didn't know," I said. "Maybe it's time we start a family." And so we did. Seth was born in 1978 and Sri returned to her true *métier*, nannying. She was an excellent nanny, and did so well we had another son, Brendan, in 1983 when we were posted in Europe. We fretted about bringing Sri to a strange country that had snow in the winter and where she did not speak the language. We decided we needed her when we learned that professional babysitters made the equivalent of $20 per hour, and double after midnight. She was delighted to travel abroad, which first required our tracking down her divorced husband, who had to give her permission to leave the country. Her first trip abroad was quite an adventure. Our Thai friend who arranged for her passport, visa, and travel bought the cheapest flight for Sri, via the Soviet airline Aeroflot, which routed her through Moscow, where she only made her connection thanks to an American who got her on the right plane. I met her flight, only to find she did not exit immigrations. Using my diplomatic credentials, I was allowed inside, where I found her being questioned, rather unsuccessfully, by the local police. They quickly released her to me.

We lived in a fashionable old apartment next to a world-famous park and garden, ideal for a young boy to sail his boat in the pond, ride a 19th-century merry-go-round, and actually grab the brass ring, or ride a small donkey among the world-class statues that decorated the gardens, all under the watchful eye of Sri.

At first we were concerned about how she would fit in the staff quarters located on the seventh and top floor of the 18th-century building. We had two staff rooms, one for Sri and the other for my dark room. Almost all of the servants in the building were young, male, black African cooks who spoke no English or Thai. Sri assured us she would be OK. Within two weeks, she had organized bathroom cleaning and garbage rosters among the seventh-floor staff. I don't know how she did it, but suspect her age (pushing 60) and easygoing manner had something to do with it. Only later did we learn that she was teaching the Africans how to cook Thai food. After a few months in town, I was approached in the lobby by one of my neighbors, a retired ambassador.

"I want to thank you," he said.

"For what, sir?" I asked.

"For Sri."

"You know her?"

"Only by reputation. But my cook from Senegal does, and he loves her, especially her food. And so do we."

Then came baby Brendan, six weeks early. He spent his first 55 days in an incubator at a famous clinic for premature babies, which probably saved his life. Seth now had a baby brother and Sri had a new baby. The following year, I was assigned as chief of station in North America and Sri was delighted to join us. She turned down an offer from her daughter to join her in London, where she and her husband owned two Thai restaurants. "She wants a nanny for free," Sri told me. "I will stay with my boys." Our boys, it was now clear, were Sri's boys too.

With Sri joining us, BJ had time to open a new business as a caterer with my sister Jenny, East West Catering, which attracted high-end clients. It did very well, as it allowed her to bring Thai food to the attention of Western clients, as well as classic European dishes she learned at a world-class culinary course she took during our European tour. Sri's English improved quickly and she pocketed all her salary to buy land and a house near the Gulf of Siam.

When I was posted back to Asia three years later, we wondered if Sri would like to join us and if she would fit in with a different culture, or whether she would like to go home after six years abroad. I called an American who had just been posted to the country to see if a Thai servant would fit in where we were going. He also had Thai experience. "Talk to my wife," he said, and put her on the phone. "Should we take our nanny?" I asked. "We have two small kids and we all love her."

"If I had had my Thai staff at our last posting, our tour would have gone much better," the wife told me. "If you don't take your nanny, send her to us." We took Sri with us. We also hired a local husband and wife team; husband gardener, wife cook. On day one, we explained that Sri was like a grandmother to the boys and that anything she said should be obeyed. The tour went fine. Sri retired in 1992, and every time we were in Bangkok she would come up from her home at the mouth of the Chao Phraya River and visit "her" boys. She was their surrogate grandmother.

Only once, when Seth was about 4, was I given pause about having a Thai nanny, who are famed for spoiling children. He was unhappy with Sri for some reason and I heard him say: "Sri, how many times do I have to tell you?"

Sri smiled as she waved me away and replied to the little fellow: "Sorry Boss!" Everyone laughed, including Seth. Thai nannies rule!

At our last posting, also in Southeast Asia, most of our staff were Christians belonging to an ethnic minority famous for their education, honesty, and competence. We had two ladies; Sun Sun, an Anglican, was the cook, and Mu Mu, a Baptist, was the maid. It was not a problem, but we learned to never expect anyone to work on a Sunday. We had a large colonial house on 2 acres with stables, and a tennis court shielded from the sun by huge rain trees that later provided the name for my consulting firm, Rain Tree International.

The junior gardener, Saw Jack, doubled as ball boy when tennis was played. We had lights for night tennis, which was popular, and when Saw Jack opened the small door of the light switch, he opened it gently with one hand while holding a lethal machete in the other. Poisonous snakes liked to curl up around the light switch, so Jack would gently remove the snake with the tip of his long blade, flip it up in the air, and slice it in two pieces on the way down.

We look back with great fondness on the staff from different cultures and countries who all provided excellent service. We kept in touch with Sri for years until she went into a Buddhist nunnery, as she told us she would. But I still worry about Jeannot and his large family, whom we left in Cambodia in 1975. I doubt the Khmer Rouge would care that Jeannot carried a French passport. They emptied Phnom Penh immediately, and I am hoping that our cook somehow made it safely to Vietnam. We tried to find him, without success. Jeannot Martin, where are you?

CHAPTER 41

Into the Enemy Camp in Cambodia

In the summer of 1990, I was put in charge of a team supporting the Cambodian resistance to the Vietnamese-installed puppet government in Phnom Penh. It was an international paramilitary program providing arms, ammunition, and logistics support to twenty thousand fighters belonging to two groups; the Khmer People's National Liberation Front (KPNLF), led by former Cambodian prime minister Son Sann, and the royalist faction known by their French acronym (FUNCINPEC), under the leadership of Prince Norodom Sihanouk.

This was a non-lethal war for the United States. We provided food, clothing, medical care, public relations programs, etc. Our Association of Southeast Asian Nations (ASEAN) allies provided all of the weaponry and training under the guidance of hand-picked, top-quality officers. The mission of the Cambodia Working Group was to force the Vietnamese to the negotiating table in Paris to end their support of the so-called People's Republic of Kampuchea (PRK) under Heng Samrin, a long-time communist and a senior official of the Khmer Rouge.

The main mission was not to kill people or take and hold ground. It was to gain the support of the Cambodian people by exposing the land grab by Cambodia's traditional enemy, Vietnam. This was accomplished through clandestine radios broadcasting into Cambodia and a growing civic action campaign aimed at helping rural areas once under the Khmer Rouge yoke. Two hospitals were built in the "liberated zone" of northwestern Cambodia as long-range penetration columns spread the word throughout the country.

On October 23, 1991, the Paris Peace Agreements were signed, bringing an end to the Cambodian-Vietnamese War and ushering in the first post-Cold War United Nations peacekeeping mission (United Nations Transitional Authority in Cambodia, or UNTAC). It was the first time the United Nations acted as the government of a nation.

Cambodian resistance disc jockey broadcasting into Cambodia from a secret location outside the country.

In March 1992, I received an invitation from the Siam Society to participate in a visit to the famed temple of Prasat Preah Vihear. The Siam Society, founded in 1904, was a center for research on the arts, literature, and history of Thailand and neighboring countries. I was a member, and in 1983 the Society published my first book, *Old Homes of Bangkok: Fragile Link*.

This was a great opportunity to visit the important and rarely visited 11th-century historical site. There was only one problem; it was in Cambodia and the PRK government still had armed troops at the temple. Preah Vihear, as the Cambodians called it, was a special site. For one thing, it was perched on the top of a cliff on the Dangrek escarpment that generally demarcated the border of Thailand and Cambodia. Thanks to a 1962 ruling of The International Court of Justice, the temple was awarded to Cambodia, possibly in part due to the good work of their lawyer, former U.S. Secretary of State Dean Acheson. The Thais were not happy about the decision, and are still not happy.

The location of the temple makes it very difficult to access from the Cambodian plain, hundreds of meters below the site. It is easier to access the site from the Thai side, and that is what the Siam Society planned to do. The good news for me was that there was no passport control when crossing into Cambodian turf, and no visa was required. There was no Thai passport control either. Arrangements were made by the Siam Society, which probably involved a small amount of money changing hands.

The invitation was a rare opportunity not to be missed. With the shooting over and the UN gearing up UNTAC, I decided that we should go and keep a low profile while entering enemy turf. About 30 signed up for the excursion, many of them old friends. No one knew I had been working with the resistance. It was not my first visit to Khmer sites with the Society. In the 1970s, I photographed a similar trip to remote Khmer ruins in northeastern Thailand guided by a retired former French ambassador to Thailand, Achille Clarac. It was great fun traveling rough through Thai provinces that once belonged to the Khmer Empire in the centuries before Siam conquered Angkor in the 15th century. Today there are still more than two million people in Thailand whose first language is Khmer. We even happened on an undiscovered Khmer ruin in the middle of a tapioca field. I published the trip in *Arts of Asia*, the Hong Kong publication revered by Asian art dealers and collectors.

The trip started with a long but pleasant overnight train ride, first class, from Bangkok to the provincial town of Sisaket. There we were met by a guide with an air-conditioned bus to take us the sixty miles south to the temple. We crossed into Cambodia without incident and walked up a decrepit set of stone stairs that were eight hundred years old, possibly older. There were no other tourists, but our reception committee comprised PRK soldiers who guarded the outpost from fortified positions inside the temple grounds. The real danger was from minefields laid by the Khmer around their positions on three sides. There were also a few Buddhist monks on hand, possibly Thai, who seemed to live there.

We walked to the high ground of the temple, now in an advanced state of decay. It must have been magnificent a thousand years ago. It was an ideal candidate for restoration, just as the French Ecole Francais d'Extreme Orient (EFEO) did for Angkor Wat and dozens of other more accessible sites a century earlier. The path suddenly ended at the edge of a red stone cliff looking out to the plains of northern Cambodia hundreds of feet below. It was a spectacular view.

We walked around the cliff-top ruin, followed by a friendly PRK sergeant who gave me the opportunity to practices my rudimentary Cambodian: "Were there any Khmer Rouge around?"

"No. They fled Cambodia when the Vietnamese invaded and were based on the Thai side of the border."

"Are there any land mines around?"

"Yes, all around. Don't go beyond the barbed wire." Good advice. Then the sergeant offered to take me on his motorbike to the nearest Cambodian town,

Anlong Veng, for a good meal. I declined his kind offer, pleading lack of time and not wanting to push my luck.

I was reminded of a story my old Associated Press boss, Horst Faas, told me after he visited Preah Vihear in 1963. Prince Norodom Sihanouk, who ran Cambodia with a stern fist in those days, organized a grand festival at the temple in honor of it being returned to Cambodia by the ICJ (the International Court of Justice at The Hague in the Netherlands). Sihanouk, ever the showman, organized the event for the Khmer elite and the diplomatic corps in Phnom Penh. Faas covered the event for the AP.

Thousands of local Cambodians gathered at the base of the cliff, where Sihanouk had a staircase constructed for selected guests to climb to Preah Vihear. They were there to see the prince, who was vastly popular among the peasantry. In return, Sihanouk adored them and organized a party they would never forget. He had an airfield built on the plain to accommodate his guests and provided lavish food and entertainment. A large campsite was constructed to house his guests, along with an outdoor cinema where Sihanouk showed films that he had produced and sometimes starred in.

Faas described the gala in detail, starting with the unfortunate death of the Soviet ambassador, who succumbed to a heart attack just as he finished the arduous climb to the top. Undeterred, Sihanouk stepped over the body of the fallen diplomat and commenced guiding a tour of the stately old ruin. After the visit to the temple, guests descended to the plain for the evening festivities.

The German photographer was impressed by the high quality of food, and especially the French wines, that Sihanouk catered for his fete, which was in two parts; one for foreign guests and another for local Cambodians. Before the food was served, guests were offered champagne and local viands. Faas noticed a very attractive Eurasian woman mingling with members of the royal family in full court dress. He caught her eye and approached. In his excellent French, he made his move, suggesting that they meet in Phnom Penh later.

"That would impossible," she said with a smile. "I don't think my husband would approve."

"Is he here?" Faas asked.

"That's him," the woman said as she nodded toward Sihanouk, who was engaged in animated conversation with guests.

Faas was talking to Monique, half-Italian, half-Cambodian, a former beauty queen and Sihanouk's latest favorite wife. Faas retreated into the crowd, hoping Monique would not report him to the Prince. She didn't.

As BJ and I strolled around the temple grounds, photographing defensive positions of the PRK, I was remined that less than one hundred miles away

Barry and BJ at the cliff-top temple of Khao Phra Viharn, Cambodia, 1991.

were twenty thousand fellow armed Cambodians who had fought the PRK to a standstill. Their Vietnamese masters were unable to continue prosecuting the war they brought to Cambodia in 1979. The Soviet Union was in disarray and about to self-destruct, and could no longer fund its far-flung wars of liberation. The UN had stationed troops in Cambodia, but so far none of them at Preah Vihear, a lonely and isolated outpost. UNTAC brought free and fair elections which resulted in a victory for Sihanouk's party. His son, Prince Ranarith, became prime minister. Sihanouk's dalliance with the Khmer Rouge was forgiven, if not forgotten.

Everyone enjoyed the Siam Society excursion, especially me. I didn't tell many people that I had taken a brief holiday at one of the least-known and visited ancient Cambodian sites, but I did share photos of the PRK positions at Preah Vihear with allies. National borders in Southeast Asia have shifted a great deal in the past few hundred years. They may shift again.

CHAPTER 42

Into the Middle Kingdom

On March 1, 1979, the governments of the United States and China established embassies in each other's capitals. After six years in Southeast Asia, I was assigned to my first headquarters tour in Langley, Virginia, in 1979. The normalization of relations with China was a watershed event in the often difficult diplomacy between the nations. Everyone was optimistic that this would foster a period of better cooperation and friendship, and, for a while, it happened.

In this spirit of a new beginning with China, I had the good fortune to be tapped to spend one month in China with an itinerary that I would create myself. The idea was to experience China as a traveler and not an official. The trip was coordinated with the embassy in Beijing and I would be in the hands of Chinese guides, with a car and driver on hand at every stop and the opportunity to get to know the Middle Kingdom on a personal level.

I welcomed this new adventure. I spoke no Chinese, and did not think my Thai or French would help me. I had very little contact with the embassy, although I started and ended my trip in Beijing, where I was cordially welcomed. There were six cities on my itinerary: Beijing, Shanghai, Guangzhou (Canton), Hangzhou, Suzhou, and Kweilin.

Before embarking on my trip, I did a lot of reading on China and what I should do there. It quickly became apparent that relatively few official Americans had visited The People's Republic, and tourism was not very developed. Landing in Beijing, I was amazed at the large number of bikes on the streets, the paucity of automobiles, and the sameness of the apparel of virtually all Chinese, regardless of gender. My hotel was adequate and inexpensive. My guide (or minder) was a young man with basic English skills and little knowledge of China before 1949.

At the embassy, the chief of station gave me two pieces of advice. When visiting the Ming Dynasty tombs, I should make sure to see one of the unexcavated tombs. And when visiting the Great Wall of China, I was to walk to the left along the wall and not to the right. The left is steeper but less traveled, and gives a better view. Both were very useful tips.

The Ming tombs are a collection of mausoleums for 13 Ming Dynasty emperors (1368–1644) in a quiet valley about twenty-five miles northwest of Beijing. When I visited, two were open to the public; one had been renovated and the other excavated. I visited both and was impressed. As I walked to the entrance to one of them, a small group of elderly American women, a rare sight in China in 1980, were just leaving. Their guide, a young Chinese male, announced with some glee: "Last chance for Happy House, ladies." He then gestured to what was a public lavatory. I heard one woman comment to a friend: "Jesus Louise, if I have to squat one more time, I'm going to die." In those days, flush toilets were a rarity in China.

After I toured the two tombs, I told my guide, a singularly uninformed fellow, I wanted to visit another tomb. "No more tombs," he announced.

"There are 11 more," I advised, "and they are nearby. I am told it is possible to visit. I want to see one, any one."

He pondered and conferred with the driver. I was right. There were tombs nearby and they were not forbidden to visit. But there wasn't much to see. I asked him to choose one and he did. About ten minutes from the excavated tomb, I was taken to a large building with huge timber columns. "Here is another tomb," he announced without further identification. An aged woman was the caretaker. She greeted me quietly. There was no entrance fee. For about five minutes, I walked around the serene site in the valley and listened to the wind pass through the trees. There were no other visitors. It was an unexpected and moving experience.

We then drove to the Great Wall of China, or more correctly to *one of* the Great Walls of China. There were quite a few of them built over one thousand five hundred years to keep would-be invaders from the north at bay. The closest wall to Beijing is only about thirty miles north of the city. Constructed in the years of the Ming Dynasty, it is relatively new and in pretty good shape.

We visited the Badaling section of the wall, a reconstructed part of the edifice with 16 watchtowers. There were some visitors, mostly Chinese, but it was not crowded. We parked and passed a Bactrian camel, where visitors, for a small fee, could don a Chinese robe and have a photo taken with the animal. I thought about it, but was daunted by a long line ahead of me.

My guide, sensing I might want to have a photo, cheerfully announced: "You can go to the head of line." Thanking him, I decided not to damage the fledgling goodwill that I hoped to achieve on my visit to China by queue

BJ in the Muslim quarter of Xian in China (taken on a later trip to China with BJ).

jumping. He seemed surprised that I would not take advantage of the perk, but led me to the Wall. I informed my guide that I would walk to the left up the steep steps of the Wall. "We go to right," he stated.

"We go to left," I responded.

"Easier we go right," he insisted. It then became apparent that this young apparatchik was lazy, in addition to being uninformed on the history of China.

"I go left, you go right," I said, "and I meet you here in one hour."

"OK," he said, and moved off for a cup of tea and a one-hour rest.

I broke out my longest lens, attached it to my trusty Nikon F camera, and started my climb on the Great Wall of China. There were few people around me; most had gone to the right. But again, my embassy information (from the chief of station) had been right. The view was quite spectacular on this side. I kept climbing and found that the wall ended shortly after it leveled off. There were no guards and no barricade forbidding movement forward.

Bromans on the Great Wall of China. (Image courtesy of Tim Carney, taken on a later trip to China with BJ)

I noticed three Chinese, two young women and one man in the uniform of the People's Liberation Army, picnicking.

They chose a perfect spot. It looked down on the wall and they were completely alone. I photographed the vista and noticed that there was a camera on their dining cloth. They were watching me intently as I operated my 300mm lens on one camera and a wide-angle 28mm lens on the other. I pointed to their camera and gestured, asking if they wanted me to photograph them with their camera. They all nodded their assent, so I arranged them carefully, with the soldier in the middle and the Great Wall behind them. I took two photos with their camera, then gestured for a photo of them with my camera. They again agreed and I snapped a few images. Then they took a few photos of me with their camera and then with my wide lens camera. Then they invited me to share their food. Not wanting to intrude, and mindful of my minder waiting for me, I just had a quick cup of tea and made my descent. Going down was trickier than going up. The steps are large and falling was a constant possibility. With minutes to spare, I located my guide just where I left him and we returned to Beijing.

BJ asked me to buy only one thing for her in China: brush painting supplies. She had studied under the well-known (in Thailand) artist Lee Boon, who specialized in large murals of horses. She was a good student and even participated in one of Lee's exhibitions. As a parting gift, Lee Boon gave BJ a scroll he had painted of one hundred horses, each in a different pose. Now BJ was running short of paper and ink. I told my guide and he nodded, saying only "Liulichang Street." It was Art Supply Central and also a good place to shop. I loaded up with paper, dry ink, ink slabs, and brushes. I also bought a few brush paintings, cheap and light. BJ was delighted.

One reason my trip was scheduled for the autumn of 1980 was to allow me to attend the Canton Fair, the oldest and largest trade fair in China, dating back to 1957. I mainly wanted to visit Canton to see the old trading port where American clipper ships, some carrying opium, would call in the 19th century. The trade fair would have been more interesting to me if I had been involved in trade, but I still found it interesting. By luck, I bumped into an American newsman from Houston and he showed me around, knowing a lot more about the fair than my guide did. In each city I visited, I had a new guide.

I told the journalist that as well as visiting and photographing the old port, I was under instructions from a China hand to have dinner at the snake restaurant in the city. The guide had heard of the restaurant but the American had not, but, being a Texan and a journalist, he was interested. The guide knew of the restaurant but said it was far too expensive. In all my travels in China, I found the food to be excellent and very inexpensive. The snake restaurant was different; it was exotic and expensive. But I was on an expense account, and so was the Tex. We decided to splurge. The guide was delighted. He calculated that his dinner probably cost three days' pay.

We were not disappointed. Even if you didn't read Chinese, you knew you were at the snake restaurant because of the live snakes on display in the front window. The place was full. All of the guests, my guide informed me, were from Hong Kong: "Guangzhou people cannot afford this."

Tex and I were the only Westerners in the place. All dishes featured snake. We started with beer to prepare us for dinner. Tex wanted to do a story, and through my guide asked a lot of questions. That led to the manager coming over to help. Then a cook appeared from the kitchen, his arms full of live snakes. Photo opportunity! In the end, it was a memorable and delicious meal. It was the highlight of my Canton visit, despite costing $60 (split with Tex).

I chose to visit Guilin in southern China for its stunning karst topography along the Li River. I arranged for a seven-hour boat ride down the river, where my car would be waiting to take me back to the city. The river boat was ideal for the trip; not too big, but plenty of room. I didn't see any non-Chinese among the tourists on board, and was surprised when a middle-aged lady approached me as I photographed the rugged mountains that looked like they had stepped out of an ancient Chinese painting.

"You 'Mellican?" she asked. I suspected she wanted to know if I was an American.

"Yes," I nodded.

"Me 'Mellican too," she informed me. "San Francisco." She was part of a group of Chinese Americans from California.

"How do you like Guilin?" I asked, expecting a positive answer.

"They really fuck Chinese from 'Mellica."

I was taken aback and also curious. "How so?"

"Everything expensive for us. Local Chinese pay little, we pay much." She went on to explain the double payment standard for overseas Chinese visiting China. It turned out we were staying in the same hotel, reserved for foreign visitors.

"Did you see sign on door of hotel nightclub?" she enquired.

"Not yet. What does it say?"

"No Chinese. But 'Mellican Chinese OK." Later that day, I saw the sign meant to prevent locals from mixing with foreign guests.

Guilin is nature's bounty and was memorable, but my favorite city was Suzhou, with its classical gardens spanning a millennium of Chinese garden design. Suzhou's beauty was man-made to mirror and improve on nature. Here I was in luck. My guide was an older gentleman, with a passion for the gardens matched only by his knowledge. He was delighted to have a client who was captivated by the gardens. I extended my visit to Suzhou and spent every available minute visiting and photographing the amazing gardens of landscapes, rivers, rocks, and water surrounding serene pavilions with doors and windows of unmatched skill and beauty.

Visitors to Suzhou today will find the gardens mostly intact but overrun with tourists. On the positive side, there is a new and vibrant art museum designed by I. M. Pei, a Suzhou native.

My month of orientation and travel went quickly. Returning several decades later with BJ, I was amazed how much China had changed, especially Shanghai, where I walked the old riverside Bund in the European enclave in 1980 with thousands of locals, all in blue Mao suits, doing their morning tai chi more or less in unison. Now the old city is mostly gone, and I miss it. I returned to Langley with a lot of fond memories, 50 rolls of shot film, and BJ's brush painting materials.

Looking back, I see how fortunate I was to be sent to China before hordes of tourists arrived. It was nice to be one of the few foreigners visiting China as it was, when people traveled by bicycle and dressed in Mao suits of blue cotton. Thank you Billy Huff for sending me.

CHAPTER 43

The Mid-Career Course

During an assignment at headquarters in 1980, I received an invitation to attend the Agency's mid-career course, something I had never heard of. It was more of a directive than an invitation, and I quickly accepted. I found that the "course" was actually a meeting of Agency employees across the wide spectrum of skills needed by the CIA. It gave people an opportunity to meet others whom they ordinarily would never have a chance to do so. I made some useful connections, but more importantly I learned a lot about the Agency and how it worked.

There are four directorates in the CIA: Operations, Intelligence, Science &Technology, and Administration. Men and women from all directorates were present, mostly in the GS-13 (military major) grade. There were about 60 officers attending the three-week course, and on the first day we introduced ourselves and said what we did. There were only three officers from the Clandestine Service, which was not surprising as we were told only 5 percent of the Agency are case officers. I knew both of the other officers attending the course; a former Marine I served with in Cambodia and a woman Soviet specialist who had served in the Soviet Union.

At our first break, the three of us were besieged by our colleagues, many of whom had never met anyone from the Directorate of Operations. They began asking questions. The Agency operates on a "need to know" basis, and one learns fast not to ask questions without good reason. We answered as much as we could.

There were no outside speakers, each participant being asked to give a one-hour presentation on what they did at the Agency. We three ops officers were told by the fellow running the course that they liked to have ops officers describe "a day in the life of a CIA officer in the field." My friend Chuck and I volunteered to jointly put together a two-hour presentation. The lady, a shy and quiet officer, offered to speak about her posting in Moscow station, the toughest and most demanding of all assignments in the DO.

Among our classmates were a cartographer ("Free maps available in the map room, drop on by"), an economist, a cabinet maker (who specialized in concealment devices for agents' secret spy gear), a submariner who spoke Russian, and a graphologist, whom I made a point of meeting and later provided with a sample of a target's handwriting. Her analysis was spot on.

Chuck set the scenario, describing the duties of a case officer in Southeast Asia working in liaison with the host country's intelligence services. He described the planning and action of a narcotics takedown raid.

I talked about a case officer operating undeclared to the host service and under State Department cover. He did his cover job in the day and worked against recruitment targets, including host country officials, at night. He was a Vietnamese linguist and was called on to handle a Vietnamese walk-in at the embassy in the afternoon. In the early evening, he met with a suspected Soviet KGB officer, who was known to have a gambling and alcohol problem and needed money. The CIA offered a solution to all his problems.

The last DO presentation was by the female officer from the Soviet and East Europe (SE) Division. Her story was the best of any of the presentations. In a soft voice that had everyone leaning forward so as not to miss a word, she described a day in the life of a case officer in Russia, under constant scrutiny by the KGB. Even her apartment had audio and video bugs planted. Important discussions with her case officer husband took place as they showered together.

She described servicing a "dead drop" loaded signal that let her know a secret agent had put down microfilm in the drop site. All this while she knew the KGB was on her. She laughed when she told the audience: "One thing that always amuses me in the spy films is how the case officer always manages to lose surveillance before making his move. That isn't how it works in real life. You need to make sure you never lose surveillance."

Then she spoke about the day the KGB grabbed her, roughed her up, and kept her in custody for a day despite her diplomatic status which forbade such behavior. "I was not doing anything operational," she said, "but they probably thought that they could break me quickly. They couldn't." She was released within 24 hours, with apologies. Such violations of civility do not pass unnoticed. A Soviet intelligence officer, somewhere in the United States, was afforded similar harassment soon after. *Quid pro quo.*

We had two field trips during the course; one to the National Security Agency (NSA) and the other to the National Photographic Interpretation

Center (NPIC, pronounced N-pick). I won't say anything about our visit to the NSA (some say the letters stand for No Such Agency).

Our visit to NPIC, however, was a treat. We were divided into small groups and given a choice of several desks to visit. I jumped on the opportunity to visit the Afghan desk to see how the CIA-supported war against Soviet invaders was going. I was not disappointed. NPIC had been tasked with finding a Russian petroleum pipeline. The problem was the pipeline was only 3 inches in diameter. The photo interpreter showed us a large sheet of satellite imagery.

"By some hard work and good luck, we found it," he said.

"What happened then?" I asked.

"Glad you asked. We sent in the Mujahideen insurgents and they blew the pipeline in many places."

For an encore, the NPIC man let us look for a downed helicopter he had spent two days looking for. The Russian Hind helicopter had been hit by ground fire and was thought to have crashed in harsh mountain terrain. He put the imagery on the table and circled an area 6 inches wide. "It's in that circle. Find it!" He challenged us. Several of us tried, but none succeeded. The man then opened a drawer and pulled out a photo of Afghan guerrillas dancing for the camera on top of the crashed Hind helicopter. "We found it," he said, "and they sent in the Muj again. They pulled out documents, maps, and assorted gear and weapons. There were no Russian survivors."

We returned to Langley happy to have seen that another little-known element of the Agency was at the top of their game.

CHAPTER 44

My Double Agent

I once handled a double agent while posted in Europe. He was an elderly gentleman with a brush mustache and a military air. I will call him Gustav. He pretended to be an agent of a communist regime and did an excellent job. Eventually we determined that the operation had run its course and Gustav agreed. We then scripted a scenario that was right out of a B-grade Hollywood spy movie.

Gustav sat in the lobby of a five-star European hotel waiting for what would be his last meeting with his communist handlers. He wore a bespoke Harris tweed jacket that fitted in with the posh elegance of the room. He was alone and had a wrapped bundle of "doctored" intelligence reports that would be his farewell "gift." He sat alone while I watched from the far side of the large lobby.

Gustav ordered a glass of wine and was joined by three men dressed in shabby off-the-rack suits of inferior quality. They looked out of place in a hotel of quality and seemed nervous to be there. Gustav rose to greet them. One of the men was Gustav's handler. The others did not speak, and probably did not understand what was being said. Gustav ran the meeting and started by presenting his case officer with the documents which had been specially prepared for passage to the enemy regime. His case officer thanked Gustav effusively. It was clear to me that he was respected and his gift was appreciated.

Then Gustav gave them the bad news. He said he was in poor health and this would be their last meeting. He said his doctor had advised him to retire immediately and seek treatment in a warm climate. Speaking Gustav's language poorly, his officer translated for the two strap hangers and then tried to dissuade him from leaving their employ. I could see them aggressively trying to change Gustav's mind. They were not happy and became belligerent. It was three-on-one, but Gustav had been in worse situations. Besides, he knew

I was nearby and prepared to intercede if the unhappy spies tried anything heavy-handed, something for which they were well known.

Gustav sought to calm them down and ordered beer for them from a hovering waiter, who could see that something was amiss. He leaned forward and said if there was any problem he was prepared to take his "gift" back and they would never see him again. He then asked to be paid, and reluctantly his case officer slipped him an envelope that contained a thick wad of U.S. $100 bills that Gustav later passed to me. He did not work for money, even from the CIA.

Attempting to turn on the charm, the senior of the trio tried to get Gustav to join them for lunch nearby. Gustav looked at this watch and said he needed to run to catch his train. He quickly rose, shook hands with each of his handlers and wished them well, and marched out of the room after informing them he had enjoyed working with them but would be moving to a warmer climate soon.

Gustav had played his part to perfection and I waited to see what, if anything, the jilted intelligence officers would do. They huddled for a meeting and ordered another round of beer. They came from a regime which did not treat failure benignly. Their first concern was their own futures. They had just lost an important source of information, and this would not go down well with their own masters. Heads could roll; literally.

I ordered a second Scotch and soda and watched, amused, for almost an hour from behind a newspaper as the other men argued with Gustav's recently fired case officer and reviewed their own situation. Eventually they paid up and departed. By the time the men left, Gustav was probably boarding a plane home to a life of well-deserved rustic ease.

I was on hand to witness the last meeting for two reasons. Firstly, I was to take action to assist Gustav if the men attempted to remove him from the room. That would have meant involving the local police and even the intelligence service, which we were prepared to do to project Gustav. The other reason was that I needed to carry the "classified" documents that Gustav was to hand over. It would have been very embarrassing if he had been searched at the border in possession of secret American documents. Gustav and I were on the same plane, and once we landed I passed the documents to him.

One small hiccup occurred that landed me in trouble with the bean counters in Langley. There were no seats in the economy section left when I tried to book my seat on the flight that Gustav was taking. Not a problem: I booked a first-class ticket for $26 more and reveled in caviar and champagne during the quick international hop, while Gustav languished alone in the cheap seats. I explained all this to the delighted deputy chief of station when I returned home. "Don't worry about it," he said. "Operational necessity." But I had broken a rule: no flying first class. The CIA can be generous in the extreme when it cares to, but must exercise fiscal responsibility and conform to government standards and rules at all times.

My accounting bounced when it hit Langley. I was amused when the DCOS gave me the bad news. "I will gladly pay the $26 out of pocket," I said. "I ate that much in caviar alone."

"You will not," he assured me. "I am going to fight this as a matter of principle." Which he did, with the approval of the chief of station. Eventually they won and I didn't have to pay for the sin of flying first class.

CHAPTER 45

Operational Golf

Mark Twain is famously quoted as defining golf as "A good walk spoiled."
I am in agreement with Mark. My favorite sport is tennis, and in my younger
years I played tennis and cricket for the Royal Bangkok Sports Club (RBSC).
Golf came later, and not easily. When a CIA officer is "declared" to a friendly
intelligence service in Southeast Asia, playing golf is almost mandatory. The
lunches that followed golf were excellent places to conduct business. This was
especially true in Thailand, where the more senior the officer you wanted to
see, the more likely he would be available on a golf course.

It is not necessary to be good at golf, but it helps. My favorite working
golf venue is the Royal Thai Army (RTA) golf club. They have two 18-hole
courses, side by side, outside Bangkok. In the early 1990s, when I was working
with four RTA generals I found it necessary to learn to play golf. I was greatly
helped by a very senior Royal Thai Police general, an old friend, who was an
accomplished golfer who had played at top golf courses around the world. In
addition to being a great fellow and close friend, the general took me on, as
a challenge I am sure, to get me to play and enjoy the sport. Many nights he
would pick me up and insist we needed to drive golf balls. I never amounted
to much as a player, but I certainly enjoyed playing the game in Thailand.

In golf, unlike tennis, you play against yourself, another thing I dislike.
But playing with Thai generals, I found, can be a lot of fun and professionally
rewarding. They play the game well and often, but differently from the way
most Americans or Europeans are used to. Take caddies, for instance. The
RTA club had 710 caddies, all female, and some very savvy on what club to
choose and how to play the army courses, which had their own challenges.
Take the par-five 12th hole on the main course. It abuts a pistol range behind
a long berm, and there is no real danger when you hear live firing nearby.
But occasionally, a ricochet can be heard zinging overhead so the girls like
to play the 12th hole on the trot.

There are a lot of caddies, but some officers will hire one lady, often a sturdy teenager who thinks nothing of toting golf clubs in lieu of construction work or planting and harvesting rice, and another to carry a sun umbrella and even a small collapsible chair. It is hot in Thailand and we usually teed off on Sundays at 0700 hours before the heat came up. We also went out in flights of six, rather than the customary four. This slows play, of course, but there are small snack bars dotting the course. The Thais are notorious snackers. We would stop for some fresh-squeezed lime juice and a few holes later have a hard-boiled egg. Thirty minutes later we could sample grilled pork skewers. Few people gain weight while playing golf, but it can happen in Thailand.

Then there is betting, a favorite Thai custom and tradition. It is always low stakes, say 10 Baht (30 cents) for a putt; or a little more for a hole, and more than that for a match. There are players who offer odds for difficult shots. They are hustlers and need watching. By the end of a five-hour morning, rarely more than a few dollars can be won or lost, mostly in good fun.

For serious betting, one needs to play the Royal Bangkok Sports Club course. The RBSC was chartered by King Chulalongkorn in 1901 as a sports venue for foreign residents of Thailand, and membership for Thais was limited to one-third of the total. That has changed, but it is still difficult to gain membership. It is always a treat to play the short but difficult golf course, which features a lot of water, in the heart of Bangkok. I loved playing lawn tennis at the RBSC, where the manicured courts are moved frequently to prevent damage to the grass. Fresh lime juice on ice is available at courtside. After a few sets of tennis or a round of golf, draft Singha beer and classic Thai food is available on the wide verandah looking out at the golf course and the horseracing track. For serious drinking, there is a dimly lit, air-conditioned bar behind the verandah, where men need to wear a coat and tie after 5pm. The club has other amenities, including an air-conditioned billiard room. No ladies please. Hopefully, that has changed.

Gambling at golf is taken very seriously at the RBSC. In the 1970s there was a famous foursome, all Thai and very prominent men in government and business, who played daily. They each put up, it was said, $10,000 on every round. It was crowded on the first tee because, in addition to caddies, there was a "forecaddie" for each golfer. It was his job to retrieve golf balls that had fallen into the many ponds and canals that abounded. The water was always shallow, and most often balls were recovered by the deft forecaddies using their bare toes to locate them in the mud. They rarely got their hands wet.

For this particular foursome there were another four caddies, whose job was to keep the score of the other players. This was serious golf-playing for big stakes. Hence the need for accurate scoring.

Thailand was not the only place where some spectacular golf was played with our liaison hosts. I was once invited to Malaysia on a quick business trip and to a round of golf at the Singapore Island Country Club. This venerable old colonial golf club first opened in 1891 as the Singapore Golf Club and allowed only British members. Women were not allowed to join, but could play on Tuesdays. They were allowed to become members in 1907.

This is a spectacular course, far greater than the tiny RBSC course, surrounded by Bangkok and surviving as a "lung" of the heavily polluted city. I was there in 1990 and played in a foursome with the chief of the Singaporean security service, with whom we had close relations. He was a delightful fellow with open disdain for the game, as was I. He would hit the ball with no care where it went, kept the conversation going, and didn't keep score. It turned out he was the only golfer worse than me out that day, and could not have cared less. I enjoyed every moment of our walk across the stunning vistas of the Singapore course.

My chief of station, Billy Huff, and I were also invited to golf in Malaysia after a trip to Singapore. While the United States enjoyed close relations with both Singapore and Malaysia, the mood was a little tense. The neighbors were having a moment of challenging relations with each other. When we crossed from Singapore to Malaysia over the causeway to Johore, it looked like a scene from the Cold War in Berlin. The Singaporean car carrying us stopped in the middle of the causeway. Billy and I got out and were met by a car from the Malaysian service. Our luggage and golf bags were transferred and we proceeded with our visit to the jungle training center of the Malaysian Army.

In Kuala Lumpur, capital of Malaysia, we were treated to a round of golf at the Selangor Club, founded by the British in 1884. Because of its mixed membership, with colonial Brits and Malay royalty, the club was known as the Spotted Dog, or just The Dog. As I was a guest and clearly a duffer at golf, I was assigned a top caddy to escort me through the round of golf with our liaison intelligence hosts. The old fellow, an ethnic Indian, was a vestige of millions of Indians who were imported by the British to work in rubber plantations or tin mines. Much like when the Brits brought millions of Indians to Burma to work in rice fields. He had a ready wit and was free with advice.

I was delighted by the opportunity to meet and have such a charming old fellow escort me around the stunning Selangor Club in the heart of Kuala Lumpur. He wore the number five on his identification badge and it rapidly became clear to me that he was no ordinary caddy. For one thing, had been at the club for decades; he casually informed me that he caddied for the prime minister and the chief of the security service. This was my lucky day.

As it turned out, the old fellow was affable and very diplomatic while giving me golf lessons as he humped my golf bag. "Just keep your eyes on the ball," he counselled when I lifted my head to follow the flight of the ball. "It is my job to look at the ball and it is your job to keep your head still and look at the ground." So it went. For the first time, I concentrated on playing golf and listening to my new coach. At the end of the day, he had taken at least 10 strokes off my normal game. I looked forward to another round of golf with Caddy number five, who once had a handicap of 10 himself, respectable anywhere in the world. Sadly, the occasion never happened.

CHAPTER 46

On the Recruitment of Spies

Espionage is more an art than a science. The key to espionage is the successful recruitment of spies. It is not easy, hence the small number of successful "headhunters" in the Clandestine Service of my day at the CIA.

The most coveted recruitment is a spy from a "hard target" country, typically a Chinese, Russian, or terrorist; someone who can provide crucial information on plans and intentions. There are many lesser fish to catch. We need "access agents" who have good friends who are hard targets. We also need safehouse and listening post agents, key support assets who have important but unsung roles to play.

There are a number of gradations within the term "recruitment." The top of the pyramid is a fully vetted recruit who will have passed a polygraph examination ("the box"), usually more than once over the course of his or her tenure with the Agency. These agents establish a track record over time and their reporting is graded. The number of agents who are fully recruited is small.

Another group are "witting collaborators." These people know they are talking to the CIA ("witting" in Agency speak) and they provide information, usually for free, based on affection for America, the CIA, or the case officer; often all three. Some of my best intelligence came from witting collaborators. The best of these was a European official of a friendly country who thought that I (and the CIA, although the initials were never used) needed to know certain sensitive things. He was right. Sometimes I would broach a topic of high interest to the CIA. He never disappointed. I judged that an attempt to formally recruit him would be taken as an insult, so I never made a "pitch." He knew, of course, that he was providing good, secret information, and in return he only expected (and got) expensive meals (with wives) that greatly exceeded my normal entertainment allowance. In every case, the meals were approved by higher authority and deemed cheap at whatever the cost.

A popular ploy, especially for hard targets, is the "false flag" recruitment. This is a legitimate recruitment, but the target does not know that he or she is working for the CIA. I once made such a recruitment posing as a European journalist. I spoke in an Asian language with the target, who accepted readily as all he cared about was the money. He didn't care who paid for the information.

Then there is the "commercial recruitment." This is also a valid recruitment that leaves the target knowing he/she is getting paid to provide confidential information but they believe that the information is going to a business, not a government. Commercial espionage is quite prevalent among businesses worldwide that are trying to get an edge on the competition. I arranged through an access agent to meet with a hard target. I posed as a businessman seeking "consultants" with access to foreign governments of interest to my firm, traveling through a town where the access and target lived. I was introduced in alias as an old friend of the access agent and went on to describe my very successful trip, where I had recruited a number of area specialists for my employer.

This all happened over dinner and no effort was made to query the target regarding his expertise or interest in outside income. Following the flow of conversation, the fellow expressed interest in how easy it would be to make extra money. He asked what kind of information we were interested in, and I told him. He asked if he could work with me, and I said no, I didn't cover his part of the world; but I knew a fellow who did. I then sent one of my officers, who spoke the target's language fluently, to meet the target. He established a rapport, said the fellow could be a good fit, obtained detailed biographic information from the target, and learned of his access to information of interest to clients. He then recruited the target, who began reporting after accepting detailed requirements. He never knew the information was going to the CIA.

During my career, I handled a hard target who had been recruited believing that he was reporting to a special group in Washington, D.C. whose job was to improve relations between the target's country and the USG. He was paid to provide confidential background information on his country's leaders, who were in factions that were anti-American or wanted better relations. He was pleased to know he was making a contribution to a better understanding between our countries. He also accepted a handsome fee for his services, which was held in an escrow account, available any time he needed it.

Headquarters was pleased with the operation but, in its wisdom, decided they wanted to take it up a notch. Langley sent a senior officer who spoke the agent's mother tongue to meet the agent. I arranged a meal at a quiet restaurant. The asset was a little surprised to see a strange face and asked if this was a turnover meeting. I said no, that the new officer spoke his language fluently and wanted to thank the agent on behalf of the "special group" on his very useful reporting. He had a few questions.

They spoke in the target's native tongue, so I don't know what was said, but I was happy to note that the agent was affable and responsive—until I heard the letters "C," "I," and "A" spoken. The agent then seemed nervous, surprised, and unhappy. He truncated the meeting, pleading a prior engagement he had forgotten about, and left. He never met with me again. I would ambush him from time to time at events I knew he would be attending, and he was always gracious, but he never accepted another lunch invitation, nor the large sum of money we were holding for him.

It was entirely possible that the agent, who was a smart and professionally successful man, knew that he was in touch with American intelligence. But he clearly did not want *to be told* that he was committing espionage. If his government found out what he had been doing, it probably would have led to prison, and very possibly his execution for treason. It also could well be that he resented being duped into working for the CIA. Whatever the reason, we received no more reporting from the asset. We learned a lesson, I hope. Not all spies want to admit they are spies, and don't need to be told that they are working for the CIA unless there is a good reason to tell them. The agent never mentioned the money owed to him.

There are also "unwitting collaborators." I knew many in this category. Some became friends in the course of my duties. These were people who liked me and the United States, not necessarily in that order, and wanted to help where they could. They provided information in much the same way as diplomacy is handled routinely and internationally. Many a state secret or discreet tidbit is exchanged over a two-martini lunch without money changing hands. It's all part of the game.

But I was ever mindful of the hoary admonition: you don't recruit friends. When you pitch a friend and they turn you down, you no longer have a friend. You may have an enemy, one who will drop a dime and possibly truncate your posting because governments (including ours) tend to expel *persona non grata* who try to make spies out of their citizens.

Even if the person accepts the pitch, the relationship is never the same. A friendship may endure, but the person then becomes an employee; one who may go to jail, or worse, if the employment comes to the attention of the new agent's government. I once recruited a senior foreign diplomat. He and his wife were very friendly, and I knew that he had financial problems finding tuition money for his children in private schools. In my role as someone who is in the business of making dreams come true, I told my friend that I could arrange for a "college fund" in return for classified information from him. He instantly knew what was happening. He hemmed and hawed, sighed and paced, and finally agreed.

I told him the only person he could tell about his new relationship with the USG was his wife. Otherwise, he would not be able to explain their newfound income. When I saw her at a social event some weeks later, she left her husband and approached me. I was nervous. The encounter could end badly for me if she didn't like the idea of her husband being made a traitor. She took my hand in both of hers and shook it vigorously. All she said was "thank you, thank you." Her dreams were coming true.

Possibly my best recruitment came after I retired from government service in 1996. He was a fellow I had known for some time and saw that he had access to information that would be welcomed by the CIA. As his access grew, I suspected that he would welcome and thrive in the dangerous world of secret intelligence collection. Eventually, I broached the subject to him. He smiled and said: "I thought you would never ask."

He knew that I had been an Agency officer, and after I outlined the role I thought he could play in the murky world I had left behind, he agreed to meet "a friend." I made an introduction to a decorated former colleague and friend whom I respected and trusted. I will call him "Jake." Jake knew a little about my friend's area of expertise and they hit it off immediately. Soon, Jake had a new recruitment. Over time, the case grew in importance. The agent became the head of a network that produced hundreds of disseminated reports. Some of them landed on desks in the White House.

CHAPTER 47

Roman Holiday

While posted in Europe in the early 1980s, I had occasion to make a business trip to Rome to meet an agent who had excellent access to an Asian "hard target" country. The agent was an academic working in Italy and was making a rare trip to the country. I was brought in to debrief him on personalities of interest in the country where I was posted.

It was a routine matter, but gave me a chance to visit the Eternal City for the first time. I first met the asset's case officer, whom I will call Bob, and then had a meeting with his agent. Bob was a Europe specialist, easygoing and affable but plagued with a history of being declared *persona non grata*. This is the bane of all case officers, being kicked out of a country. It suggested that Bob was an unguided missile when it came to running operations, and I was on guard.

Bob told me that after our meeting he would be hosting a dinner for the asset, FIREFLY, and I was invited. This was an opportunity for FIREFLY to meet the chief of station, whom I will call Eric. The dinner was to show FIREFLY how much the CIA appreciated his cooperation and demonstrate the importance of the relationship. It was all fine with me. While I looked forward to meeting the COS, a mandarin of Europe Division with a reputation of being a martinet, I was mainly interested in eating a meal at a famous restaurant. The dinner was primarily social. Business matters would be handled in our meeting with FIREFLY earlier in the day.

The meeting took place at an outdoor osteria, with a table well away from others. FIREFLY spoke fluent French, the language I would speak with him. His Italian was excellent, a language Bob spoke well. FIREFLY's English was not strong. The meeting went well. I was introduced as an expert on the hard target (something of an exaggeration). FIREFLY seemed delighted to have a visitor come to meet him and he answered all my questions fully, to the extent that I ended up with some disseminable intelligence in addition to a lot of useful operational information on target personalities and installations. Bob and I levied some requirements on him and promised more before he left for Asia.

I was impressed with FIREFLY, whom I found informed, well connected, and engaging. We shared an interest in the restaurant chosen for dinner. This venue exceeded the modest expenses normally allowed for such entertainment. But Bob would not have to worry about the bean counters who frown on such extravagance. The COS's presence would keep them at bay. I was rather surprised when I saw our table was in the crowded main room, with little chance for private conversation. I would have chosen a less conspicuous table, especially with the COS on hand. I would have selected a private room, but this was not my party.

Bob arrived with FIREFLY, who seemed delighted and a bit overwhelmed at the opulence of the room. The budget of an academic, even a senior one like FIREFLY, did not extend to dining in a Michelin-starred restaurant. Eric arrived soon after. He also seemed not to like the choice of table. He was grumpy at first, but knew the mission that evening was to be affable to the guest of honor. Eric's focus was on FIREFLY, but his Italian was mediocre and French nonexistent. It soon became clear that Eric had a hearing problem, an issue that was exacerbated by the noise all around us.

Drinks were ordered. I had a glass of wine, following Eric's lead. FIREFLY and Bob ordered dry Martinis. As the alcohol began to take effect, we all relaxed a little, including Eric, who chatted with me about mutual friends and past postings. It didn't take long to realize that FIREFLY could not hold his liquor. After his second martini, and before the food was ordered, FIREFLY began toasting. First it was "to our friends across the sea." No danger there. He sounded like a businessman with foreign clients.

Then he toasted "Our American friends" in robust Italian. A few heads turned. Eric looked nervous. I was steeling myself to hear the three initials which cannot be spoken. Mercifully, they never came. The COS stepped in with an appropriate and gracious toast of his own that suggested he was in some sort of transatlantic business—which, of course, he was.

The food arrived, and it was sublime. I thanked Bob for choosing a great restaurant and FIREFLY chimed in his agreement while savoring a truffle. When ordering dinner, I was not extravagant, unlike FIREFLY, who ordered the best, without abandon. If the intent of the meal was to bond with FIREFLY, it worked. As our secret agent sipped a fine Barolo, he became increasingly happy; and voluble. I had some difficulty understanding his rapid French, and

Bob has the same problem with FIREFLY's Italian. All had to be translated for Eric.

Fortunately, no classified information was discussed. At no time was I worried about the security of our operation, but the bizarre matter of two languages in play, both having to be translated, gave me a wine-induced epiphany. I saw our overly public entertainment of a clandestine source as a skit being performed by students of the CIA's Basic Ops Course at the end of their six months of intense training for the benefit of the staff at The Farm. The whole thing was farcical until you considered the serious security implications of what could happen if things went wrong. *Saturday Night Live* could have had a field day with the theme.

Eric, the often-grumpy chief of station, was not amused. He didn't see the humorous side of the evening, but I hoped he saw the positive effect it was having on FIREFLY, a man at the top in his field of study who also possessed a massive ego. I suspect he was not salaried, which made the evening even more important. Over an aged grappa after dinner, Eric leaned over and said to me: "This is the most fucked-up agent meeting I ever saw." I had to agree. This is not the way it was taught at The Farm. I answered: "That may be, Eric, but I think, despite everything, it went well. Thank you for inviting me to Rome. The meeting went well and dinner was exceptional." Eric may have been right about the meeting. It was a mess, but it worked. FIREFLY was happy, and that's what counted. But I hoped I would never have a meeting like that again, and I never did.

CHAPTER 48

Tehran Hostage

On November 4, 1979, 52 American embassy personnel in Tehran were taken hostage by Iranian students in support of the Iranian Revolution that toppled the regime of Shah Mohammad Reza Pahlavi. This began a 444-day saga until the hostages were released. I knew two of the hostages.

One was Victor Tomseth, who was serving as Deputy Chief of Mission, the number two man in the embassy. Vic was an Asian specialist. He had served in the Peace Corps in Nepal and embassies in Thailand and Sri Lanka, and was married to the vivacious Wallapa from Thailand. Vic was one of the heroes of this ordeal. He was at the foreign ministry when the embassy was taken and spoke to his Thai cook, Somchai, in Thai, requesting that Somchai help hide embassy staff not taken at the embassy. Somchai arranged for the Americans to be sheltered by the Canadian embassy.

The other fellow I knew was a CIA case officer, whom I will call Isaac. He was a rough-hewn officer with whom I had served in Cambodia during the 1970–75 war. Isaac was one of our upcountry officers assigned to provincial centers to report on what was happening in the countryside. It was hazardous work, as most cities were surrounded by the Khmer Rouge. Each officer assigned spoke French or Cambodian, had military experience, and was handpicked.

Isaac was treated harshly by the Iranians and spent much of his time in solitary confinement He was subjected to torture, which only hardened his resolve and dislike of the revolutionary Iranians. His life was made more difficult because he was Jewish. Isaac was the hostage who was quoted by journalists, to whom he spoke briefly upon his release, saying: "Buy Israeli war bonds." He hadn't lost his sense of humor.

While in confinement, Isaac was able to secretly and securely contact CIA headquarters. One message was addressed to POTUS, the President of the

United States. It read: "Exercise the military option." I don't know if this influenced President Carter, but on April 24, 1980, Delta Force launched Operation *Eagle Claw* to rescue the hostages in Tehran. Bad weather and bad luck forced the operation to be aborted, with the loss of eight American lives.

I was posted to CIA headquarters when the Iranian crisis took place. One night, while at a dinner party in Washington, D.C. hosted by a senior Canadian diplomat, the host took me aside and said: "We are sheltering six American diplomats in Tehran who the Iranians did not capture." I thanked him and thanked Canada for their help. Early the next day, I made my way to the Iran Task Force in the headquarters building, not knowing if they were aware of this development. The room was crowded and very busy. I asked to see the chief of the task force. "I'm sorry, he's busy. Who are you and what do you want?"

I replied: "I'm from East Asia Division and last night a Canadian diplomat told me their embassy in Tehran was hiding six Americans from the embassy. I just wanted to make sure you were informed." He walked me to the chief's office, where he was on the phone.

"This officer has some information you should hear." I repeated my story. The chief thanked me for dropping by, adding: "We are aware and are working the problem. Today we are sending officers up to Ottawa to work with the Canadians. Please keep this under your hat." I did. This operation, known as the Canadian Caper, led to the eventual spiriting out of the six Americans with Canadian passports on January 27, 1980. Later, a film called *Argo* was made in Hollywood telling the story of the joint CIA and Canadian operation. The film won three Academy Awards, including the Best Picture of 2012. As often happens, Hollywood didn't quite get it right. In this case, the crucial role of Kenneth Taylor, the Canadian ambassador in Tehran, was played down. President Carter called Taylor the "main hero" of the operation. It was Taylor who took the initiative to hide the Americans in his own residence and oversaw the operation. President Reagan awarded Ambassador Taylor the Congressional Gold Medal in 1981.

After the Canadian Caper succeeded and the public were informed, the business building opposite the Canadian embassy in Washington, D.C. hung a huge banner on the face of the building. It read: "Thank you Canada." A nice gesture from a grateful nation.

In the 1980s, both Isaac and I were assigned to CIA stations in North America, but not the same one. A friend in the FBI, Bob, told me that Isaac was greatly admired and respected by the FBI officers he worked with, and told me a short story:

One day "Isaac" needed to pay a call on an FBI one-man office not far from the big city. When he got there, our man asked to see identification. "Isaac" had ID but not in his true name identifying him as a CIA officer. Our guy said he couldn't talk to him until he was certain he was a CIA officer. So "Isaac" said, "You know Bob, don't you," and our guy nodded. "Let's give him a call." So they called me. Our guy said, "A guy is claiming to be from the CIA and says you can vouch for him." I could have just put "Isaac" on the phone but decided to play with our guy. "Describe him," I said.

"He looks like a sack of shit."

"Yep, that's him."

In fairness to Isaac, Bob was just joking. Isaac believed "casual Friday" was every day. It was true that he looked a bit like an unmade bed, but that was part of his charm.

CHAPTER 49

Singapore Incident

Singapore is one of my favorite countries, cities, and islands. I first visited it in 1974, escaping the war in Cambodia for a week and spending much of that time at the Orchard Road Car Park maze of food stalls. Laksa noodle soup and pork sate sustained me. I sampled the mandatory Singapore sling cocktail at the Long Bar of the Raffles Hotel, but decided after one sampling to switch to something guaranteed to keep malaria at bay: gin and tonics.

I once asked an American oil man in Jakarta, after a few sets of tennis at the Petroleum Club, what he liked most about Indonesia. Without thinking, and in all honesty, he immediately said: "Singapore." The city-state was the destination for all shopping, medical treatment, vacations, and cuisine. Singapore at Christmas was a marketing masterpiece. Who knew the city Mr. Raffles founded had so many Christians.

My only rap on the island nation is the expulsion of a friend of mine, a bona fide State Department Foreign Service Officer who was erroneously thought to have been a CIA officer getting too close to a member of the loyal opposition in Singapore. If the officer had actually been a CIA case officer behaving over zealously, the matter would have passed quietly. But for a State Department officer, and a good one, to be declared *persona non grata* demanded immediately retaliation. So it was that a top Singaporean diplomat in Washington, D.C. was kicked out. But that was long ago and almost forgotten.

I was on a visit to Singapore in 1991 with a small group of RTA senior officers to discuss regional security matters with the Security and Intelligence Division (SID). After a useful meeting on areas of mutual interest, the agenda moved on to an area of vital interest: golf. No meeting of ASEAN intelligence organizations is complete without a round of golf, and Singapore boasted one of the finest venues at the Singapore Island Country Club. Walking the old course at the Singapore club is memorable, with its stunning vistas and view of Singapore harbor. I also admired the SID chief, whose style was to hit the ball and not let golf get in the way of a good conversation. Let someone else keep score.

And then there was the food. Singapore has unparalleled cuisine, with a local touch built on a tradition of Chinese, Malay, and European flavors. Seafood is central to this mélange, and hairy crabs from Shanghai are a treat. I would time meetings to the hairy crab season. Our Singaporean hosts outdid themselves with hospitality, marking the event as another example of SID in action; efficient but always under the radar. My kind of intelligence service.

At the end of our visit the next day, tired but in good spirits, we were at Changi Airport heading back to Bangkok. Changi is probably the prettiest airport in the world. If the taxi ventured more than one kilometer per hour over the speed limit, soft music erupted, signaling a speeding offense to the driver and a hint of impending doom if he did not slow down. This, I suspect, would have pleased the hyper-efficient rulers in the novel *1984* by George Orwell.

I was catching up on my reading in the lounge with my boss and our Thai allies, led by generals who were graduates of Sandhurst, the British military academy, and the Virginia Military Institute. Suddenly, a man arrived, clearly in a hurry, and huddled with the Thai officers. He was a Thai official, probably military, and spoke rapidly in low tones. Something was up and it didn't look good. I immediately thought of a coup d'état in Bangkok, something I had witnessed more than once in the past.

The generals were all huddled to hear the man out. Then they looked over at me. It was not a happy look. One general walked over.

"There has been an incident," he said.

"In Bangkok?" I asked.

"No. In Singapore. Someone has attacked the Singapore policemen guarding the residence of the Thai ambassador. Then he broke into the residence while the ambassador's wife and daughter were there."

"That's bad," I said. "Are they OK?"

"Yes. He surrendered and is in custody. He is an American."

"That's bad too."

"It gets worse. He is an American Marine."

The general now had my full attention. All Thai eyes were on me. Apparently, a drunk U.S. Marine had pitched up at the ambassador's residence on Orchard Road and injured two Singaporean police before breaking into the residence, where the ambassador's wife talked him into giving himself up.

"I know the ambassador," I said. "We served together in Europe. Is there anything I can do?"

"We are informing our headquarters. You may want to inform the ambassador in Bangkok."

I phoned the American ambassador in Bangkok and briefed him on the situation. I told him the Marine was looking at a court martial and possible jail time, but that the ambassador's wife had quickly defused a bad situation. I told the ambassador that the Thai ambassador and his wife were old friends of mine and suggested I call them to apologize on behalf of the U.S. Government and the U.S. Marine Corps.

"Make it so," he directed.

I then called the Thai ambassador and told him I was in town briefly with a few Thai generals. He thanked me for the call and said the issue had been resolved quickly and there were no hard feelings. The press didn't get involved and we made our flight back to Bangkok as scheduled. I was glad I was not the Marine's commanding officer. He was having a bad day; but not as bad as the Marine.

CHAPTER 50

Thailand and the CIA

Few countries have had such a close and continuing relationship with the Central Agency as Thailand. In fact, it dated long before the CIA was created in 1947. In World War II, Thailand was a focus of the Office of Strategic Services, the forerunner of the CIA, when they supported the anti-Japanese resistance movement, the *Seri Thai* (Free Thai), led by M. R. Seni Pramoj in the United States.

Operating inside Japanese-occupied Thailand, the OSS also worked closely with Thai Prime Minister Pridi Panomyong, who had led opposition to the Japanese and was an Allied agent with the code name Ruth. After the war, a number of former OSS officers lived and served in Thailand. Probably the most famous was William Donovan, founder of the OSS and a Medal of Honor winner. He was ambassador to Thailand from 1953–54. Other prominent OSS alumni in Thailand were Alexander MacDonald, founder of the *Bangkok Post* newspaper, Jim Thompson, who became known as the "king of Thai silk," and Robert "Red" Jantzen, who served as CIA chief of station from 1959–66.

Throughout the Cold War, Thailand was a strong American ally, especially in support of American military and intelligence operations in Vietnam and Laos. Thailand was particularly helpful in Laos, where Thai Border Police were heavily involved in the training of paramilitary forces, mostly Hmong tribesmen, to fight Vietnamese military invaders. CIA men like Bill Lair and Dan Arnold were closely identified with these secret operations. Dan was deputy chief in Thailand and later COS in Laos, with thousands of guerrilla fighters, more Thai Army "volunteers," and 200 unarmed aircraft belonging to the CIA's airline, Air America, under his command. Dan, a Marine wounded in World War II, was twice decorated by King Bumiphol of Thailand, who was personally involved with some of CIA intelligence operations, especially with his beloved Border Police, who were active in

King Bumiphol of Thailand, left, and Queen Sirikit, right, attend the funeral of Phra Suth Lekhyananda in Bangkok in 1978. On the right is Group Captain Sudhi holding the hand of his son, Piwat. Next to him is Sudhi's brother, Police Major General Sumedh, and behind him in black is Sudhi's wife, Siripong. Sudhi and the king were classmates in elementary school.

the mountains protecting the kingdom from communist subversion within Thailand and from China and Laos.

His Majesty wanted to commission two CIA officers, Lair and Jack Shirley, as officers in the Border Police. Under American law, this was not allowed. In the case of Bill and Jack, President Eisenhower agreed with the king; Bill became a lieutenant colonel and Jack a captain. Both served long years with the Thai fighting in Laos and both were decorated by the king. Such was the degree of trust and confidence that the CIA earned in the 1950s.

One of the many American military officers caught up in the Cold War support of the Thai military was my father, U.S. Air Force Major Harry Broman. He was assigned to Thailand in 1962 as a civil engineer advisor to the Royal Thai Air Force, and was heavily involved in the construction of air bases which later housed USAF bombers and fighters during the fighting in Indochina.

In 1970, when I was the Military Assistance Command Vietnam liaison officer in Thailand as a first lieutenant in the Marine Corps (i.e., an R&R officer), I was invited to dinner in Bangkok by Pappy's old friend, Sudhi. At the dinner, in a private room of a Chinese restaurant, were Sudhi, his wife,

Sue, and some siblings, including a brother who was a general in the police and another who was a successful businessman. Another brother was the king's cardiologist. I was seated next to the host, who tapped his water glass and announced loudly: "Now we speak English." Without missing a beat, everyone seated who had been speaking Thai, switched to English. Except me. I kept trying to practice my Thai.

While the CIA enjoyed great clout and influence at the highest levels of Thai government and society, one of the problems facing them came from the U.S. Department of State. The president's senior man in any foreign country was the ambassador. He spoke for the United States and all other official Americans, including the CIA—on paper. In Thailand for decades, Thai officials, starting with the king, looked to the COS as the man they preferred to deal with. The CIA knew Thailand, its ways, and its history. In more than a few cases, CIA officers married into Thai high society, while others spent much of their careers in Thailand or nearby Laos with Thai military or paramilitary. It was all too cozy for some ambassadors.

One ambassador in the 1970s disliked the Thai prime minister, a general with strong links to the CIA. He also disliked the chief of station and felt the CIA officer was usurping his powers. The ambassador, a man who no experience in Asia, let alone Thailand, managed to offend the prime minister, who informed the chief of station at one of their weekly breakfasts that he intended to declare the ambassador *persona non grata* and kick him out. This would have been a very bad move for U.S.–Thai relations, which the COS quickly and forcefully stressed to the general. In the end, the general relented and the ambassador stayed at post, unhappy with both the general and chief of station. He probably never knew how close he was to having his career saved by his *bête noire*.

My best friend at the Basic Ops Course at the Farm in 1972 was Johnny K., who had finished a tour in Laos as a paramilitary officer on contract to the CIA. Johnny worked with the famous (most would say notorious) Anthony "Tony Poe" Poshepny, a hard-drinking Marine survivor of the battle for Iwo Jima in World War II and much-decorated jungle fighter in northern Laos, where he was married to a Hmong princess. Tony was somewhat larger than life and the role model for Johnnie's career, which was to spend as much time as possible in Thailand and Laos.

After his Lao tour, Johnny was elevated to full staff status and sent to the Farm for training. We had plans for serving together in Thailand down the road. As it happened, I was sent to Cambodia and Johnny went back to Laos. While I was in French language training, I received word that Johnny had been killed in southern Laos while working with a battalion of Royal Thai Army "volunteers." Years later, I was drinking with a Thai army general on the Cambodian border at a time when, once again, the Thai were working very closely with the CIA on a small war of mutual interest.

The general, who later rose to command the army and then the country, was a man of great integrity and ability, but one of few words. We were talking about the war in Laos and I mentioned the loss of my friend Johnny. "Was that on the Boloven Plateau?" asked the general.

"Yes, sir," I said. "Do you recall the incident?"

"I do. My best friend was the battalion commander and he was killed by the same artillery round that killed your friend Johnny."

CHAPTER 51

The Interior Gang

In the 1950s, a group of young officials of Thailand's Ministry of Interior (MOI) became friendly with a number of young American diplomats assigned to the U.S. embassy in Bangkok. The group became known as The Interior Gang, with some lasting friendships forged and useful professional contacts cemented. Over the years, the Thai side of the gang aged and grew powerful. The Americans rotated home or to a new embassy, to be replaced by another young officer. Eventually, the gang broke up, as gangs often do.

By 1976, the gang was history, until a young second secretary newly assigned to Bangkok met an elderly and very senior officer of the MOI. I will call him Lek. The MOI is large and it is powerful. For one thing, the MOI controlled the police, a national institution larger than the army. For another, all of Thailand's 77 provinces are directed by governors working for the MOI. Over drinks at a government reception, the old Thai told the young American about the Interior Gang and how it had prospered a generation before. "Now we Thai are all old, and some of us are very powerful. Our American friends are all gone and some of them are now ambassadors. We should revive our old gang," he said. The American, a Thai language speaker, sensing an opportunity to meet important Thai officials, agreed. He was also a case officer of the Central Intelligence Agency working under diplomatic cover.

Following the chance encounter with the American, Lek went to work. He contacted a few surviving Thai members of the old gang and got their concurrence to host an evening with American diplomats. Disregarding their own high rank, it was decided to invite junior-grade Americans, just as it was done in the past. I will call Lek's new American friend William, who reported his meeting with Lek to the chief of station. He liked the idea of the new initiative by the Thai to revive the Interior Gang and told the ambassador so. Ambassador Charles S. Whitehouse also liked the idea.

Whitehouse was not your average ambassador. He was born in Paris in 1921, where his father was a career Foreign Service Officer. He grew up in Europe and South America, but dropped out of Yale University in 1942 to join the Marine Corps. He was a dive-bomber pilot in the Pacific and won seven Distinguished Flying Crosses, along with 21 Air Medals, an extremely distinguished war record. He returned to Yale after the war and graduated in 1947. He did not immediately follow in his father's footsteps after the Marine Corps, choosing instead to join the fledgling Central Intelligence Agency, as many "Yalies" did in those days. He served four foreign assignments, including one as chief of station in Cambodia, and in 1956 moved to the Department of State, where he specialized in Southeast Asian matters. Whitehouse had two tours in Vietnam before being named ambassador to Laos and then to Thailand in 1975.

Whitehouse supported the idea of resurrecting the Interior Gang, including the participation of junior officers, and attended several of the social gatherings. This helped even out the imbalance of the sides, as the Thais badly outranked their American counterparts. The Thai parties were always great fun and carefully arranged, as local provincial governors were usually tapped to host the events. Of particular fun was the evening on the banks of the Chao Phraya River in Nonthaburi, a province just north of Bangkok. The governor arranged dinner al fresco on a large riverside deck festooned with flowers and decorations, with a sumptuous buffet of Thai delicacies, all of which were delicious. No Thai party is complete without an assortment of alcoholic beverages. Mekhong whiskey was on hand, and also ice-cold Singha and Chang beer. Ambassador Whitehouse led the American delegation, which was mainly junior and middle-grade officers. The ambassador brought a few bottles of Johnnie Walker (Black) whisky, a favorite of the Thais.

The Thai like to mix their business with pleasure, and that night in Nonthaburi was no exception. The young Americans made connections with senior interior ministry officers, who were delighted to rekindle the old "gang" with new Americans. Whitehouse set a good example. He joined in with toasts, tested foods that lesser ambassadors might have avoided, and told stories of his years in the region, letting everyone know that he was a bona fide Old Indochina Hand.

For dessert, a selection of Thai fruit was offered. It included some of the world's best mango, papaya, lychee, pineapple, and jackfruit, but the main attraction—and test for the Americans—was durian. This Thai favorite was disdained by many foreigners in Thailand due to the sharp and even obnoxious odor given off by most strains of the expensive fruit. It was clearly an acquired taste, and Thai hands quickly learned to seek out the two most expensive of the dozens of durian strains on the market. These were the "golden pillow" (*mon thong*) and "long stem" (*gan yao*) varieties, firm-textured fruits with little or no odor. Ambassador Whitehouse, with years of experience in Cambodia, Vietnam, and Laos, jumped right in with the durian and gained a lot of "face" for the American side. One note of caution: never mix durian with Cognac—they don't get along.

At the end of the evening, everyone was fully satiated by the food and noticeably intoxicated by the assortment of drinks. The embassy officers were all happy that we had cars with drivers to take them home safely. As Ambassador Whitehouse made his way to his waiting car, which was flying the American flag, a tipsy Thai host next to him said: "You know Mr. Ambassador, in the old days we ended our evenings with a visit to one of Bangkok's better known massage parlors." He may have been joking. Or more likely, it was the alcohol talking. But Whitehouse didn't miss a beat.

"Let's go," he said.

Junior officers around him couldn't believe their ears. Neither could the old Interior Gang members. "Of course tonight is out of the question. We need to make a reservation for such a large group," said the man responsible for the Thai prison system.

"Not a problem," said the ambassador. "Maybe next time."

There never was a next time, but Ambassador Whitehouse had made his point. He was not a man to be toyed with and was ready to stand up with his men. Never mess with an old Marine with seven Distinguished Flying Crosses.

CHAPTER 52

Wild Bill Casey

At times during my decades in the CIA, leadership at the highest level was lacking. Serious damage was done, for example, by Admiral Stansfield Turner, a director (DCI) appointed by President Jimmy Carter. In 1979, Turner eliminated more than 800 positions in the Clandestine Service, a hatchet job that has been dubbed the Halloween Massacre. It probably did more damage to the CIA than the KGB ever did. President Clinton similarly downsized the Directorate of Operations in the 1990s, further damaging morale and the Agency's ability to forestall events like 9/11.

Happily, the damage done by Carter and Turner was somewhat reversed with the appointment by President Reagan of William Casey as DCI in 1981. Turner characterized Casey's appointment as "the resurrection of Wild Bill," an accurate but probably backhanded reference to William Donovan, a winner of the Medal of Honor as an army officer in World War I. He was the dynamic and brilliant head of the Office of Strategic Services during World War I, the precursor of the CIA. Donovan was known by friends and foes alike as "Wild Bill," a title he earned and enjoyed. Casey, also a prominent New York lawyer and great fan of Donovan, gave up his law practice to join the OSS, an outfit often operating behind enemy lines conducting espionage and sabotage. He became the chief of the OSS's Secret Intelligence Branch in London and undoubtedly enjoyed being nicknamed "Wild Bill."

Casey was just what the CIA needed: adult leadership bent on taking the offensive in the Cold War against the Soviet Union. He had served as Reagan's presidential campaign manager and oversaw the rapid expansion of the Clandestine Service and human intelligence (HUMINT) reporting. The recruitment of spies once again found favor in the White House. Morale soared and the Soviets found themselves in shooting wars around the world, from Afghanistan to Nicaragua and Cambodia.

I only met Bill Casey twice, and he only called me once.

The first time I met Casey was in the early 1980s, when I was assigned to a large station in Western Europe. One of my main duties was to make connections at the highest level of the Cambodian resistance. Having served in Cambodia and Thailand, I knew the main players in the fight against the Khmer Rouge and later the Vietnamese. I was well placed to get America back in the "game" in Southeast Asia. Casey knew this and took me aside at a reception in his honor. He only wanted to talk about Cambodia, to roll back the advances of the Vietnamese and Chinese. He also wanted to bleed the Soviets, who were the major backer of the Vietnamese.

Casey told me that a new wind was blowing from Langley in support of President Reagan's attack on the "Evil Empire." After years of inaction and retrenchment during the Carter years, Casey assured me that Cambodia would be part of the global effort. I would be on the team. He was supportive of American engagement in Southeast Asia after a decade of disinterest by Washington, despite the genocidal practices of the Khmer Rouge.

Casey was in France in 1984 with President Reagan as part of the 40th anniversary ceremonies commemorating D-Day, June 6, 1944, when Allied forces landed in Normandy. While posted in Europe, I had a support asset who put his vacation villa at the disposal of the CIA in support of a sensitive operation I was running. I will call the agent Caleb. He was an Ivy League aristocrat who had served with Bill Casey in the OSS in England. He was a charming fellow, active in business in Europe and influential in New York. When I was introduced to him, it was soon apparent that he was interviewing me, rather than me interviewing him. It seemed he wanted to know if I was the "right sort." Apparently I was, because he welcomed me to his remote villa, gave me the keys, and said the liquor was free, as was the villa. This operation was the only time I flew in helicopters operationally (not counting Air America in Asia). It was the quickest and easiest way to reach Caleb's hideaway.

At one meeting, I informed Caleb that Casey was coming to Europe. He already knew. "There will be an OSS reunion in Paris," Caleb said. "I will put in a good word for you."

"Thanks for the offer," I said, "but you know that is out of the question. Casey has no need to know that you are assisting the Agency, and it would be a breach of security for you to mention it to anyone, including Mr. Casey."

"Of course you are right," Caleb answered. "Mum's the word."

I suspect that at the gathering of OSS greybeards, with a glass of malt scotch in hand, Caleb took Bill aside and said something like, "I'm back; but can't talk about it."

The last time I saw Bill Casey was in the mid-'80s in the Pacific Northwest, where I was assigned as a chief of station. Casey came to town to give a speech and took advantage of the visit to meet his local officers. We were in two groups: one overt and one covert. I ran the covert office. With my assembled officers, we met with Mr. Casey in the local federal building. Casey gave a pep talk to the assembled Agency officers, then took me aside.

He wanted to talk about Cambodia and said that progress was being made in giving support to the non-communist resistance. I told him that I had recently made a recruitment of a former Cambodian military officer who had been in liaison with Phnom Penh station and had now gone back to Asia to fight the Vietnamese. Casey then told me the name of an officer whom he was about to name Chief of East Asia Division. I knew of the man by reputation only, and it was not good.

Casey then said: "Keep this to yourself. I haven't made the announcement." I promised to tell no one, and kept my word.

Two days later, my secretary entered my office and told me that Mr. Casey was on the phone. That was the only time Casey phoned me. I immediately suspected a prank or a lapse in our security. I knew it was Mr. Casey on the line due to his mumbling, which made comprehension difficult. "Barry," he said, "I want to thank you for the job you are doing and your latest Cambodian recruitment. That isn't what I am calling about. Do you remember that I told you who your next boss would be?"

"Yes, sir, I remember."

"And do you remember that I asked you to keep it to yourself?"

"Yes, sir, I told no one."

"That's good because I made a mistake. That guy is going somewhere else." He then gave me the name of the new Chief/EA, and I told him I thought it was a good choice. Casey said I could talk about it as it was now public. Then he rang off.

Casey continued his service with gusto in going after the Soviets and became involved in the Iran-Contra affair, a scandal involving the facilitation of arms to Iran, with proceeds going to help the anti-communist rebels in Nicaragua. On December 15, 1986, the day before he was scheduled to testify before Congress on Iran-Contra, Casey suffered two seizures and was admitted to hospital. He was operated on for a brain tumor and died on January 29, 1987. Despite his quirks, I enjoyed working with him. Mr. Casey was the last of his breed.

CHAPTER 53

In the Marine Reserves

I joined the Central Intelligence Agency in June 1971, several weeks after I left the Marine Corps. I learned that the Corps had a reserve unit inside the Agency. I joined it, a Voluntary Training Unit (VTU) composed of a few dozen officers, mostly from the DO where I worked. We had monthly meetings of little merit and were expected to participate annually in two-week active duty training. This put us back in the Corps, in uniform, with pay, doing something useful.

It was often difficult to conduct active duty when posted in the field. In my two years in Cambodia, 1973–75, a country ravaged by a war that ended the week I was evacuated, I gave little thought to the Marine Corps or my status as a reserve captain. Not long after the fall of Cambodia, however, I did go on active duty with the Royal Thai Marine Corps (RTMC), which conducted annual training with the U.S. Marines. As a Thai-speaker, I was assigned to be one of the umpires for the war "games." The mission was a raid exercise in which a combined force of U.S. and Thai Marines made an amphibious landing, blew up a target installation, and returned to the offshore ships.

My first stop on board the task force command ship was to pay a courtesy visit to the task force commander, a U.S. Navy rear admiral. The visit was not to exceed 15 minutes. The admiral was a short, rotund fellow with a steel trap mind and full of questions. He had been told that I had served in the American embassy in Phnom Penh, but did not know that I worked for the CIA. He had been involved in the evacuation of the embassy in April 1975 and wanted to know about Cambodia since the Khmer Rouge took over. I answered his questions, trying to be as brief as possible.

Then the admiral asked for a briefing on the political situation in Thailand.

"At your pleasure, sir," I replied. "When would you like it?"

"Now. You have one hour."

The briefing went over an hour due to the admiral's many good questions. I gave him a comprehensive view of a complex situation, along the lines of my briefings to Congressional visitors and their strap hangers.

The raid exercise went very well. The landing force went ashore in the dark and avoided aggressors on the ground as they made their way to the objective, which was blown without incident or casualties. My role was to observe and work with the Thais as an umpire. I view the RTMC as Thailand's elite, but unsung, fighting force and a pleasure to serve with. They are patterned closely after the USMC. I trained with two of the best young officers at The Basic School in Quantico in 1968, and kept in touch with them.

On another occasion when I was on active duty with the Thai Marines, we made a landing in southern Thailand at Prachuap Khiri Khan on the Gulf of Thailand, the narrowest part of Thailand, with Burma only a few miles away. Again I was an observer and umpire. A joint U.S.-Thai landing force in amphibious tractors hit the beach at a coconut plantation, which closely resembled beaches in the South Pacific during World War II. This time there was only slight resistance from designated aggressors firing blanks. I was with the attacking force as we crossed the main north–south highway and moved inland. Soon, a Thai jeep with two agitated officers roared up and halted the attack. It seems the Burmese border was not far away and the Thais did not want to provoke an international incident by inadvertently invading Burma, their traditional enemy. Otherwise, the exercise went well. As a result of my working with the RTMC, I published a photo essay with text, "Asian Amphibians: The Royal Thai Marine Corps," in the November 1980 issue of the *United States Naval Institute Proceedings*.

Back in Langley after three tours in Southeast Asia, I resumed my reserve duties and went on active duty with the Office of Naval Intelligence for two weeks to write a paper for the Marine Corps derived from sensitive HUMINT regarding Soviet military intentions. I was selected to write the paper not because of my expertise on the Soviets and the Warsaw Pact countries, but due to my holding high security clearances above TOP SECRET that allowed me to read, and write about, the documents. The final paper could only be read by a few senior Marine officers, and could not be kept overnight at Marine Corps headquarters. As I exited the building, in uniform, I was stopped by a Marine lieutenant colonel whom I knew from Basic School.

"Is that you, Broman?" he said, with a look of disbelief in his eyes.

"Yes, sir," I said as I snapped to attention and saluted, noticing the Silver Star and Bronze Star ribbons on his uniform.

"Are you still in the Marine Corps?"

"Just the reserves, Sir. I've been writing a paper for the Corps while on active duty."

"What's your day job?" he asked, visibly relieved.

"I work for the State Department; just returned from six years in Southeast Asia." He had no need to know I worked for the CIA.

"Keep up the good work, Captain" he said as he moved on, probably wondering if I really worked for the State Department.

On 23 October, 1983, two truck bombs destroyed buildings in the Lebanese capital, Beirut, where U.S. Marines and French military were billeted: 241 Marines and 58 French were killed. I was posted in Europe at the time and asked to be assigned to Beirut for my two weeks of active duty to serve as a liaison officer in the aftermath of the bombings. The Marine Corps said "yes," the CIA said "no."

Instead, I went to Mons in Belgium. A friend of mine was a senior civilian intelligence officer at the NATO Supreme Headquarter Allied Powers Europe (SHAPE), located near Mons. He knew I was looking for two weeks of active duty and said he needed me in Mons to write a paper similar to the one I had written for the Marine Corps. The source documents for the paper required someone with my clearances, as before. This time the Marine Corps and Agency agreed that I could go. As far as I know, no one at SHAPE, apart from my friend, knew I was CIA. I had known him for years, and his wife, a CIA officer, once worked for me. The assignment was straight forward, the resources documents impressive, and the results important for future NATO planning.

The Marine Corps' birthday, November 10, took place while I was in Mons. There were a few Marine colonels assigned to SHAPE, and one of them hosted a small event to mark the anniversary. I was invited, and was the youngest Marine present. Therefore, I shared the first piece of the birthday cake with the oldest colonel. I had sometimes been the oldest Marine on hand at birthdays, but had never before been the youngest.

When I returned to my station, I was surprised to learn that my VTU had been abolished. Apparently, the Agency had a deal with the Marine Corps that if the U.S. went to war, officers in the VTU could be recalled into the Marine Corps, but they would not leave their CIA jobs. At some point this became contentious, and the Marine Corps decided to drop their VTU at the CIA.

That was the end of my affiliation with the Corps. I think it is a shame, as the few officers with special skills and clearances made a very inexpensive contribution to the mission of the Marine Corps.

I phoned my friend in Mons and informed him my VTU had been disbanded. I no longer was in the Corps. He commiserated with me, thanked me again for the paper, and said that he would send me a copy of my fitness report, a glowing document that was written by a senior NATO officer who was not cleared to read my paper. He also sent me my pay.

CHAPTER 54

Montana Trek with a Merc

Some men seek danger and adventure. Employment with the Central Intelligence Agency is often seen as a means to that end. But usually, the CIA does not want such men, for various reasons, most of them good. Such a man was Guillaume Vogeleer, better known in Asia as Jimmy the Merc—as in mercenary.

Jimmy was a Belgian who earned his spurs as a parachute NCO in the army, with service in the Belgian Congo in the 1960s. That led to several gigs in Africa as a mercenary, including service in Nigeria's Biafran War, *circa* 1967, where Jimmy was paid 60 Krugerrand gold coins per month. He pitched up in Southeast Asia in the 1970s, where he became a fixture on Pat Pong Road in Bangkok, where his Thai girlfriend, Daeng, ran the Madrid Bar. Long before Jimmy showed up, the Madrid was a CIA watering hole, notably for the paramilitary men working with the Thai army and police in Thailand and Laos.

I knew Jimmy for several decades in Asia, Europe, and the United States. He was an engaging rogue with a nasty temper when provoked, and carried a knife in his belt buckle. He was short and stocky, but moved like a cat. I met him through a colleague who Jimmy had befriended. Jimmy let it be known that he wanted to work for the CIA, but the Agency saw him, correctly, as trouble on the hoof. He had no access to any target of operational interest, but did have a few connections in the drug and *demi-monde* world of Bangkok's underworld. He was always looking for action and sometimes worked *pro bono* with a rebel Karen ethnic group in Burma, the oldest-running insurgency in the region if not the world. He was also friendly with the anti-communist resistance in Laos and Cambodia and maintained a cordial relationship with the Royal Thai Army.

Jimmy spoke little about his background but once showed me photos of himself with British actress Jacqueline Bisset. His Belgian wife was her cook

Barry with former Belgian mercenary Guillaume "Jimmy" Vogeleer in Glacier Park National Park, Montana, 1981.

and he was a part-time bodyguard. Jimmy left his wife and Hollywood when he sought more action and greater freedom in Asia.

Back in the late 1970s, I trekked in Nepal with The Bear, former Air America pilot George Taylor, and DEA officers Peter "PT Tomaino" and Dick Kempshall, the latter a former Marine. PT dubbed the group of trekkers, all Vietnam veterans, "Eagles" and had plastic badges made to identify us. I was originally Eagle 5, but we liked one of the Sherpas on the trek so well we presented him with the Eagle 5 badge. Then I became Eagle 6.

A few years later, George Taylor, known to his friends as "Big George," was working in Whitefish, Montana, flying medevac helicopters. I once asked him how he chose the mountain town near Glacier National Park. "I came to town," he explained, "and read the front page of the local newspaper. It read, 'Grizzlies 2, People 0.' I instantly knew I would like this town." We arranged a second trek of the Eagles in Glacier Park in June 1981. George, PT Tomaino, The Bear, and I had been on the Nepal trek. For Montana, we invited a British businessman based in Bangkok, Tim Hughes, to join us. We also invited Jimmy who was eager to become an Eagle. We rendezvoused in

Seattle and drove to Whitefish, where George made arrangements for us to make day hikes into the park while spending the nights in luxury in towns around the stunning national park. George had been a senior Air American pilot in Vietnam, Laos, and Cambodia, and flew one of the last missions of the old CIA airline at the evacuation of Saigon on April 30, 1975. He was now a landowner with 10 acres of timber overlooking the park. A sign posted on adjacent property read: "Trespassers Will be Shot. Survivors Will be Shot Again." Welcome to Montana! Jimmy felt right at home.

One night we were in Browning, home of the Blackfoot Nation reservation. As usual, we told old stories from Vietnam, Laos, and Cambodia. Like wine, they got better with age. Late in the evening, our waitress brought a large pitcher of beer to the table. When we said that we had not ordered the beer, she pointed to a truck driver sitting alone at the bar. "It's on him," she said.

George walked over to the bar, thanked the fellow, and invited him to help drink the beer he had just given us.

"No thanks," he said. "I've got to get back on the road. I have a schedule to keep. No beer for me."

"May I ask why you bought a pitcher?" George persisted.

"I didn't serve in Vietnam myself. But listening to your stories, I wish I had."

We waved him goodbye as he headed for his rig.

A few nights later, we were at East Glacier. We hiked up to a lake with ice on it, and forded a stream that flowed out of the lake, heading ultimately for the Mississippi River. It was brutally cold. We took off our boots, rolled up our jeans, and crossed the fast-flowing stream. The Bear was in great pain as he dried off his frozen feet. But the short walk up to the spine of the Rockies was worth it.

At a hiker-friendly bar in East Glacier, we fell in with some young Canadian ladies. They ran the Alberta Visitors Center nearby to lure Americans north to Waterton Park in Canada, a continuation of Glacier. They were a generation younger, but very friendly and eager to try an upside-down margarita suggested by our urbane English trekker, Tim. With the grudging concurrence of a fretful bartender, Tim gently guided the girls, one at a time, into position. They leaned backwards over the bar and Tim carefully poured a shot of tequila into their mouths, followed by a shot of lime juice. The young Canucks were athletic and thirsty, and enjoyed the drinks. Tim, once a Brit rock and roll star, and an accomplished Hash House Harrier runner from Bangkok and Hong Kong, quickly made some new friends.

On our last morning, we walked unsteadily into a rustic restaurant promising hearty breakfasts. They weren't lying. An elderly waitress walked up. She sized up our motley crew, pulled out her pad and paper as we looked at our menus, and said "Go!" Soon, large plates of fried eggs, hash brown potatoes, and elk sausage links appeared with large mugs of coffee. All were outstanding. When it came time for dessert, Jimmy ordered first.

"I'd like a piece of pee," he said in his strong French accent.

"I beg your pardon," answered our waitress, none too happy.

"You know," Jimmy insisted. "Pee, apple pee."

"I'll take that as pie," said the relieved woman. "You want vanilla ice cream with that, Frenchie?"

"*Oui, madame,*" said the old merc. "And I am Belgian."

CHAPTER 55

My Friend the Narc

The Drug Enforcement Administration (DEA) and the CIA have had their differences. This may be a cultural issue. DEA agents are essentially cops who go after narcotics traffickers. The CIA is an intelligence organization without powers of arrest. The DEA seeks to destroy drug traffickers by identifying their leadership and working closely with friendly foreign intelligence and police departments. The DEA gets paid by the "bust" of drugs seized and traffickers jailed. The CIA, on the other hand, gets paid by the recruitment of sources, to run them and not to get them arrested. Their job is to provide intelligence on the bigger fish. On assignments in Asia, I worked closely with the DEA. One of them, Dick Kempshall, was a Marine veteran of Vietnam and one of my trekking buddies in Nepal. Dick and I became close when he was assigned as supervisor of the DEA unit working at Honolulu's international airport. In those days, I was often posted to Southeast Asian stations and often spent home leaves on the Big Island of Hawaii, BJ's home.

Before one trip, I wrote to Dick telling him that we would be passing through Honolulu en route to Hilo, Hawaii, and hoped we could meet for a coffee. Dick wrote back welcoming a coffee, and instructed me to seek out a DEA agent as soon as we arrived in Honolulu. We arrived after a long flight across the Pacific with two tired young sons and four pieces of checked luggage. The international terminal was a madhouse of multiple flights from Asia arriving at almost the same time. We got in line with our bags to go through immigration and customs.

There were at least 200 people ahead of us. I spotted a uniformed official and said that I needed to speak to an officer from the DEA. One minute later, a man in plain clothes approached me with the uniformed officer.

"Can I help you, sir?" he asked.

"Is Dick Kempshall here today?" I replied.

"Yes, sir, he's the boss."

"Please tell him that Eagle 6 would like to talk to him."

"I will pass the message, sir," said the DEA officer, thinking, perhaps, that this was an official business matter.

Two minutes later, Dick arrived with his agent in tow. He was all business. Instead of a friendly welcome and a handshake, Dick said somewhat brusquely: "Welcome to Honolulu. Please gather all your luggage, hand me your passports, and follow me."

Dick then walked us to the head of the line, gave our black diplomatic passports to the customs agent to be stamped, and said to the Customs officer, "They're with me," nodding in our direction. The passports were stamped and handed back to Dick. That saved us at least an hour waiting in line. There was plenty of time to make our connection to Hilo at the domestic terminal nearby.

Once outside, Dick broke into a big smile and said: "No need for a distinguished spy such as yourself to wait in line. Welcome home, Marine!"

He then walked us over to the domestic terminal, where we had a cup of coffee while waiting for our flight. Dick's assistance was thoughtful and very much appreciated. We chatted over old times, especially the week-long trek in the mountains of western Nepal. I invited him for dinner if he could make it to the Big Island.

Over the years, Dick helped us get through customs a few more times, always with the same initial brusque manner and always with immediate cooperation from the Customs people. I wonder if he told his own people that Eagle 6 was really a CIA officer.

Dick's story is not quite over. I retired from government in 1996 and was living in Seattle. We made plans to visit BJ's family in Hilo and had no need of Dick's assistance in getting through customs, since we were already in the States. But I wanted to give Dick an update on my status and called his number. Dick was still in Hawaii, but was no longer working at the airport. He was in charge of an interagency task force.

"We don't get to Honolulu at all these days," I informed Dick. "Do you ever come to the Big Island? We will be in Kona with BJ's brother later this month."

"I do, since my new job takes me to all the islands," Dick replied. "We are supporting local antinarcotics operations and as you are aware the south Kona coast is a major source of marijuana. To help identify and suppress growing ops, we have just been given a twin-engine German helicopter. I think I need to make a familiarization flight on the Big Island. Do you feel like another chopper ride?"

"Sounds great; when and where? I'll be there." We settled on a date. Dick said he and his chopper would pick me up at Kona airport at 3pm.

BJ dropped me at the airport and took the boys to a beach further down the Kona coast. I was on my own. She wished me luck. I approached a large uniformed Hawaiian security guard and told him I was expecting a helicopter in a few minutes.

"No choppers come in here," he said.

"I'll wait," I replied.

Three minutes later, I heard the familiar sound of a helicopter. Coming in low out of the sun was a large, black, unmarked chopper. It landed nearby and Dick got out wearing aviator's dark glasses and a flak jacket.

"That will be my ride," I informed the guard.

Dick greeted me warmly and handed me a DEA baseball cap. We were in the air 30 seconds later.

"We wear flak gear," he explained, "because of ground fire. We won't take any fire today because this is not an operation. This is an 'orientation flight' with our new bird and I hope you enjoy it. You can't buy rides like this baby provides. I've got 30 minutes to show you places you have never seen on the Big Island."

He was right. He put me in the co-pilot's seat for the view and we launched. We headed south about twenty feet over the water along the Kona coast at over one hundred miles per hour. It was like the opening sequence of the *Magnum PI* television series, skimming the waves of Hawaii. Suddenly, the chopper lifted as we gained altitude heading for the snow-capped Mount Mauna Kea.

"We won't go to the top," Dick said. "It's over thirteen thousand feet high. We can see some snow close up." And we did; very close up.

"We normally stay low over the marijuana-growing areas," Dick continued, the chopper descending at a rapid rate, "so the bad guys can hear us but not see us. No need to give the growers a target. We coordinate units on the ground and guide them to the sites we identify. Great fun but a little dangerous."

After dipping down into lush gullies with waterfalls, I wished I had brought a camera. The scene was like the Napali coast of Kauai we had visited some years before in a commercial chopper. All too soon, Dick told me the ride was over and asked where I would like to be dropped off.

"My brother-in-law, Ken, is the Bank of Hawaii manager in Kealakekua, not far from where Captain Cook was killed and eaten by Hawaiians in 1799. There's a baseball diamond near his house, you can drop me there."

The big bird dropped me effortlessly on the ball field. I thanked Dick for the ride. With my new DEA hat on, I walked up the hill to Ken's house two minutes away as the chopper lifted off. I had a key to the house, and just as I walked in the phone rang. It was Ken calling from the bank, not far away.

"What are you doing?" he asked. I told him I had been on a great helicopter ride courtesy of the DEA.

"My neighbors are calling me saying you were dropped off at the ball field. They are flushing their stashes. They think BJ is married to a narc."

"Close, but no banana," I told Ken. "I sometimes go after heroin dealers, but marijuana is of no interest to us."

CHAPTER 56

A Short Sojourn in Saudi Arabia

The temperature on the clock tower in al Khobar registered 50 degrees Celsius. That's 122 degrees Fahrenheit, a personal worst. I was in eastern Saudi Arabia consulting for a Thai client and was wondering what I had gotten myself into.

Two weeks earlier, I received a call in Seattle from an old friend from days in Cambodia. Warren Hoffecker, now a businessman, from Al Khobar. He had a hot tip on a major construction project in Saudi and knew I had construction contacts in Bangkok. I called Bangkok, and my client was indeed interested and asked me to represent him in negotiations in Saudi. I called Warren and he put wheels in motion.

Warren was a Princeton graduate and an Army Special Forces officer in Vietnam, where he was wounded and decorated. I met him in Phnom Penh in 1973 when I was on my first posting for the CIA and Warren was working for Catholic Relief Services. Now he was an Arabist, speaking fluent Arabic and working for a large American company in Saudi. Despite the stifling heat, Warren enjoyed working in the Middle East, where he acquired a serious collection of textiles and rugs. His wife, Andrea, and two children stayed home in McLean, Virginia.

Warren told me I needed a visa to Saudi, which he would expedite and arrange through a broker in Washington, D.C. Normally this would take a few days, but he said I could get a visa quicker as the Crown Prince of Saudi Arabia was involved in the project. Warren invited me to stay in his Virginia house and had already alerted Andrea that I was on my way.

I arrived late at night, but Andrea was waiting and told me that she had arranged a small dinner party with old friends from Cambodia the next day.

"Warren told me I would get my visa in one day," I said. "I might not have time for a dinner."

Warren Hoffecker, left, with Barry in Saudi Arabia on business for a Thai client.

"It always takes two or three days," she answered. "Early tomorrow, go to the visa broker in DC. He will take care of it. Dinner will be at seven. I have invited the McCarthys and Carneys." They were old embassy colleagues I had not seen in years.

The next morning, the visa broker warned me: "This could take a few days. I hope you are not in a rush."

"Warren told me the visa would be handled by the Crown Prince's office, so I am expecting it sooner."

"Good luck with that," he said, as I handed over my passport and a $100 bill.

I drove back to McLean with a bottle of wine, looking forward to the dinner ahead. Around 3pm, the visa man called: "I've got your visa. You are booked on a 6pm flight to Al Khobar via Amsterdam. Please come and pick up your passport and visa. I have never seen things move so fast with the Saudis."

I apologized to Andrea for missing the party.

"No need," she said with a wistful sigh. "Maybe next time. Give my love to Warren."

Warren was waiting for me in Al Khobar and briefed me on the need to move quickly to negotiate the deal on behalf of my Thai client. A meeting was arranged, and en route to the meeting Warren swung by the clock tower to see that it was indeed 50 degrees. "Gets hotter," he said, "but not much."

Our meeting was with an Egyptian businessman who was the general contractor for the large housing project. He was connected with both the Egyptian and Saudi leaderships. A tall and elegantly dress Saudi walked into our elevator. He was in his mid-40s, bearded, and wearing robes of deep red; clearly a man of importance.

Warren spoke to him in Arabic. The man laughed and replied. They held a quick, animated conversation. The gentlemen got out with a flourish of friendly gestures to Warren.

"Who was that?" I asked.

"Beats me," said Warren.

"It sounded like you were old friends. What did you talk about?"

"I recognized his clan from his clothing and said 'with this heat you must wish you were back home in the mountains hunting with your falcons.'"

"What did he say?"

"You got that right," he said. It was typical Warren Hoffecker. An ability to make friends easily in several languages. As much as he enjoyed the Middle East, and made a very good living, his first love was Cambodia. Warren would take annual leave from his job in Saudi to vacation in the war zone of Cambodia, helping the royalists. He was especially tight with General Toan Chay, a very capable leader of the royalist faction who led from the front.

I stayed with Warren in his house in a gated community, with a "club" that was essentially a bar serving homemade beer and moonshine alcohol, a substance totally forbidden in Saudi Arabia (along with women driving automobiles) but permitted for some foreign workers. Another friend working at Aramco, the large petroleum company in Saudi, was given a 60-page booklet on how to operate a still, a skill he soon mastered. Warren's little pub offered a variety of drinks flavored with small vials that were labeled "whiskey," "gin," "rum," etc. It was a poor substitute for the real thing, but it was intoxicating and that was the main purpose of the drinks.

Our meeting with the Egyptian went well, and within a few hours we had negotiated an agreement that my client needed to sign. There was a problem. No Thais were allowed to fly to Saudi Arabia, thanks to an ugly scandal in 1989 when a Thai employee of a Saudi prince stole 200lb of gems and absconded to Thailand, where he was eventually caught. The problem came when it was found that half of the returned gems were fake and the most important item, the 50-carat Blue Diamond, was missing.

This very embarrassing and expensive scandal, known as the Blue Diamond Affair, resulted in the murder of four Saudis in Thailand, including three diplomats, the eventual imprisonment of several Thai police officers (including a three-star general), and the expulsion of tens of thousands of Thai workers in Saudi Arabia. The affair soured Thai–Saudi relations for years and cost the Thais billions of dollars in lost remittances from Thai workers.

The problem was solved by meeting in Bahrain, a small island nation in the Persian Gulf and connected to Saudi Arabia by a 25-kilometer (16-mile) causeway. Bahrain is everything that Saudi is not. Although it was the site of the ancient Dilmun civilization, Bahrain converted to Islam in the 7th century. It is modern, sophisticated, and very Westernized. Alcoholic drinks are permitted, and our hotel suite was much more comfortable than Warren's stoic compound quarters in Al Khobar. Before our meeting, Warren spirited me to meet his favorite rug merchant, a jovial Persian who sprinted the length of his large and sumptuous showroom to greet Warren. They chatted briefly in Arabic, then Warren introduced me and proceeded to give me a 30-minute tutorial in tribal rugs.

Over tea, the rug man leaned forward and whispered: "You are a lucky man to know Meester Warren. He is a wise man and appreciates our culture."

"And rugs," I added.

"Of course rugs, but more than that. He is a scholar and gentleman. And not an oil man." He stopped, afraid he may have gone too far. Maybe he thought I was an oil man. I quickly informed him that I was a retired diplomat and that I knew Warren from the Cambodian war. "Ask him to show you his collection of old Cambodian silk," I advised. That brief encounter led to my interest in tribal rugs and my modest collection, mostly Baluch from Afghanistan.

The Bahrain negotiations went well and we all made money on the project. Warren insisted on buying me an Arab headscarf, a *ghuthrain*, not for the negotiations, but as a souvenir. My week in Saudi went fast.

That was the last time I saw Warren. A year later, he was recruited to work as an interpreter in the Iraq War and I lost contact with him. A few months after that, a mutual friend called to say that Warren had suffered a heart attack and died. He is buried in the Arlington National Cemetery in Virginia.

CHAPTER 57

Cambodian Water Festival

In 2007, I was in Cambodia shooting photos for a book, *Cambodia: The Land and its People*, that was published in Singapore. I had amassed a large collection of photos of the country, starting in 1963, and continued my collection during my posting to Cambodia from 1973–75 and on numerous later visits when peace finally returned.

Accompanied by our friend Kim McDevitt, I visited new areas of Cambodia that had eluded me in the past. A highlight of my visit was the opportunity to photograph the Water Festival, not to be confused with the Cambodian New Year celebration held in April and featuring widespread water throwing, but nothing rivaling the excess of the festivals in Thailand and Burma at the same time. The revival of the Water Festival in Cambodia is a three-day event taking place at the end of the monsoon at the time of a full moon, in October or November, in Phnom Penh. It is officially called Bon Oum Touk, the Water and Moon Festival.

The population of the city grows substantially as more than a million people from the countryside flock to Phnom Penh to see two thousand five hundred rowers racing in four hundred narrow boats, some of them seventy feet long with a hundred rowers and, in some, a young lady on the bow urging them on to victory, vying for prizes and glory. Revelers line the banks of the Tonle Sap River opposite the Grand Palace. The festival is also timed for the annual change in the flow of the river, which flows from the Mekong River upstream to the Tonle Sap (Great Lake) and then flows back to the Mekong as the river level drops.

The Tonle Sap River is the only river in the world that changes its course annually. When water from the Mekong meets the Tonle Sap, the river flows upstream. As the water level drops, it changes its course and flows out of the Great Lake, which triples in size annually as water pours in. At times the river

A woman giving encouragement to boat racers on the Tonle Sap River at Phnom Penh, Cambodia, during the Water Festival in 2007.

can be treacherous, and even small waves can sink the fragile, thin hulls of the long racing boats. Fatalities have occurred when boats capsize and standing oarsmen are caught in the strong currents.

I was lucky to be at the races in 2007. Three years later, the huge throng of visitors stampeded, resulting in the deaths of 347 people and injuries to 755 more. That caused the festival to be cancelled for the next three years.

Kim, an English-educated Cambodian aristocrat, was educated with the Khmer royal family. Her best friend was HRH Princess Bopha Devi, the Minister of Culture and the daughter of the late King Norodom Sihanouk. Using her palace connections, Kim arranged for me to photograph the second day of the festival from the king's personal viewing stand. This was not the first time that Kim called in favors for me at the palace. I was permitted to photograph the royal ballet training school, the national museum, and areas in the palace for *Architectural Digest* that required special permission.

I recalled Princess Bopha Devi vividly from my days with the Associated Press photographer when I was assigned to cover the state visit of Chinese President Liu Shaoqi to Cambodia in 1963. At the time, the princess was the young prima ballerina of the Royal Khmer Ballet, tiny and absolutely beautiful. I photographed the ballet performed for the Chinese guests at an open-air pavilion

Young girls training for the Royal Khmer Ballet in Phnom Penh, Cambodia.

in the palace and greatly regret that I have none of the photos that I took. The AP writer covering the event was Pulitzer Prize winner Malcolm Browne from Saigon. He noticed my infatuation with the lithe princess. Taking me aside, Mal whispered: "Be careful, that is not just another Cambodian dancer; that's Sihanouk's favorite daughter." I heeded the warning and did not actually talk to the princess until decades later. She kindly led a small delegation from the palace at my book's launch in Phnom Penh in 2009. Kim was on hand. We first met in Phnom Penh in 1973, when Kim was married to a French coffee planter. They divorced at the war's end in 1975. She later married Tony McDevitt, a Scottish accountant. BJ and I were witnesses at their wedding in Brussels.

King Sihamoni, the son of Sihanouk and Monique, was crowned in October 2004. He was classically trained in ballet and the piano in Prague. He later taught ballet in Paris and in 1991, after the Paris Peace Agreements which brought an end to the war of resistance to the Vietnamese puppet regime of Heng Samrin, Sihamoni was named Cambodia's permanent representative to UNESCO in Paris. Sihamoni is sophisticated, charming, and well liked. But because his mother was not a royal wife, he was not in line to succeed Sihanouk. I was told that Monique made a deal with Hun Sen, a former Khmer Rouge who took power in 1997 through a coup d'état against the democratically elected government, to have her son put on the throne.

The king opened the water festival on day one and presided over its closure on day three. That left day two open, and Kim, with the help of

Prince Norodom Sihanouk embraces Chinese President Liu Shaoqi in 1963 in Phnom Penh.

Prince Norodom Thomico, got me into the royal enclosure exclusively. Armed with my longest lens, it was a perfect venue to photograph the long thin boats, loaded to the gunnels just offshore in choppy water. The viewing stands on both sides were filled to capacity, while there was only Kim, Prince Thomico, and me in the royal belvedere. The photos turned out well and were used in the book.

The final problem was getting out of the royal enclosure, through the huge crowd of revelers in a partying mood. Fortunately, the young Thomico prevailed on a few of the security officers to form a wedge and guide us away from the river to a Spanish restaurant, where we had dinner reservations. It was a great pleasure to see so many happy Cambodians enjoying the centuries-old festival and witness life returning to normal after years of genocide under the Khmer Rouge.

CHAPTER 58

Up the Rajang River of Borneo

It has been my pleasure to photograph the great rivers of Indochina for Pandaw River Cruises, a leading Asian river cruise company. I was therefore pleased to receive an invitation in 2009 from Paul Strachan, the owner of Pandaw, to photograph the company's latest cruise on the Rajang River. Great! Now where's the Rajang? I knew the Mekong, Irrawaddy, Chindwin, even the Ganges in India, but had never heard of the Rajang.

Turns out it is the longest river in Malaysia, located in the state of Sarawak on the island of Borneo. This is Rajah Brooke country, which immediately interested me. Sir James Brooke, the "White Rajah of Sarawak," was a British soldier and adventurer in the mid-19th century who ruled as Rajah of Sarawak from 1841 until his death in 1864 after helping the Sultan of Brunei put down a rebellion. Brooke, however, was best known for his successful efforts to suppress the scourge of piracy in the region and the pacification of local head-hunting Dayak tribesmen. The Brooke family reigned as the white Rajahs of Sarawak with good sense and benevolence until after World War II, when Sarawak was turned over to the British crown as a colony, eventually joining the Malaysian Union in 1957.

I accepted Paul's invitation with alacrity and suggested I bring along an old friend, retired Canadian Ambassador Manfred von Nostitz, who had joined a local bank in Malaysia. Paul was delighted to have Manfred on board, so I booked a flight to Kuala Lumpur and began my adventure. Manfred was no ordinary ambassador. For one thing, he was the great grandson of Otto von Bismarck, the founder and Chancellor of Prussia, modern Germany. He was born in 1941 in Paris, where his father was a German diplomat. As a refugee from Germany, he emigrated to Canada with his stepfather, Baron von Richthofen. After representing Canada as a renowned international fencer, he became a diplomat specializing in Asian affairs, with postings to Hanoi,

Saigon, and Can Tho, where he headed the Canadian International Control Commission supervising the withdrawal of American troops from Vietnam. He was named ambassador to Pakistan, Malaysia, Thailand, Laos, Burma, and Brunei. In Pakistan, he headed a Canadian military mission overseeing the withdrawal of Soviet troops from Afghanistan. We served together three times: twice in Southeast Asia and once in Washington, D.C.

The Rajang is a good river, but not a great one. For one thing, it is only 351 miles long and the jungle portion is too shallow for large boats. The Pandaw fleet is patterned after the boats of the Irrawaddy Flotilla Company (IFC), a Scottish company that once had more than four hundred boats plying the waterways of colonial Burma. Paul's little fleet follows in that tradition.

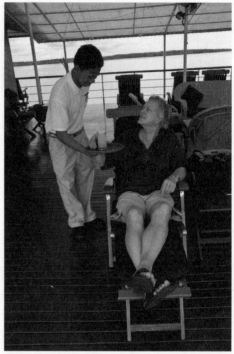

Retired Canadian Ambassador Manfred von Nostitz enjoying a cool drink on a Pandaw cruise up the Rajang River of Malaysia.

The newly hired skipper, a Brit who had once worked on the *QE II*, although not familiar with the rough-and-tumble of Indochina river seamanship, was able to put into a riverbank without a quay by nosing up to the shore, where a crewman would leap ashore and have a rope thrown to him. Within a few minutes, the boat would be tied up, fore and aft, and a gangplank would be run ashore, where crewmen would then cut steps into the riverbank. There is a steep but quick learning curve on the Pandaw fleet, just as there were in the days of the Raj with the IFC. You learn fast or move along.

While there are no towns of note on the Rajang, there are a few old Dayak villages, which evoked the violent past of the river, especially the human skulls in the long houses, evidence of the Rajang in wartime. The Iban or Sea Dayaks are known for their ferocity, especially their penchant for taking human heads, an activity that was suppressed by Rajah Brooke with some success but later permitted by the British when it suited their interests in the war against the Japanese. In World War II, the Allies recruited 1,000 Dayaks from the Kapit division on the Rajang to serve as guerrillas and sources of intelligence behind Japanese lines. More than a thousand Japanese were killed or wounded. The British relaxed similar rules against head hunting among the Naga hill tribes of Assam and upper Burma, so long as the heads taken were Japanese.

During the Malayan Emergency, fighting communist insurgents after the war, Dayaks were again called into service as Sarawak Rangers, active as scouts and sources of intelligence. Head hunting was again permitted and photographs were published in 1952 of Royal Marines posing with Dayak scouts holding severed heads.

Most recently, during the Indonesia–Malaysia conflict known as the Konfrontasi between 1963 and 1966, when Indonesia sought to separate Sarawak from Malaysia, Dayaks along the Rajang were again recruited as border scouts to counter the invading Indonesians from Kalimantan, the Indonesian side of Borneo. As usual, Indonesian heads were taken, and when we visited Dayak long houses on the Rajang we invariably found friendly tribesmen happy to share their home-brewed alcohol with us and proud to display severed heads of unlucky Japanese, communist Chinese, or intruding Indonesians.

A most interesting fellow traveler on board the MV *Orient Pandaw* with us was a lively and elderly English woman, Lady Elizabeth Janion—"call me Monica"—the widow of Rear Admiral Sir Hugh Janion. The admiral served in the Royal Navy during World War II on the frozen and extremely hazardous Murmansk run through U-Boat wolf packs and Luftwaffe bombers en route to the Soviet Union. For his services, Admiral Janion ended his distinguished career as captain of Her Majesty's Yacht *Britannia* from 1975–81.

Lady Janion was the life of the party afloat and the first to dance with Dayak girls ashore. I recall one evening at sundown on the upper deck when, gin and tonics in hand, Monica told Manfred and I about the time when she was a very young girl, in a staff car in the Khyber Pass of the Northwest Frontier of British India, when the car came under fire from Pathan rebels in the hills above: "My Indian nanny threw herself over me to take a bullet that was meant for me. But the threat soon passed, no one hurt, and we moved on."

Monica was a classy lady, always up for a bit of fun with the locals, but serious and sedate when the occasion called for it. She was one of a dying breed, a daughter of the Raj and a sailor's wife, with all the baggage and responsibility that those positions bring. When I think of Lady Janion, I recall the Royal Navy toast, "Here's to the wind that blows, Here's to the ship that goes, And to the lass that loves a sailor."

Lady Elizabeth Janion dancing with indigenous Dayak girls on the *Orient Pandaw* on the Rajang River in Malaysia.

Manfred had his own stories which he shared with me over the years. My favorite dealt with his two grandmothers. On his father's side, Helene von Nostitz struck up a lifelong friendship with the sculptor August Rodin and was featured in a number of books about him. Rodin always wanted to sculpt her in the nude, which she refused, but she agreed to pose for a number of busts now featured in several museums. As a niece of President Hinderburg, she was invited to tour and lecture in the United States in the 1930s, forming friendships *inter alia* with John D. Rockefeller and Thomas Watson, an early head of the technology firm IBM.

Manfred's great-grandmother, Sibylle von Bismarck, had successfully managed the Bismarckian estate of seventy thousand acres in Varzin, Pomerania, for over forty years after her husband, Otto von Bismarck's second son, Wilhelm, had died in 1901.

When Soviet forces approached in January 1945, she organized and accompanied a refugee trek to the west on horseback to convince the populace to leave, including Manfred and his family, who had taken refuge there from the war.

She turned back to receive the general heading the Soviet forces arriving at Varzin, circumspect in taking over the estate because of Russian deference for Bismarck's close relationship with Russia. Greeting the Soviet general, she led him around the estate and, after asking him for a glass of water in the manor house kitchen, swallowed a cyanide pill, killing herself in front of the general. At 81 years old, she refused to start a new life as an impoverished refugee in the West.

Manfred also gave a talk to the guests on board the *Orient Pandaw* on modern Malaysia and the current challenges facing a mostly Islamic country with a large and prosperous Chinese minority, as we slowly cruised on the quiet river, passing miles and miles of sago palms that have replaced the jungle with a cash crop. At night, we were sometimes entertained by troupes of Malay or Dayak dancers, some warlike with spears in hand, but mostly attractive youngsters in ornate dress, following the Pandaw tradition to entertain as well as inform.

The *Orient Pandaw* no longer plies the Rajang. Bigger rivers with more attractions are in favor with river travelers these days. But the Dayaks are still there, more or less intact, ready to defend their land and with a long knife in hand to remove a head or two, if needed.

CHAPTER 59

On the Burma Pipeline

The Yadana natural gas field lies in the Andaman Sea about forty miles from the coast of Burma (known also as Myanmar). A pipeline was completed in 1998 that runs two hundred and fifteen miles underwater to Daminseik, and from there another forty miles underground to the Thai–Burma border at Pilok. The gas powers as much as 10 percent of Thailand's electricity and 50 percent of Burma's largest city, Rangoon (Yangon).

In 2002, my consulting firm, Rain Tree, was hired to travel the length of the pipeline onshore and document life in the villages along the route on the Burma side. This was a rare and welcome opportunity to visit the Karen villages along the pipeline's path as it wound through thick jungle, where tigers still roam. The only real problem was passing through Karen country. The Karen are an ethnic group that has been at war with the Burmese government since the country achieved independence from Great Britain in 1948. The Karen military arm, the KNU (Karen National Union), were active in the rugged mountains along the border and the pipeline was a lucrative target as revenue from the sale of gas helped fund Burma's various wars with dissident minority groups.

The assignment called for traveling the length of the pipeline both in Thailand and in Burma. The Thai side was relatively easy, and made easier when a major general in the Royal Thai Army offered to drive me to the Thai–Burma border where the pipeline entered Thailand. I accepted his kind offer, and with another Thai friend we headed west from Bangkok for the pipeline.

We spent the night near the bridge on the River Kwai, made famous in film. The bridge linked Japanese-held Thailand with Burma during World War II. In the film it was blown up at the end by Allied saboteurs, led by William Holden. In reality, the bridge was never blown, but some spans were dropped by Allied bombing which also hit the prisoners' camp, with great loss of life.

I first visited the bridge, which is still in operation, in 1963 as the Associated Press photographer in Bangkok covering the state visit of Princess (later Queen) Beatrix of the Netherlands. Her visit to Thailand included a trip to the immaculately maintained cemetery for Allied war dead. About two thousand Dutch soldiers were buried there, along with some five thousand British and Australian prisoners of war. In 2002, the town and bridge were tourist destinations, although rail traffic no longer runs to Burma.

Heading west from Kanchanburi, we went easily through several RTA checkpoints with a general at the wheel. We climbed into forested and thinly populated mountains until we pulled into the RTA compound at the highest point, which demarcated the border. A large pumping station nearby was under heavy guard by Thai soldiers. I received a detailed briefing from the young RTA captain in charge of a company of troops. He spoke excellent English and told me that relations with the Burma Army were good.

We toured the pumping station and then walked to the end of the road on the Thai side of the border. As I walked ahead to enjoy the view, looking into Burma and down the other side of the mountains, the Thai officer warned me: "Stop, you are going into Burma. Thai is not allowed."

Pumping station on the Burma–Thailand gas pipeline in southern Burma.

I stopped and looked up at a large, fortified bunker, where a man wearing a battle jacket of the Burmese Army and a *longgyi*, a man's sarong, looked down at me.

"That's the battalion commander," said the Thai captain. I waved at the man and he waved back.

"*Mingalaba!*" I called to the officer in Burmese. Good day.

He returned the greeting and said "*La bee*" (come here). I asked the captain if he had ever seen the battalion command post.

"No," he said, "it is forbidden."

So I walked up the hill alone to meet the Burmese major. He greeted me in good English and asked how I knew Burmese. I explained that I had lived in Rangoon and spoke a few words only.

"What are you doing up here?" he asked in a friendly way.

"I work for the oil company," I said, more-or-less truthfully.

"Come have some tea," he offered. I looked down at the Thai officer watching us. "What about him?" I asked.

"OK, invite him up." I called to the captain in Thai, a language I knew much better than Burmese.

"You speak Thai too?" the major asked.

"I spent many more years in Thailand than Burma," I said, and thanked him for inviting the Thai captain for tea. We sat in a well-built bunker with good fields of fire covering the pumping station just below the structure on the Burma side of the border. We enjoyed good Burmese black tea, and the Thai captain clearly enjoyed the stunning view he had never seen of the jungle and the all-weather road that wound down to Burma's coast on the Andaman Sea parallel to the underground pipeline.

We chatted for a few minutes and I asked the major if it was all right to take photos from the bunker. He looked sternly at me and said: "No photos."

"No problem. In a few days I will be coming up that road," I said, pointing to the pipeline access road. "What would you like me to bring you?"

The major pondered and at length said: "A bottle of Mandalay rum." That ended our tea break and I returned to the Thai side of the border with a very happy RTA captain, who had finally been inside the Burmese Army command post. My trip on the Thai side of the border concluded, the general drove me back to Bangkok. Mission partially accomplished.

My next stop was Rangoon for meetings with French petroleum company Total, the operating partner of the international consortium that owned the pipeline. I knew a little about Total and its work building the pipeline offshore and through the Burmese jungle. The boss in Rangoon briefed me on my assignment and put me on the next helicopter flying down to Daminseik, where the pipeline comes ashore south of Rangoon.

I was met by the chief of security, a tough-looking ex-military officer with long experience in oilfields. I will call him Pierre. He was happy that I spoke French and said he would be my guide. I traveled the length of the pipeline in Burma with Pierre, photographing life in villages along the route. There were basically two kinds of villages: Burmese in the low country and Karen in the mountains.

The Karen are a major hill tribe in eastern Burma, with their own state north of the pipeline. Their abiding goal since 1948 has been achieving independence from Burma. The Karen are unlike most other minority groups in Burma in that they are generally well educated, after being converted to Christianity in the 19th century. Their main school in Rangoon, Judson College, evolved into the University of Rangoon. There were numerous Karen villages along the pipeline, and elements of the Karen army, the KNU, were active in the jungle. This threat to the pipeline was met by the deployment of two battalions of the Burmese Army to provide security. I had already met one of the battalion commanders on the Thai border.

Total had organized a comprehensive program dedicated to the welfare and prosperity of the civilians along the length of the pipeline and employed a number of trained Burmese, notably doctors and teachers, to run the program. I was impressed. The program reminded me of civic action projects I had seen in Vietnam when I was in the Marines. I spent a full day visiting villages in the low country, accompanied by Total staff and Pierre. The medical facilities were well staffed and equipped. The schools were the best I had seen anywhere in Burma. There was a nursery for fruit trees, where locals could select whatever they wanted to plant without charge. We visited a prosperous fishing cooperative on the beach. I had read that there were human rights abuses in villages along the pipeline, but I saw no evidence of it. On the contrary, as I later told Burmese friends, if I knew anyone who wanted to live in a place where medical care and schools were free, I would tell them to head for the pipeline.

At the end of the busy day, we stopped for tea at an open-air shop on the main north–south road that crossed the pipeline. It was a crowded truck and bus stop. A middle-aged woman served us hot tea or ice-cold soft drinks. She also brought tasty Burmese Indian snacks such as samosas and a fish-based soup called *mohinga*, a Burmese staple. Everything was delicious. When I went to pay, a Burmese physician who was part of our group laughed and said: "There will be no charge." I assumed that Total was hosting me, but I was wrong.

"That lady," the doctor told me, "owns this shop. She said there will be no bill."
I found this strange and asked why. "Because she has a loan from a micro-bank
that Total organized and has made a lot of money here," the doctor added.
"She knows we are Total people and wants to thank us."

Back at the base camp in the late afternoon, Pierre showed me around the
camp, which looked more like a military base than an oil camp. Security was
tight at the entrance and the whole camp was surrounded by coils of barbed
wire, watch towers, and lights of illumination at night. I was again reminded
of Vietnam. My quarters were spartan but clean and had air conditioning.
The mess hall was basic, but the food was excellent, with a choice of French or
Burmese food. I had both. When I asked if beer was available, Pierre apologized:
"I am afraid no alcohol is permitted in the camp." I was surprised. I told him
that I had been a guest of Mobile Oil in Indonesia at a major natural gas
field in northern Sumatra some years earlier. "They had modern houses for
the American and Indonesian staff, a club with a swimming pool and tennis
courts, and a dining room with full bar and French wines," I explained to
Pierre. "This is the only camp I have ever seen that did not have wine." He
replied: "We need to be ready for terrorist attacks at all times. We don't worry
about the Karen here. We worry about Karen who might move down from
the Karen state and blow the pipeline. You will see more soldiers when we
get into the mountains."

So I washed dinner down with a chilled bottle of French sparkling Perrier
water. I also took a bottle with me to my room. I decided I didn't need to
tell Pierre about the bottle of Johnnie Walker (Black) scotch that I traveled
with back in my room.

The next morning, after an early breakfast of omelette, hot French baguette,
and *café au lait*, Pierre drove us east along the pipeline into thick forest,
scattered Karen villages, and Burmese Army patrols along the paved road that
followed the pipeline. We made numerous stops for me to photograph the
villages, where I recognized the colorful dress of the Karen ladies. I noticed
that all the villages had churches, mostly Baptist. Everyone was friendly.

As we moved higher, the heat of the base camp was gone and the mountain
air was almost cool. Pierre pulled off the road and stopped at a fast-running
stream. I wondered why we stopped. "Bring your camera," he advised, and
I obeyed. We had walked along the stream bed for less than a minute when
Pierre stopped. "Have a look," he said, pointing to fresh footprints in the
mud next to the stream. "Tiger tracks," he said. "Good photos." I took
a few photos and trusted Pierre knew what he was talking about. "This
morning," he explained, "we had a report of a tiger around here from the

army. These are fresh. The army not only keeps the KNU away, they protect the tigers from poachers, usually Thai."

At length we arrived at the border, just past a large pumping station. I had seen the station a few days earlier from the top of the hill. As we arrived at the command post of the battalion I had visited from the Thai side, the major was waiting for us. This time he was in full dress uniform with numerous decorations. No *longgyi* this time. This was business and he was waiting for us. I greeted the major, who was accompanied by members of his staff. After he welcomed us to his mountain-top bunker, the major pointed down the mountain and said: "Photo OK." I took a few snaps of the pumping station and the winding road down to the sea.

Then he looked at me, waiting. On cue, I presented him with a small woven cotton Karen shoulder bag with a wrapped gift inside. It was the bottle of rum I had promised.

CHAPTER 60

Searching for a Locomotive
on the Silk Road

For more than twenty years, I lived outside the United States and traveled widely on four continents. One area that was *terra incognita* to me was Central Asia, until an old friend, Chris Andrew, showed me the error of my ways. Chris is an American businessman with more than a decade in the Middle East based in Istanbul. He was responsible for sales in 40 countries. His favorite country in the region and his current home is Uzbekistan.

Chris urged me numerous times to visit him after extolling many of the charms of this former Soviet republic, starting with his favorite product of the country: melons. That's right, melons. Huge, sweet melons from the Ferghana Valley, the most fertile in all of Central Asia. In September 2018, I accepted his kind invitation.

But first, he said, I needed to see the fabled Silk Road that passes through Uzbekistan, the overland link between China and Europe for centuries and taken by such notables as Genghis Khan, Alexander the Great, Tamerlane, and a Venetian traveler named Marco Polo. These visits (Marco Polo excepted) caused great pain and suffering to the locals.

The three great cities on the "road" are Samarkand, Khiva, and Bukhara. There was no need for camels these days, Chris assured me. Excellent roads, airlines, and high-speed trains link the cities with Tashkent, the capital of Uzbekistan, a bustling commercial center with a magnificent subway system that puts American cities to shame.

I casually mentioned to Neil Hollander, my film partner based in Paris, that I was going to visit the Silk Road. Neil immediately replied: "Uzbekistan is great. You've got to go. I almost made a film there. It's a long story." It was a long story I wanted to know.

It transpired that in 2004, Neil was hired to direct a feature film in Uzbekistan based on a true story from World War II. It was the tale of a

Barry sits with movie extras in Khiva, Uzbekistan, in 2018 while searching for a locomotive for another film.

Polish Jew of the communist persuasion who fled the German invasion in 1939 and was accepted as a refugee by the Soviets. He was a medic and was sent by train to Uzbekistan, where he spent much of the war working under the supervision of a Muslim doctor. He fell in love with the doctor's daughter. A Jewish–Muslim marriage was not as farfetched as one might think. For centuries, Jews lived in harmony with Muslims along the Silk Road.

The working title of Neil's film was *The Last Stop*, and the opening shot was to be the Pole arriving in the Ferghana Valley on a steam train loaded with fellow refugees. The film was to end with a train headed west. I won't spoil the ending, as the film might still be made. Neil said the one thing he needed for his film was a steam train, but he didn't know if they still existed. His project, he said, began in 2004 with a trip to Uzbekistan, where he met with film and finance people. The problem came in May 2005, when anti-government protests broke out in Andijan in the Ferghana Valley. Several hundred protestors were killed in the violent government response. That put an end to Neil's film project. He hoped I could revive it, but the sponsors were long gone. I was not optimistic, but said I would do my best.

Chris was on hand to meet me when I flew into Tashkent, the multicultural capital of Uzbekistan. Tashkent is an ancient city with a modern and attractive look. It has tree-lined boulevards that are broad and flow smoothly, a sign of a well run metropolis. Uzbekistan was previously a part of the Soviet Union until independence in 1991, when the USSR self-destructed. The Russian population of Tashkent has shrunk, but other minorities give the city a cosmopolitan look, a crossroads of East and West. Armenian and Georgian Christians live peacefully with Buddhist Chinese and Koreans, and a potpourri of moderate Central Asian Muslims, notably Uzbeks, Tajiks and Kazaks. Of the five 'stans' of Central Asia, Uzbekistan vies to be the most developed and best governed.

Chris had my itinerary all planned. For two weeks I would visit the three main Silk Road cities—Khiva, Bukhara, and Samarkand. Then I would go to the Ferghana Valley, since the melon season was on us. Uzbekistan produces 160 varieties of melon. Among the best are the melons of the Ferghana Valley.

I mentioned Neil's abortive film project to Chris, and to my surprise, he and his Russian-and English-speaking Uzbek buddy, Sanjar, loved the idea. Sanjar was a savvy, fun-loving, well-connected businessman. He made a few calls to set up meetings with Uzbek film producers. All went well. One producer was familiar with Neil's project and expressed interest. It helped that I had produced nine documentary films with Neil and that I had worked on a Tarzan film in Thailand, a Hollywood feature film, in the early 1960s.

But there was a problem, I noted from the outset. There was a need for a steam locomotive that would open and end the film. The potential producer who liked the idea of resurrecting the film thought such a train still existed. We all went to work looking for it.

Our visit to the Silk Road started with a quick flight to Khiva. It is the farthest of the cities from Tashkent and the smallest, with a population of fifty thousand. It is also the newest, dating from only one thousand two hundred years ago. It is the best preserved too: an open-air museum of architecture

An Uzbek carries ripe melons to market in Samarkand, Uzbekistan, 2018.

Sanjar Rasulov, left, our guide, center, and Chris Andrew in Tashkent, Uzbekistan.

populated almost exclusively by ethnic Uzbeks in a country rich with ethnic diversity. We stayed in a hotel that had once been a Muslim school, a *madrassah*, the only hotel of its type in the world. I was struck by the friendliness of the people. Photography was not shunned, as it sometimes was elsewhere in the Middle East. Children did not beg, demand money for photos, or press us to buy trinkets, which I have seen in some Asian cities. Khiva was quiet, evocative of its great history, and ridiculously inexpensive.

By sheer luck, we walked into an Uzbek feature film being made. The city is one huge location for historical films. Sanjar leapt into action and introduced me to the film's producer, who welcomed us and let me photograph while the crew were setting up. I mentioned my interest in reviving Neil's film project. He listened politely, then leaned forward and said in a low voice: "I believe there is a steam train still working in the Ferghana Valley." The game was afoot.

Our next stop via bullet train was Bukhara, a city of a quarter of a million people and a history more than two thousand five hundred years old. For centuries, Bukhara was a center of trade, scholarship, and religion. The Muslim majority lived in harmony with Bukharan Jews, who had lived in the area since Roman times. The city is a UNESCO World Heritage site, with more than 140 architectural monuments. The funky hotel where we stayed could have been one of them. I jest, but in a lesser city it would have been a landmark itself.

Bukhara is a prime example of the ethnic mosaic that is Uzbekistan. Originally it was heavily Tajik, but over time Uzbeks and Russians moved in. The Russians were the last conquerors of the Bukhara Khanate in the 19th century. The tsar got into the "Great Game" with the British, carving out Muslim states in Central and South Asia for their empires.

Traveling east, we reached Samarkand, the jewel of the Silk Road. The name alone evokes romantic images of camel caravans carrying goods in both directions, linking Asia with Europe. Samarkand is right in the middle of the long link between China and Europe. The city paid a stiff price for its location and status as a major trading center for more than two millennia. It has the dubious distinction of hosting three of history's greatest conquerors, all of whom took their toll on the city and its inhabitants.

The first was Alexander the Great, a Macedonian from the west who arrived in 329 BCE. He destroyed the city, then rebuilt it with the help of thousands of laborers and artisans. The city flourished under its Hellenistic influence.

Genghis Khan appeared from the east with his Mongol horde in 1220 CE. His horsemen sacked and pillaged Samarkand, but the Khan later imported men to rebuild it. More peaceful visitors were the Venetian traders Niccolo and Maffeo Polo, who visited the area in 1271 with their 17-year-old brother,

Marco, who kept a diary. Marco Polo described Samarkand as follows: "A very large and splendid city. It is inhabited by Christians and Saracens. They are subject to the nephew of the Great Khan."

The third great ruler was Tamerlane, known locally as Timur, who conquered Samarkand in 1370 and founded the Timurid Empire. He was a nomadic ruler from the Central Asian steppe and led military campaigns across the region, reaching as far as modern Russia, Egypt, and Turkey. He was known as the "Sword of Islam," killing millions in earning that title. But Tamerlane was also a builder and some of his greatest works were in Samarkand, where he brought craftsmen from afar to create a magnificent city known for its architecture.

Tamerlane rebuilt Samarkand into a vibrant city of 150,000 people, the foremost trading center in Central Asia. Today, the city has a population of half a million, many of them ethnic Tajiks. Perhaps the finest collection of restored tombs in Asia is found in Samarkand, with the Shah-i Zinda necropolis, where a number of Tamerlane's family are interred. It is a monument to the great ceramic stone artists of the age, and also those of the present, who have restored the site with incredible skill and attention to detail. I was much taken by my visit and wrote an article on the necropolis that appeared in the September/October 2020 issue of *Arts of Asia*, the Hong Kong magazine for serious Asian art collectors and dealers.

After our fascinating sojourn on the Silk Road, we relaxed in Tashkent to plan our visit to the Ferghana Valley. Chris showed me the city, starting with its world-class subway system. For years, photos were forbidden because the subway was also used as an air raid shelter. It is a work of underground art. A wide variety of foods are available in Tashkent, reflecting the many minority ethnic groups in Uzbekistan, starting with Uzbek cuisine and its most popular dish, *plov*. The name is not very alluring. Let's call it by its international cousin's name: pilaf. My favorite version features a combination of rice, onions, dried fruits, and pine nuts. I was introduced to kofta, a grilled dish of spiced lamb balls, and acquired a taste for Georgian, Armenian, and Korean cuisine. There is a sizable Korean community in Tashkent, thanks to Stalin, who removed thousands from the far eastern border of the USSR for security reasons. Their version of Korean food is not quite the same as I remember from Seoul, but it is a welcome departure from standard Central Asian fare. Melons were available, but the season was young. We were saving ourselves for the Ferghana Valley.

A favorite son of the valley was Babur, another conqueror, with blood lines descending from both Genghis Khan and Timur; quite a gene pool. Among his conquests was India, where he established the Moghul Empire in the 16th century. His grandson was Shah Jehan, builder of the Taj Mahal. Babur only lacked the one thing he craved: melons from his homeland in the Ferghana Valley.

While melons were on our minds, our first order of business was to find the elusive steam locomotive. Sanjar arranged a meeting with a senior train executive in Ferghana, a pleasant woman who succumbed to Sanjar's charm. It transpired that there was a locomotive in Khoqand, not far from Ferghana, and it was available for rent for a film. Could we see it? No, it was on military property which was off limits to foreigners. Could Sanjar visit the train and take photos? Yes.

A military officer drove us to the base, in a remote part of the valley. Outside the base, the officer departed with Sanjar in a waiting vehicle, while Chris and I cooled our heels. Chris briefed me on the sites to see in the fertile valley, which produces a variety of crops in addition to melons, notably cotton, other fruits, and vegetables. The valley is also a center of the colorful Central Asian *ikat*, woven resist-dyed fabric.

Sanjar returned with the photos. The train existed and was available, but the film project ultimately ran afoul of the biggest issue of filmmaking: money. It only needs the right backer, and the rest is easy. Of course nothing is really easy in film making, especially on location in Central Asia. But who knows? Uzbekistan today has an enlightened president, a reformer who is reaching out to the West, so there is still hope.

Our quest to find the ideal melon was also a success. It is a long camel ride to the Ferghana Valley, and the melon season is short. Fortunately, camels are no longer needed. We traveled on an express train from Tashkent just as the season was getting started. The melons were worth the wait. Now I am no melon man, and was raised on cantaloupes and honey dew melons; fine, but no match for the melons of the Ferghana Valley. They are of a higher order in the world of melons. They are the best I ever tasted; sweet, juicy, and huge. Now I could understand Chris's enthusiasm. And I can also see why Babur was so sad in Delhi, far to the south, dreaming about the melons in his homeland.

CHAPTER 61

Travels with Neil Hollander

If Neil Hollander ever had a calling card, it should have read: "Dr. Neil Hollander Ph.D." And under that: "Author, Film Director, Adventurer."

Neil was one of my best friends, and there is no good explanation of how this happened. In 1964, I was a Navy midshipman destined for the Marine Corps when I met Neil on the campus of the University of Washington. He was a self-proclaimed leftist, an anarchist by preference, and aficionado of the late Marxist theorist Leon Trotsky. Neil was no fan of the U.S. Government, and I was no fan of the Far Left.

We did have some common ground. We both loved to travel, had lived in Southeast Asia, and enjoyed adventures which usually involved taking risks, Neil probably more than me. His father, an engineer, had built airfields in Alaska in World War II, but was black balled as a pro-communist during the shameful McCarthy era of American politics in the early 1950s and could not find work. So he became a sculptor, and his wife, a mathematician and later publishing executive, was the family breadwinner. Neil pretty much raised himself.

When we met, I was working on a bachelor's degree in political science while Neil was studying for a PhD in communications. Neil had recently returned to America after teaching at the International School of Bangkok, where one of his students was my sister, Jenny. I was busy working for the Associated Press in Bangkok at the time and did not meet him.

Eventually, Neil and I shared a houseboat in Seattle with my girlfriend (now wife of 53 years), BJ. I was then working on a master's degree in Southeast Asian studies and Neil was a teaching assistant while still working for his doctorate. Our three-bedroom houseboat had an outside moorage on Lake Union, looking out at Seattle's Space Needle. Our monthly rent was $80. It was probably so low because the boat was condemned by the city of Seattle. Its roof leaked and it listed on the port side.

Our first trip together was during Christmas break 1966. It was cold in Seattle, and Neil wanted to see the sun. He drove a Peugeot 404 with a sunroof, which was perfect for the trip. We agreed Mexico was the natural destination, and after a little research decided to aim for the old port city of San Blas on the west coast, one hundred miles north of Puerto Vallarta in the state of Nayarit. In the 18th century, San Blas was an active shipbuilding port, with vessels traveling to and from the port of Cavite in the Philippines. When we visited, the town was down to about eight thousand souls. The port had silted up long ago and the town was quiet—perfect for us, especially the weather, which was dry and in the low eighties. It was a good time not to be in Seattle's rain.

My Spanish was pretty good in those days and everyone was friendly. We checked in at the Buccaneer Hotel and purchased a gallon of Bacardi rum in a wicker cask that set us back U.S. $5. It lasted most of our trip. On our first night, we walked around town in the dark, drinking rum and enjoying the balmy climate. Our wandering found us at the ruins of the Church of Our Lady of the Rosary, built in 1769. Somehow, we climbed to the bell tower, which was minus the bells and stairs. We fell asleep, and at sunrise awoke to find that we not only didn't know how we got up, but didn't know how to get back down. We slowly and gingerly made our way down, to the delight of a crowd of small children. The rest of our holiday was spent on the beach and in numerous cantinas.

In 1968, with my MA in hand, I went on active duty as a first lieutenant in the Marine Corps, married BJ, and headed for Vietnam and later the CIA. There was almost a 30-year hiatus in my friendship with Neil. After my retirement from government service in 1996, I heard that Neil was alive and well and living in France. We made contact.

At our first meeting in Paris, Neil filled me in on the years we were out of touch. He finished his doctorate in Seattle, traveled the world, wrote books, directed films, married a French academic, and settled in Paris. One of his early adventures was buying a vintage teak Burma-built ketch named *The Milky Way*. He sailed for years in the Med, Atlantic, and Pacific with his German friend and fellow mariner Harald Mertes. In 1974, they sailed from Spain to the Canaries and across the Atlantic to Brazil. They then sailed north into the Caribbean Sea and across the Pacific from Chile to Tahiti. They were at sea for three years. Neil and Harald wrote a book, *The Last Sailors: The Final Day of Working Sail*, and produced a three-part documentary film, *The Last Sailors*, narrated by Orson Welles, who also wrote the foreword of the book. It was the first of three films that Orson narrated for Neil.

Neil's wife, Regine, was a writer, novelist, and academic at the University of Paris. She met Neil in Paris in 1980. Their story is a case of love at first sight. Neil, a carefree vagabond with a doctorate and no fixed abode, pitched up in Paris. He was living in a cold-water apartment near the flea market. One day, Clarisse, a French academic we all knew from our days on the houseboat in Seattle, arrived in Paris, where she had arranged to stay with Regine while doing research. She arrived at Regine's apartment in the 15th *arrondissement*, with Neil in tow.

Neil invited the ladies to dinner at his humble apartment and served coq au vin accompanied by bleu d'Auvergne cheese. After dinner, Regine invited Neil and Clarisse to her apartment for drinks. Neil somehow missed the last Metro home. Regine had cots prepared for Clarisse and Neil. Clarisse was shocked in the morning when she brought tea to Regine and found Neil in her bed. It was a quick courtship. Later that day, Neil moved his typewriter and small suitcase into Regine's apartment. He never left. They later married, and over the years expanded their apartment by acquiring adjacent properties. Dinner guests were treated to a nocturnal view of the nearby Eiffel Tower, with its nightly light show perfectly framed by the dining room window.

My first Asian travel with Neil took place in 2002, when I was invited to attend the gathering of Naga hill folk in the mountains straddling the Burma–India border. I had been invited to the event the year before by my French/Burmese friends Patrick and Claudia Saw Lwin Robert. We had a marvelous time visiting one of the great hill tribes of Asia in an area normally off limits to foreigners. This time I was able to arrange a stipend from the Jim Thompson Foundation in Bangkok to photograph and film the event. *Into the Naga Hills* was my first film with Neil.

Most Naga live in India in rugged hills where a low-intensity war of independence has smoldered for decades. The Naga tribes on the India side are heavily Christianized, but the Burmese Naga mostly remain animist and largely unchanged from the colonial days of the British, when the Naga were famed for their custom of taking human heads and raiding lowland villages to take slaves. This usually led to punitive columns of British forces attacking the offending village and burning it.

Early British writers wrote of the "Naked Naga," as they often eschewed clothing. The story is told of an English woman, wife of a colonial officer in Nagaland in the 19th century, who employed Naga men as gardeners and various household servants, all of them nude. Just another story of the Raj making the best of a hardship posting.

The gathering of the tribes in 2002 was at the remote mountain village of Lahe, not far, as the hornbill flies, from the un-demarcated border with India. Some groups walked for days for the annual event, prompted by promises of free rice from the Burmese government. Sadly, the army handed out T-shirts for the topless girls and males were given soccer shorts. There was inter-tribal dancing at night around 6-foot-high fires. The purpose of our short film was to record Naga textiles and their music from the dancers. The film was made to accompany a traveling exhibit of my photography shown at Jim Thompson's silk outlets around the world.

The senior Burmese intelligence officer, who gave us permission to film in Burma, arranged for us to exit Nagaland down the Chindwin River, an unexpected treat. While descending the shallow river, with jungle on both sides, we passed a large gold mining camp and stopped to photograph and film women panning gold along the shore, while dozens of dredges brought upriver sands laced with gold. One miner told us she had made $60,000 panning gold during the past year. We had the subject of our next film, *The Golden Road to Mandalay*. In antiquity, the land that now is Burma was known as *Souvanaphoum*, "The Land of Gold."

The Irrawaddy and Chindwin rivers bring gold dust down from the mountains of northern Burma, the eastern end of the Himalaya range where the motherlode of Burma's gold remains undiscovered. We spent several weeks on a 60-foot river taxi we rented and converted into a floating film platform as we filmed gold camps along the upper Irrawaddy. We filmed the gold being smelted in Mandalay and pounded into gold leaf to be placed on images of the Buddha. A word of warning: don't eat fish out of the Irrawaddy. Cyanide is used in processing the gold, and many fish contain traces of cyanide.

In 2004, Neil and I were allowed to visit and film jade mining in the Kachin State of upper Burma. For centuries, the finest Asian jade has come from a narrow belt of jade deposits along the Ulu River around the Kachin town of Hpakant, an area off limits to foreigners. That does not include Chinese miners, who have made deals with the Burmese military. When we went in, there were tens of thousands of Chinese using heavy equipment and explosives, raping the country's "Stone of Heaven" and shipping the jade overland, sometimes huge stones weighing tons, directly back to China.

It was my privilege to address a Sunday service of Kachin Baptists next to the village jade mine, while Neil filmed the event and the choir sang "Amazing Grace" in Kachin. Many Kachin, a warlike tribe who were largely converted by American missionaries to the Baptist faith, saw service in World War II with the American OSS against the Japanese invaders. Ten thousand Kachin served

Neil Hollander entering the shaft of an underground jade mine at Hpakant, Kachin State, Burma.

Burmese girls jump on a beach in Arakan State, Burma.

in OSS Detachment 101 behind Japanese lines. As one old Det 101 survivor told me: "Japanese survivors of that campaign could hold their reunions in a phone booth." After suffering atrocities at the hands of the Japanese, the Kachin rarely took prisoners.

True to his penchant for taking chances, Neil accepted the offer of a Burmese jade mine owner to go underground to film. Most jade mining was done above ground, but a few underground mines followed jade "pipes" in primitive and very dangerous conditions. I urged Neil to stay on the surface, but he saw an opportunity for rare footage and descended with the mine owner, delighted to have a Western visitor. I photographed Neil as he prepared to descend.

"For Regine," I said, "in case you don't come back."

"I always come back," Neil retorted. And so he did.

We finished the quick visit with great photos and footage. I published jade images in *Arts of Asia* and several books. But none of our jade footage, unique and historically important, ever made it into a film. Today, the jade mines are in an active war zone, as the Kachin Independence Army is again in arms against the Burmese and entry is forbidden.

Most of the films Neil and I made were of a cultural nature. After the Naga and gold film, we made a film on the iconic woman's cosmetic of Burma, *thanaka*, followed by a series of silk weaving films in northeastern Thailand. When our Burmese intelligence officer friend, who was also a general, suggested we make a film about opium in Burma, I was surprised and skeptical. I had spent years fighting drug traffickers in Southeast Asia and knew that the trade was largely in the hands of tribal warlords at war with the Burmese Army. Making a film would be difficult and dangerous. Neil loved the idea.

The so-called "Golden Triangle," where the borders of Burma, Thailand, and Laos intersect, was the major source of heroin in the world in the 1990s, most of it coming from Burma in remote mountains controlled by various rebel groups, the most important being the Wa. Travel by foreigners was dangerous and forbidden. I mentioned this to the general, a fact he knew well. I knew the Wa well, having mounted intel operations against them for years. The American Drug Enforcement Administration has offered large rewards for the capture and prosecution of the Wa leadership. Now I was in danger of meeting them. Neil relished the opportunity.

"The Burmese Army does not go into those hills," I told the general, another fact he knew well from painful experience fighting the Wa, a tough tribal group that straddle the China–Burma border in the north of the Shan state. The Wa, known to the British as the "Wild Wa," who were never subdued by them, were foot soldiers of the Burma Communist Party (BCP) in their long insurgency against the Burmese that ended in a ceasefire, but not surrender, in 1968.

"If I say you can go, they will let you film, the Wa will let you film," added the general.

"Where will we stay? Who will help us?" I still was not sold on the idea.

"The United Nations," the general replied. "I will make it happen." And he did.

The United Nations Office on Drugs and Crime had a program in Burma designed to wean opium growers off opium and to grow other crops. They were active in the northern part of the Shan State with a 72-person team comprised of numerous ethnic minorities in the area, including Shan, Kachin, Wa, Lahu, and Akha. All were under the direction of a very experienced and capable Frenchman, Xavier Boulain. They agreed to host our visit to the remote and rugged Wa Hills, known to the Burmese as Special Region 2, where, under a peace agreement, the Wa were allowed to carry arms and grow opium.

No Burmese Army troops were in the region and no Burmese currency was accepted, only Chinese yuan. No Burmese flags were flown, only the flag of the United Wa State Army. During an interview with the Wa leader, he asked: "When are you going back to Burma?"

"I'm in Burma," I answered. That was a mistake.

"You are not in Burma. You are in the Wa State." I didn't argue. He had twenty thousand men under arms. But he did welcome our visit and we were not bothered by the Wa State Army. With cameraman and editor Kevin Chapados, Neil and I spent a very fast two weeks filming the opium fields and meeting many of the cultivators who made, on average, $12 per month. The big money went to the Wa leaders and their Chinese friends.

We visited a Lahu village, where most of the men were former BCP members. We spoke with an old village leader who directed his granddaughters to show us how raw opium is obtained. In the morning, the poppies are "scored" with an implement with five blades. The raw opium oozes out of poppies, and in the afternoon the opium is scraped up ready for smoking. Neil and Kevin filmed and I photographed. Afterwards, the old fellow offered us a pipe of opium. Not to seem rude, I accepted. But I didn't inhale.

The drug of interest to the U.S. and other foreign governments is not opium. We are after heroin, a product trademarked by the German pharmaceutical company Beyer derived from opium, but 10 times more addictive.

Our sojourn with the Wa resulted in the film *Flowers of Death*. It was quite an adventure and happily lacked danger. As the Burmese military regime became more repressive, we decided to make an anti-regime documentary.

I was sure it would be my last visit to Burma. This time we did face danger. Without telling any of my Burmese friends what was afoot, Neil and I made several trips to Burma, filming without any permission or assistance. It was "shoot and go" filming. Neil was in his element.

After filming in refugee camps along the Thai–Burma border, we were invited to go into Burma with elements of the KNU. We traversed a minefield on foot while on a KNDO patrol not far from a Burmese Army military strongpoint. We got our footage, photos, and made it back to Thailand without incident.

In Chiang Mai, we were given access to the extensive footage of the Free Burma Rangers (FBR), a humanitarian group run by Dave Eubank, an ordained minister and former U.S. Army Green Beret. The FBR sends medical teams into Burma to help minority groups, especially the Karen, who are suffering at the hands of the military regime there. The Eubank family, including children, travel inside the mountains of upper Burma, often on horseback, to minister to the local people.

Our final interview for the film *Burma: A Human Tragedy* was with Aung San Suu Kyi, aka The Lady, a winner of the Nobel Peace Prize and the symbol of democracy whom I had met earlier and respected greatly. She spent much of her adult life in prison or house arrest after winning a free and fair election in 1988, much to the chagrin of the military, who refused to let her take office.

We met her at her office in Rangoon, which was under constant surveillance by the military junta. She was very friendly to us and candid in her remarks. With the interview in hand, we went straight to the airport and left Burma safely. Our film was financed by an internationally known cinema star who was a big fan of Suu Kyi. Our son, Brendan, edited the film, which was graciously narrated *pro bono* by Hollywood actress Anjelica Huston. By the time the film came out, the political world in Burma had changed. To everyone's surprise, the military became friendly and Suu Kyi was allowed to run for office. She won a landslide victory.

The army backed down. Suu Kyi's party, the National League for Democracy, formed a government and she was suddenly in power. Political prisoners were released from jail and a free press appeared in Burma for the first time in decades. Things were looking good. But it did not last. The military had never yielded power fully, and after losing the national election in November 2020 they seized full power on February 1, 2021. The Lady was back in jail and civil war broke out in Burma. It was back to square one—or worse.

Our last film was *Who Killed Jim Thompson: The Thai Silk King*. In it we claim to have found the killers of the American businessman, a hero of the OSS in World War II, who disappeared on Easter Day 1967 while on vacation in the Cameron Highlands of Malaysia. We believe Jim was murdered by the Malayan Communist Party and credit Thai businessman Xuwicha "Noi" Hiranpruek with solving the mystery. He had two sources, both of whom we interviewed. The film debuted at the Foreign Correspondents Club of Thailand in 2019 to a packed room. It won awards in Asia and the United States.

In all our years of partnership at Adventure Film Productions, there were only two unfinished film. One deals with the jade mines of Burma and the other with the pre-Buddhist spirit worship of *nats* in Burma. In 2005, we attended the annual week-long *nat* festival at Taungbyone, about twenty miles from Mandalay. Two of Burma's 37 *nats* are propitiated there through mediums (*nat kadaws*) who dance while imbibing large amounts of alcohol to please the Taungbyone brothers, who were real people like the other 28 *nats*. All of them died violently. We have great footage of *nat kadaws* in action and interviews with the Burmese faithful who somehow adhere to Theravada Buddhism while also keeping an eye out for the *nats*.

But Neil won't be on hand to guide it to the screen. He passed away in Paris in June 2021 after a long battle with cancer. Regine was at his bedside. Neil was 81.

CHAPTER 62

The Girl from Yaroslavl

There is a girl in Yaroslavl, Russia, who I am worried about.

She would have been about ten years old when, in 2015, BJ and I took a cruise in Russia up the "Waterways of the Tsars" and stopped in her city. It was a delightful week-long river trip from St. Petersburg to Moscow through the largest lake in Europe, passing villages with ancient wooden churches and off-the-beaten track towns and cities. One of them was Yaroslavl, an ancient city of half a million inhabitants at the confluence of the Volga and Kotorosl rivers, one hundred and sixty miles northeast of Moscow.

In the 9th century, Viking rowers from Scandinavia established a settlement nearby on a major trade route on the Volga founded by Yaroslav the Wise. These men were known as the Rus ("men who row"), which evolved into Russians. It was an independent state in 1218 and was incorporated into the Grandy Duchy of Moscow in 1463.

Our cruise boat stopped for a day in Yaroslavl and we enjoyed a day ashore in this beautiful old city that, in the 17th century, was the second-largest city in Russia. One of our first stops was at an Orthodox church and a monument to the victims and victors of World War II, known in Russia as the Great Patriotic War. As we strolled around the well-kept memorial on a warm day, a family of Russians arrived to pay their respects to Soviets lost in the war, both civilians and military. I watched the father take out a camera and pose his young blonde daughter in front of the memorial, with the grand church in the background.

I was quite taken with the young girl posing quietly for her father. I wanted to take a photo of her too. Not speaking much Russian, I gestured to the father that I would also like to take the young girl's picture. He understood, agreed, and asked the girl if she would pose for another photographer. She shyly nodded her agreement. I placed her in front of a statue of a fallen Soviet

A young girl in Yaroslavl, Russia, waves at the camera in 2015.

soldier to the left, with the gilt onion-domed church in the background. I took my photo as she stood unsmiling for the camera. Then I asked for one more; she smiled and nodded. As I took the photo, she raised her right hand and waved. That was the photo I was looking for. I thanked her and her family, and we moved on.

Another stop in Yaroslavl was at a large school, where we were treated to Russian folk songs from young girls. It was delightful, if a bit touristic, and I suspect that the school made a little money this way. But before we heard the songs we were taken up to see a wall on the upper level of the school. This was a shrine to the teachers and students from the school who died in the Great Patriotic War. The war is remembered as if it was a recent memory, not sixty-plus years before. Few families were not touched by the twenty million dead from the war.

There were dozens of photos of people from the school on the wall, mute testimony to the magnitude of the city's loss. Then we saw a smaller selection of photos separately, and I asked our guide, Tanya, who they were. She said they were the fallen heroes of the war in Afghanistan where the Soviet Union lost more than fifteen thousand soldiers killed in action in the incursion that failed

Barry stands in front of a statue of Felix Dzerzhinsky in a Moscow park, 2015. Dzerzhinsky was known as "Iron Felix" and was the founder of the Soviet secret service, which in Barry's day was the KGB. (Image courtesy of Tim Carney)

to add the rugged mountainous country to the Soviet Empire in the late 20th century.

Finally, there was a small number of photos at the end of the wall. "Who are they?" I asked Tanya.

"They are the fallen from Chechnya," she said, naming the long-running conflict between 1994 and 2017 in the North Caucasus mountains that left many thousands dead.

"Where is the memorial to the fallen Russians in the Ukraine invasion?" I asked, referring to the 2014 attack that resulted in the Russian annexation of Crimea and the occupation of parts of eastern Ukraine. Tanya was not happy.

"There are no dead from Ukraine," Tanya insisted. "The fighting was short and is over."

Of course, the fighting was not over. Russian-funded separatist military operations culminated in the February 2022 full-scale invasion, which led to heavy fighting and massive support from the West in halting the Russian advance. Russian losses have been heavy.

This has led me to thinking about the little girl in Yaroslavl. She would be about seventeen or eighteen now, and may have a boyfriend. He would likely be of military age, and since 2022 many thousand young, poorly trained, and even more-poorly led Russian men have been killed in the Ukraine war. I assume there is now a portion of the school's memorial wall that is devoted to the rising number of Russian dead in Ukraine. I hope the girl's boyfriend, or even husband, is not among them.

—